MANAGING COLLEGES AND UNIVERSITIES

Issues for Leadership

Edited by
Allan M. Hoffman
Randal W. Summers
Foreword by Dean L. Hubbard

BERGIN & GARVEY
Westport, Connecticut • London

AAN6264

Library of Congress Cataloging-in-Publication Data

Managing colleges and universities : issues for leadership / edited
by Allan M. Hoffman, Randal W. Summers ; foreword by Dean L.
Hubbard.
   p. cm.
  Includes bibliographical references and index.
  ISBN 0–89789–645–9 (alk. paper)
  1. Universities and colleges—United States—Administration. 2.
Educational leadership—United States. I. Hoffman, Allan M. (Allan
Michael) II. Summers, Randal W., 1946–
  LB2341.M2779 2000
  378.73—dc21   99–37688

British Library Cataloguing in Publication Data is available.

Library of Congress Catalog Card Number: 99–37688
ISBN: 0–89789–645–9

First published in 2000

Bergin & Garvey, 88 Post Road West, Westport, CT 06881
An imprint of Greenwood Publishing Group, Inc.
www.greenwood.com

Printed in the United States of America

The paper used in this book complies with the
Permanent Paper Standard issued by the National
Information Standards Organization (Z39.48–1984).

10 9 8 7 6 5 4 3 2 1

Contents

Foreword

Few will challenge the underlying thesis of *Managing Colleges and Universities: Issues for Leadership*: The world is changing rapidly and these changes will have an inevitable and profound impact on higher education. Even those who disagree with Allan Hoffman and Randal Summers' prognostications regarding the exact direction this change will take, must agree that institutions that fail to respond to the trends taking place around them will not likely survive with significance very far into the new millennium.

Regardless of one's position in the academy, the experienced practitioners who have contributed to this book provide a wealth of hands-on knowledge of the inner workings of the traditional academic institution. Their insights and suggestions have been honed in the trenches and, therefore, merit careful consideration. Another strength of the book is that it not only outlines some of the forces impacting the academy, but also delineates successful change management strategies.

While not every reader will find every chapter equally enlightening, all will come away with a greater appreciation for the challenges facing higher education and with a renewed sense of urgency to get on with figuring out how to ensure the continued relevance and vitality of American higher education.

Dean L. Hubbard

Introduction

We are probably all familiar with the old cliché "the only constant is change." Fortunately or unfortunately, in reality, it is more than a cliché. We are reminded in our daily work and our social lives that the demands of change are not only continuous but also becoming increasingly complex. The hallowed halls of academe are no stranger to this "complex change" phenomenon. Let's review the challenges facing higher education:

- There is new competition in higher education—the rise of "for profit education."
- Traditional institutions are facing shrinking budgets and enrollment challenges.
- There are major technological advances in education methodology—the information age is here.
- There are shifting demographics in the higher education workforce—graying of the instructor/tenured professor; the new breed of college professor with different values, attitudes, and work ethic.
- There are shifting demographics in the higher education student body—increasing adult and minority and off-campus enrollment (via distance learning).
- There is a greater demand by organizations for skill-based education to prepare graduates for the challenge of the workplace in the global marketplace in the new millennium.

In essence, the cultural context of higher education has changed but our management paradigm has not. As a parallel, American industry in the 1980s found itself faced with new formidable competition, a changing workforce, and a world characterized by rapid change. In order to succeed, management had to change the way it conducted its business. Similarly, with sweeping changes in the healthcare system, administrators found themselves floundering in a new world—they had to change or become anachronisms.

Unfortunately, what we, as managers/administrators in higher education, have been doing for many years is no longer working. In fact, the high turnover in higher education administration is but a symptom of the importance of our addressing the future now.

In this book, we will provide both a conceptual framework and practical approaches relevant to leadership issues in higher education. It is our intent to help in the transition from:

- traditional manager/administrator to a valued leader in higher education;
- being accountable for delivering cost/effective education to a responsibility that focuses on changing student behavior in order to impact the organizations where they will work;
- being viewed as a higher education institution to being valued as a partner to industry and government in achieving a competitive advantage in the global marketplace.

The chapters in this book cover a wide range of topics that relate to leadership issues in higher education. The contributing authors are from many walks of life—professors, administrators, and consultants. They were selected for their expertise in a particular topic and they were given latitude in respect to their approaches and writing style. What follows is a brief summary of each of the chapters.

This book contains 12 chapters. Chapter 1, "Organizational Structure, Management, and Leadership for the Future," explores academic organizations with hierarchical structures. The authors indicate that these organizations once thrived but now face serious setbacks in market share and operating resources. They challenge the status quo of leadership in colleges, asserting that they are slow moving, change resistant, with static organizational structures and systems-driven management. The chapter describes new competitors and the organizational strategies they use to enter the higher education marketplace. The authors point out common principles for restructuring higher education organizations and the impact this would have on management and leadership in the future.

Chapter 2, "The Practitioner's Dilemma: Understanding and Managing Change in the Academic Institution," focuses on the imperative of managing change for the future survival of academic organizations. The forces of change that affect academic institutions are identified along with outdated conceptions and responses to change. The author contends that by understanding the academic institution as a dynamic human environment, practitioners will be ready to manage change.

Have you heard from Prince Machiavelli lately? Well, chapter 3, "A Memorandum from Machiavelli on the Principled Use of Power in the Academy," is a memo to you from him. The memorandum captures the view that the ability to make changes begins with an assessment of the type of organization and then an understanding of the decision makers, the decision-making process, and the implementers of change. This is a "must read" chapter.

Chapter 4, "Higher Education Management in Theory and Practice," explores what we teach students about management in higher education. The authors suggest there is no agreement about the implications of what we choose to teach. An assertion is made that all theories regarding organizations can be categorized into structural, human resource, political, and symbolic groups. The author takes the position that simply learning an espoused theory will not guarantee that it will become someone's "theory-in-use" or actualize in management practices/behavior.

Chapter 5, "Successfully Managing Higher Education Consortia/ Partnerships," looks at the historical development of consortia, the nature of consortia in higher education, and how to be successful in creating them.

Chapter 6, "The Financing of Higher Education," reviews the trends in higher education that have had major impact on the economics of higher education. The authors indicate there has been continual growth in enrollment, which will continue to the year 2005. They point out that the demographics of the student body have changed, there is now less federal government support resulting in diminished revenue, and there is an increasing demand on colleges and universities for greater accountability. The authors suggest a number of approaches to determine the monetary value of higher education to individuals and society as a whole.

Chapter 7 is a case study of the actual process of tuition setting at Arizona and Kansas public university systems. The authors present an overview of the issues and forces affecting tuition levels. They highlight the relationship between the board and campus management in the tuition-setting process.

Chapter 8, "Collective Bargaining," explores the context in which collective bargaining functions in higher education. It examines the issues around organizing for education management and leadership during the process. Third-party intervention and the impact of collective negotiations upon higher education are reviewed.

Chapter 9, "Student Development: Its Place in the Academy," points out the emergence of student affairs as a prominent player in academia. The author presents an interesting historical overview of the student personnel movement and the role of student development in the college environment.

The chapter explores organization development and planning issues in the context of continuous improvement leadership for student practitioners.

Chapter 10, "Managing with Diversity in Colleges and Universities," emphasizes the creation of an environment where people of varying age, gender, ethnic origins, life experience, worldview, and education can build a community together and enjoy success. The chapter explores diversity in the workplace in the context of four megatrends that influence higher education organizations: adjustment to a global economy, adoption of sophisticated technology, abandonment of the traditional organization, and development of a multicultural/multiethnic workforce. The chapter concentrates on the fourth trend.

Chapter 11, "Managing Evaluations in Higher Education," looks at the evaluation system at the University of Illinois at Urbana-Champagne. The chapter highlights the evaluation programs/activities of the Office of Institutional Research, which is responsible for the design and management of evaluation programs to help campus decision-making.

Chapter 12, "Evaluating Collegiate Administrators," begins with the premise that the main reason for evaluating administrators, as is the case for faculty, is to improve administrative performance. The authors describe the characteristics of effective administrator evaluation systems, outline the operational guidelines for administrator evaluation, and provide a six-step process for employee-employer assessment. They also discuss a step-by-step process in handling a termination.

This book was developed by experienced academic leaders/managers and is intended to help academic administrators develop strategies to effectively deal with the issues and challenges of leadership in higher education.

Allan M. Hoffman
Randal W. Summers

Organizational Structure, Management, and Leadership for the Future

Richard Alfred and Scott Rosevear

The postwar decades were boom years for management in colleges and universities. A generation of presidents, deans, and top-level managers welcomed the development of organizational structures and management processes designed to help them deal with the rapid pace of growth. Bureaucratic structures, academic divisions, presidential cabinets, master planning, planning-programming-budgeting systems, management by objectives—tools like these brought control and precision to management at both department and college levels. Leaders seeking to manage growth added administrative divisions that reflected a growing need to coordinate staff and resources. New units such as strategic planning, enrollment management, and research and assessment came into being and added to the complexity of administration while expanding the layers of bureaucracy. Although the market in which colleges and universities operate has changed dramatically, approaches to management and leadership have remained remarkably constant. Despite much talk on campuses about the need to prepare for rapidly changing needs by becoming more flexible and responsive to change, colleges and universities adopt innovations very slowly.

The pace of global competition and technological change now threatens to render organizational structures and management obsolete. As external markets move faster and faster, college leaders are finding that the academic organization—departments, administrative units, and staff—is static and slow. Management and leadership have also become problematic at the institutional level. Since the end of the higher education growth era in the early 1980s, it has become apparent that colleges and universities have diminished their competitive position by centralizing decision making in larger and more complex structures. As new, less hierarchical competitors have begun to emerge, colleges are faced with the potential for powerful setbacks in market share and operating resources.

Not surprisingly, new ways of managing and leading have been proposed to address the deteriorating competitive position of colleges and universities. Many are focused inward. The lessons from Peters and Waterman's "excellent" companies have led the way, closely followed by total quality management, reengineering, and the learning organization. Each approach has made its contribution, but none of them have resulted in profound changes in how colleges and universities work. The result: each has amounted to tinkering when, in fact, fundamental change or restructuring may be necessary to make them more competitive. Walls between departments continue to exist, decisions continue to be made at the top of the organization, planning and budgeting continues to be centralized, and the structure of the organization—and divisions within—remains hierarchical. Leaders continue to place emphasis on top-down planning and control. By virtue of their training and experience, they favor systems-driven management models that repress innovation and forestall the development of people-centered entrepreneurial models essential to competing in today's fast-moving markets.

In this chapter, we begin with the observation that colleges and universities are slow-moving, change-resistant organizations with static organizational structures and systems-driven management. We then describe new competitors and the organizational strategies they are using to enter higher education markets. Creating "value" through new approaches to cost, program design and delivery, and customer service will be a critical challenge for management. We acknowledge this challenge and outline new organizational models that colleges and universities need to consider in order to create value. Finally, we extract common principles from these models that can serve as a framework for restructuring postsecondary organizations and cite their implications for management and leadership.

COMPETITORS: MOVING TO A DIFFERENT BEAT

Competitors are at work reshaping the postsecondary education market. Five competitors in particular are having a significant effect on educational design and delivery, yet have not been met with adequate institutional responses: (1) companies and corporations providing on-site programs for current and future workers; (2) corporate giants in the communications industry with a capability for distance delivery into homes, workplaces, shopping centers, and areas where people congregate; (3) supplementary education providers, such as private tutoring companies, which use proven techniques to produce positive learning outcomes in students; (4) K–12 schools partnering with business and industry to prepare work-ready youth; and (5) temporary service agencies using training programs to prepare flexible workers for many different jobs.

What are these competitors doing, or could they do, to challenge the preeminence of colleges and universities? They are creating *value* in ways that surpass colleges and universities. Value can take many forms, including some that have not been considered by college faculty and administrators. It can be created in the form of *cost*, which makes education more affordable for students through operating procedures that control costs. Community colleges, for example, can build a competitive advantage in relationship to higher cost four-year colleges because they have multiple funding sources and instructional strategies that enable them to keep student tuition low. Or value can be realized as *convenience*, which makes access easy by bringing courses and services directly to the customer. Potentially, telephone and cable companies are in a strong position to make education convenient for students through distance delivery into homes, community centers, shopping malls, and just about anywhere people congregate. Or value can be created in the form of *great programs and services*, which attract students because of their distinctive design and delivery. Take, for example, the skill of corporations with high-powered training programs (e.g., Motorola and General Electric)—first in identifying employee needs, next in high-quality program design, and then in fast program development. These capabilities transform otherwise pedestrian training programs into niche programs that can be delivered outside of company walls and bring the corporation that developed them into the business of education. Or value can be achieved through *customer intimacy*—operating practices that distinguish one institution from another because they reach out and identify beneficiary needs and find ways to help them achieve important goals. Some proprietary schools have succeeded in competition with established colleges through student intake procedures (i.e., admissions and financial aid), which are custom crafted to students, and support services, which provide a direct linkage between education and work. Finally, value can be created in the form of *maverick ideas*, which provide a competitive advantage to organizations that invent totally different ways of delivering education and surprisingly outstrip traditional institutions. K-12 schools partnering with business and industry in the primary grades to introduce children to technology and education/work linkages could potentially reshape college enrollment patterns by preparing students directly for work in corporations. These students would appear on college campuses as part-time learners already engaged in a career, not as full-time students seeking a career.

Value, whatever its form, will be the vehicle that determines success for organizations in the postsecondary education market. Organizations that succeed will find new ways to create value that enable them to deliver

Figure 1.1
Forms of Value in Postsecondary Education

programs, courses, and services better and more economically than other organizations. Motorola, for example, possesses a range of resources that could yield a competitive advantage in the delivery of postsecondary education. Using the interplay of values described in Figure 1.1, Motorola could choose to partner with a telecommunications firm and deliver high-quality courses to "customers" in homes, workplaces, and other locations. It could establish its own form of credit for these courses and circumvent the traditional accrediting apparatus by connecting credit with important outcomes (e.g., jobs, job skills, and advanced technology training). The academic semester and credit hour would become irrelevant and so would when, where, and how a course is taught. Most important would be value created for the customer. Success would be determined through creating competitively distinct value and deploying it in a well-conceived strategy.

What is astonishing about these competitors is their focus on the "customer" and their speed in serving new and existing markets. Research has shown that six factors contribute to their success (Senge 1990; Prahalad and Hamel 1990; Schein 1993):

- Well-developed core competencies that serve as launch points for new services.
- An ability to fundamentally renew or revitalize by periodically changing the services they deliver and delivering new ones.
- A focus on "operational excellence," which in some way distinguishes the programs and services offered by the organization from those offered by other organizations.
- A flattened decentralized organization that enables staff to identify and respond quickly to changing needs.
- A dedication to "customers" and "suppliers" that enables the organization to "live" the customer's problems; it understands that the best program or service

isn't the best value if the customer is unable to use the program or service effectively.

Competitor organizations have ways of creating and delivering *value* that set them apart from colleges and universities. They focus on *learning* required to make *transformational changes*—changes in basic assumptions needed to succeed in today's fast-moving, often turbulent market.

A brief comparison of the organizational development paths followed by colleges and universities and competitor organizations since the late 1970s may provide valuable insights into management and leadership for the future. In their search for continuing growth and resources, colleges and universities adopted centralized planning and decision support systems. With increasing size and complexity, executive officers delegated many operating decisions to deans, department chairs, and a growing number of management specialists. Senior administrators cast their own jobs as making strategic decisions, developing structure, and allocating resources to support programs and services. The role of resource allocation in that series of tasks was crucial. As the department and division structure first made growth possible and then competitively necessary, resource allocation and information systems became the essential tools that executive officers used to understand and control their expanding enterprise.

This management model enabled colleges and universities to grow for more than two decades. But, while presidents and vice presidents see centralized planning and resource allocation systems as controls that link them to increasingly diverse departments and services, faculty and staff deeper in the institution see them as inhibitors to creativity and initiative. Lacking resources to pursue individual initiatives, faculty engage in behaviors that meet minimum expectations, but fail to advance the institution. At best, the resulting organizational culture is passive. Faculty and staff perform functions that meet department goals and implement institutionwide initiatives out of necessity, not interest. The "institution" is reduced to the department or service unit and the concept of a boundaryless organization—an institution without divisions or "walls"—is fantasy. At worst, the top-down management culture triggers antagonism and disengagement. Coping mechanisms are developed to adapt to organizational life and precious human resources are lost.

Contrast this management model with models implemented by high-performing organizations that seek to engage the mind of *every* employee in ideas that promote growth and change. Leaders in high-performing organizations are committed to developing the organization through unleashing the creative potential of staff. By developing a management philosophy based on a more personalized approach, leaders attempt to empower staff to develop their own ideas. This does not mean stripping the organization of all of its formal systems, structures, and procedures. It does require redefining them so that they support top management's ability to focus on staff.

Leaders in high-performing organizations have downplayed their strategic decision-making roles and delegated much of that responsibility to managers and staff who are closer to the business. Top administrators still influence long-term direction, but they recognize that they have their greatest impact by working internally to develop the organization's resources as strategic assets. Personal relationships are used to communicate complex information and information systems support, rather than dominate discussions about core issues. The challenge goes beyond creating communication networks. Leaders in high-performing organizations have found ways to ensure that all staff have access to information as a vital organizational resource. In a time of intensifying competition and advancing technology, an organization's success depends on its ability to gather intelligence, transform it into usable knowledge, embed it as organizational learning, and diffuse it rapidly throughout the organization (Bartlett and Ghoshal 1995). High-performing organizations succeed not by abstracting and storing information at the corporate level, but by gathering and distributing it through staff and exploiting it as a source of competitive advantage. This amounts to a reversal of the traditional institution-staff contract in colleges and universities. High-performing organizations see their responsibility not in terms of ensuring long-term job security as is true of colleges and universities, but as providing opportunities for personal and professional growth.

In the new age of competition, colleges and universities will no longer be well-served by the hierarchical organization or its implicit employment contract. In an environment with competitors trying to deliver new forms of value, the critical resource is knowledge—composed of information, intelligence, and expertise (Bartlett and Ghoshal, 1995). Unlike capital resources, knowledge is most valuable when it is controlled and used by those in direct contact with students and service markets—faculty teaching courses, middle managers recruiting and serving students, and staff meeting student needs. In a fast-changing, competitive environment, the ability to gather and exploit knowledge quickly is what gives organizations a competitive advantage.

The implications for management and leadership in colleges and universities are profound. If faculty and staff are vital to information gathering and using resources instead of personnel who teach and deliver services to students, administrators can no longer afford to isolate themselves from staff. Top executives will need to find ways to restructure their institutions through delayering, breaking down walls, and reallocating strategic roles and responsibilities to faculty and staff deeper in the organization. In short, colleges and universities will need to adopt new organizational structures and people-centered approaches to management that virtually redefine academic and administrative divisions and faculty and staff roles. This will result in an organization that moves faster to create value and focuses on improving and exceeding past performance. The life blood of this organization will be constant innovation generated and carried out by faculty and staff.

VEHICLES FOR CHANGE: NEW ORGANIZATIONAL MODELS

The traditional college and university organizational model—a pyramid with a president on top, several vice-presidents or deans reporting directly, some senior or middle managers below them, and so on down the line until the people are reached who actually do the work—is fine in a business where things don't change quickly. The pyramid structure, by definition, is slow to react because it evolved in a time when markets didn't change quickly (Ross and Kay 1994).

Increasingly, colleges and universities need to respond quickly. Like businesses and corporations, they face stiff competition and students who want what they want and when they want it. In this kind of environment, the slowness of the pyramid structure gets in the way. What is needed is a new kind of organization, one that responds faster and is more flexible. But this organization should not reinvent the wheel; it should borrow from the learning that has taken place in organizations that have undergone transformation. In this section we present a number of different organizational models that are possible designs for the future. Each model has inherent strengths and limitations and each has advocates who view it as a preferred model. Our position is not to advocate, but to examine all of the models as part of a total picture and to apply this knowledge to leadership and management in colleges and universities.

The Distributed Organization

Professional schools in some universities are structured as organizations in which departments and programs report directly to associate deans, who control the resources and are expected to manage them in a fashion consistent with the academic and research mission of the professional school. Each of the departments and programs pursues its distinctive specialty and is given the freedom to service its customers.

This example describes what Galbraith (1994) has labeled the "distributed organization." The center of the organization, the headquarters or senior management, distributes strategic initiatives and operations to the individual units. The units then assume accountability for the organization's mission and their own objectives and responsibilities. Distributed organizations form when "local expertise is superior to central expertise."

Thus, they are characterized by aspects of both centralization and decentralization. The organization centrally controls long-term strategies and policies. On a decentralized basis, however, the units have the autonomy to make operating decisions that satisfy the organization's goals.

The distributed organization gains a competitive advantage through the empowerment of units. Each unit wraps itself around a particular product or market, thereby enabling the organization to adjust quickly to changing needs. There is no confusion in roles played by the units and there is no duplication of effort—a characteristic of bureaucracies. Each unit directly meets the needs of its customers while pursuing the goals of the organization.

The strength of the distributed organization emerges when different units work constructively together. Galbraith (1994) concedes that managers must effectively coordinate relationships between units that serve the organization's goals. This organization is most efficient when "dependence is balanced and reciprocal between units." Cooperation among the units fosters mutual dependence. As a result, beneficiaries are serviced across business lines. This relationship can be seen in university business schools when different units work together to educate corporate executives on the effectiveness of new systems in their organizations.

The Molecular Organization

According to Ross and Kay (1994), the molecular organization represents how enterprises will have to be structured in order to realize success in competitive markets. Organizations that react faster and are flexible enough to address multiple demands will achieve performance goals. The ultimate goal of this organization is to satisfy the customer as quickly as possible.

Ross and Kay explain the molecular organization by breaking it down into levels. Every level contains a "strategic nucleus," which represents senior management. The executive officer has a simple role in this organization: to establish corporate priorities, clearly articulate the corporation's vision, and protect its culture. The molecular organization releases senior managers from the headaches that accompany daily operations. They are able to perform a more critical function by focusing on long-term, big-picture corporate strategies. Moving around the nucleus are "clusters," or the operating staff. These front-line personnel are closest to the customer and the pulse of the market. The front line foresees changes in the market and can shift priorities quickly to adopt new strategies. All operating units work closely with customers in order to ensure fast and appropriate service.

Middle management in the molecular organization is a vastly smaller segment than the traditional workforce. They manage linkages between the operating units and senior management, allowing for clear communication of customer needs and the organization's vision. *Teamwork* is an important part of the molecular organization. Comprised of separate departments, teams wrap around the customer to satisfy a common goal. Blending the skills and ideas of all team members results in the high-speed delivery of products and services. Above all, teams are empowered to make decisions that affect the customer. Ross and Kay (1994) characterize these teams as working networks, or "communities," that are more integrated than the recent emergence of "cross-functional teams."

The molecular structure, with all facets of the organization focused on the market, is primed to utilize its speed and flexibility to secure new customers. Nissan is a good example of a company that has successfully earned its own niche in the automobile market through the timely introduction of specially styled cars that appeal to a small market. The company has recognized that small markets exist for customized cars if the cars are introduced quickly and in small quantity. In contrast, if one of the Big Three automakers entered this market, their inflexible structure would force them to mass produce the car on a long-term basis, thereby overserving the need.

The Learning Organization

According to Nonaka (1991), the only lasting competitive advantage of organizations is knowledge. Organizations that are able to generate new knowledge and transfer it to the customer will thrive in an increasingly complex market. Learning organizations strive to create new knowledge, communicate it throughout the organization, and rapidly build upon this knowledge to innovate and create market advantage. The great learning organizations, such as Honda and Canon, are recognized for their responsiveness, market foresight, ability to quickly deliver products and services, and their capacity to get ahead of the competition in designing innovative products.

There is no single organizational chart that represents a learning organization. It is, however, an organization completely focused on the creation of knowledge. All strategies and structures are based upon mining the organization's human resources to create new knowledge. This can be accomplished, for example, through open meetings, small group discussions, or social functions. Dynamic working relationships between senior management, middle managers, and employees closest to the product and customer propel the knowledge cycle. Managers massage differences in knowledge interpretation among organizational units to stimulate knowledge creativity. Senior management frames knowledge with metaphors and symbols to communicate the organization's vision of creating new innovations. By conceptualizing knowledge as a vision, senior management communicates to the organization the common elements of knowledge that run across all units. Armed with this information, operating units are able to synthesize their unique compartmental perspectives into new knowledge while continuing to learn from the markets they serve. In this way, knowledge is derived simultaneously from two sources: the organization itself and service markets.

Middle management is responsible for combining the tacit knowledge from both the front-line and senior management into explicit knowledge. Middle managers bridge the visionary ideals of top executives and the chaotic market reality of those on the front line. Innovation results from the interaction of "explicit" knowledge and "tacit" knowledge. Explicit knowledge is formal and systematic, such as the plans for building a plant. Tacit knowledge is ingrained in an individual (or group) and cannot be directly communicated to others. It is the "know how" that results from being committed to an organization or task.

The key element in a learning organization is redundancy—a situation that occurs when "overlapping" processes foster shared goals and tasks across different functional units. Utilizing the talents of individuals from separate departments, such as engineering and marketing, brings "multiple perspectives" to a project. More employees are informed and, therefore, knowledge is more "fluid" in the organization. Finally, open access to all corporate information creates redundancy. If employees understand the same information, they can apply common knowledge to the development of products and services.

The Mosaic Organization

Management pundits and writers have declared that rapid change is the new reality in service markets. Customer attitudes are changing—products and services must be better, they must be delivered faster, and they must be reasonable in cost. Hierarchical organizations will not be able to keep pace with rapid change. A new type of organization is needed that empowers operating units to meet needs by providing distinctly different services to customers. This is the "mosaic organization" (Alfred 1995) and its organizing principle is customer-focused delivery.

Mosaic organizations are "self-transforming" and "decentralized around small entrepreneurial units." These units are able to rapidly deliver services without interruption and to adjust quickly to sudden changes. External alliances with customers and suppliers enhance this capability. Among the many characteristics of mosaic organizations are the following:

The Mosaic Organization is

Agile: it turns quickly and accelerates rapidly in responding to customers.

Lateral: it is comprised of lateral units which share information and power across the organization.

Personal: staff have an "owner" mind-set; customers feel as if they are dealing with an owner wherever they tap into the organization.

Social: it is comprised of teams which lead to a different work experience; a sense of community and social connection to the organization.

Learning-Focused: it develops a competitive advantage by learning faster than competitors.

Self-Transforming: it has the ability to change from within to meet customer needs; a "strategic readiness" to anticipate fluctuations and change accordingly.

Collaborative: it establishes relationships with customers and suppliers that allow it to continuously develop unique products and services.

Forgetful: it is always looking beyond today's successful product, service, or idea to something entirely different tomorrow; it is forgetful of the present before it strangles creativity.

Ultimately, mosaic organizations depend on the factor of *speed* to develop new products and services to gain a competitive edge. In a global marketplace loaded with restructured companies, it is speed that separates high- from low-performing organizations.

Modular Organizations

Many private-sector organizations have shunned vertical organization for a lean, nimble structure centered on what they do best. The idea is to nurture a few *core competencies*—designing and marketing computer software, or educational programs, for example—and let outside specialists deliver the service, meet with clients, or do the accounting. These organizations avoid becoming monoliths laden with plants and bureaucracy. Instead, they are hubs surrounded by networks of suppliers. The suppliers are modular—they can be added or taken away as needs dictate.

The streamlined structure of modular organizations fits today's tumultuous, fast-moving marketplace. Outsourcing noncore activities yields two advantages. First, it holds down unit costs and investment needed to turn out new products and services rapidly. Second, it frees organizations to direct scarce resources where they hold a competitive advantage. Typically, that means more money for market research, designing new services, hiring the best staff, and training service personnel. Organizations using the modular model can achieve rapid growth with small amounts of capital and compact management. Personal computer marketer Dell Computer, microprocessor designer Cyrix, and apparel and footwear company Nike have leveraged small investments into big fast-growing enterprises. One reason is that they do not have to invest in fixed assets.

Modular organizations work best when they achieve two critical objectives: collaborating smoothly with suppliers and choosing the right specialty. Reliable vendors must be found who can be trusted with inside organization knowledge. If market activity increases, they also need assurances that suppliers will stretch and rapidly retool to push out new products. Like other companies, modular organizations also need vision to identify what customers will want.

Maverick Organizations.

Semler (1993) described a radical approach to organizational design in a publication documenting the transformation of a Brazilian manufacturing company from a declining family business into a fast-moving, multinational corporation. Semco was a large, stagnant company struggling amid difficult economic conditions when top leadership changed. After implementing traditional strategies during times of crisis, such as removing the "dead wood," the new executive team determined that radical changes in management were needed if Semco was to survive. New management strategies were established that significantly reduced the fragmentation and bureaucratic nature of the company. Walls were eliminated from offices, memos were limited to one page (including strategy plans), the dress code was thrown out, and employees were encouraged to decorate their own work areas. All corporate financial information, including balance sheets and employee salary information, was available to any employee. These and other radical management changes broke down bureaucratic barriers and opened communication at all levels.

These changes, however, were not enough to improve Semco's market share. More had to be done to restructure the organization to move faster in response to market needs. The organizational chart was eliminated and one does not exist today. Semco is now a *circular organization* made up of three concentric circles, rather than the traditional hierarchy. Job titles at the company have been reduced to four across all employees. At the center of the organization is a group of six employees called Counselors (see Figure 1.2). Counselors are the executive officers of a traditional organization—those responsible for setting policies and developing organizational strategy. A second group or "circle" consists of Partners or the business unit heads. The third "circle" includes most other employees, from clerical staff to sales associates. Known as Associates, this group carries out the work of the organization. Its members work in clusters reporting to Coordinators who present the first layer of management in the organization. In this design, the Counselors serve as the organization's catalyst resulting in decisions and actions by the Partners, who actually drive the company. Coordinators then lead teams of Associates in fulfilling specific functions.

The circular organization eliminated the bureaucratic hierarchy at Semco. Twelve layers of management were reduced to three. Other than

Figure 1.2
Maverick or "Circular" Organization

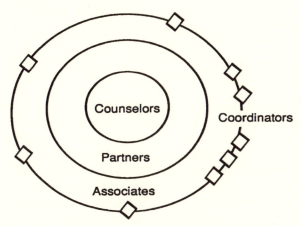

Counselors, personnel with similar job titles do not report to each other. Throughout the company, employees have escaped the grip of hierarchical management and have the freedom to express their views and take leadership positions. Other than global corporate decisions, an employee at any level can make a decision without consulting a superior. Combined with changes in management style, this organizational design has empowered employees by rewarding independence and creativity. It has also resulted in a higher level of performance for the company by enabling it to constantly generate new ideas and move them quickly to the market.

In its ultimate expression, the circular organization has become a series of organizations, each operating at a greater distance from the parent organization. This has happened as individuals or teams of workers have "left" the company to start their own businesses. For example, as Semco's operating costs grew and flexibility declined, it had to make large staff reductions to compete against other manufacturers. It created a "satellite program" comprised of former employees to reduce fixed costs and respond quickly to the market. In this program, Semco provides excess employees with compensation above severance pay and a support system to successfully launch their new enterprises. In the beginning, the satellite company works for Semco, but the new company is always able to broaden its customer base. Semco provides the satellites with work space within its own factories and cuts lease payments for the use of heavy equipment.

The satellite program has served to reduce Semco's payroll and cut inventory and operating costs, while at the same time giving the company an an advantage of having subcontractors that are knowledgeable about its operations. Several years after the satellite program was launched, Semco's 500-person workforce had been reduced to 200. Half of its prior manufacturing business had been contracted to the satellites and a number of employees carry dual affiliations with both the parent company and a satellite. In effect, the satellite program has created a "borderless" organization in which flexible teams work independently.

Open-Book Organizations

Case (1995) argues that open-book management is a new way for organizations to structure their operations and be profitable. The practitioners of open-book management argue that the best known of new managerial methods have a spotty record. Quality efforts, for example, often improve quality, but they don't always improve the business. Staff can become so obsessed with quality-related measures that they fail to remain abreast of customer needs. Reengineering can help organizations cut costs—except that this is often seen as a euphemism for layoffs, with predictable effects on morale and productivity. Teamwork and empowerment programs have their success stories so long as the organization stays with the program. Each of these methods has benefits and liabilities, but none of them present a new paradigm or comprehensive rethinking of management.

Open-book management encourages staff to think differently about the organization. It changes—fundamentally—the link between the employee and the organization. Yet the organizational chart does not need to be altered and staff do not need continuous training to get started. There is no standard set of rules for implementing open-book management, but there are a few basic principles. Chief among them is the need for staff to become familiar with the factors that determine the organization's performance, much like that of a major stakeholder or owner. In open-book organizations, staff perform like a businessperson rather than an employee. They understand why they are being called upon to solve problems, cut costs, improve quality, and give customers better service. And, as *stakeholders* in the organization, they have a reason to do so—they share profits and losses and, thereby, have a direct stake in the organization's success.

Four principles are uniformly employed in open-book organizations. First, information is disseminated and shared widely throughout the organization. Staff are taught how to do their jobs effectively and how to gauge the performance of the company. The ultimate goal is for employees to understand the financial data that are most critical to the business. Sprint's Government Systems Division, for example, measures revenue per employee. This information provides employees with a clear picture of the company's business conditions. Second, open-book organizations teach basic business concepts to their employees. Employee ignorance of business knowledge limits the organization's performance through poor decision making and by eliminating the "fun" in business. Manco, a fast-growing distributor of consumer products in the Midwest, sells a large volume of inventory to Wal-Mart and a dozen other large companies. In the past, its sales personnel—like salespeople everywhere—competed for top-line revenues. Profitability was someone else's worry. Then Manco began producing and distributing monthly account books that broke the company's numbers down by every conceivable category—including profits generated by each salesperson's accounts. The company's sales compensation system was reconfigured to take profitability into account, and sales personnel were taught profit and loss concepts and how to read balance sheets. Quickly, salespeople were motivated to think about ways to improve profitability as well as sales.

Third, open-book organizations empower staff to make decisions based on what they know. Three methods to empower workers are commonly used. The "huddle-system" holds departments accountable for their particular financial and performance numbers. Results are periodically communicated to corporate officers and the departments are required to solve identified problems. Turning an organization into a group of smaller organizations is another proven tactic for empowerment. These "subcompanies" operate as if they are independent companies or "business centers." These centers are responsible for their own performance and utilize business concepts to manage their operations. Published Image, a financial newsletter publisher in Boston, has established teams called "little Published Images." Unlike traditional teams, Published Image's teams act like self-contained businesses. Each has its own editor, art director, salesperson, and a couple of junior staffers. They line up clients and negotiate prices. They take responsibility for producing their clients' newsletters from start to finish. They collect their own accounts receivable and keep their own books. Veteran managers oversee the teams and set companywide policies. But the teams' autonomy encourages members to think like owners rather than like staff.

Finally, open-book organizations enable all staff to share gains and losses. Employees know how the organization is performing through information they receive and use about performance. Manco, for example, sets annual targets for net earnings and return on operating assets. When staff hit both targets, the company is in a "bonus condition," meaning that staff collect payouts ranging from 10% to 50% of their total compensation.

Open-book organizations advocate ownership and responsibility. They teach business principles and they provide staff with the tools they need to be stakeholders. They expect staff to know the big picture and to do what needs to be done to achieve important organizational goals.

COMMON PRINCIPLES IN NEW ORGANIZATIONAL MODELS

College and university administrators do not find it easy to import new organizational models to campuses. Under the best of circumstances, they cannot envision new organizational structures that decentralize power and make the institution more productive. Under the worst circumstances, they resist parallels between profit and nonprofit organizations and refuse to consider corporate management models. But even if they could envision new structures and buy into corporate models, transformation is a complicated undertaking. It is like trying to fit a new management model to a classic bureaucratic organization. One must know a great deal about the new models and the organization's culture to begin the process of transformation.

To aid administrators in thinking about the value and utility of new models, we have identified common principles that are reflected in almost all of the models (see Table 1.1). First, we describe these principles in some depth to determine the context in which they evolved and the magnitude of change implied for colleges and universities. We then draw contrasts between the new organizational models and those in colleges and universities. The final step is to determine the extent of change colleges will need to undergo if, in fact, change is necessary to achieve a higher level of performance.

Competitive Organizations

To what extent are colleges and universities organized to compete effectively for new and continuing markets? Future markets will become increasingly complex with new competitors and technologies forcing organizations to adjust to dynamic changes. Competitive organizations value constant change in products and services to get ahead of the competition. They value innovativeness and benchmarking as normative behaviors for producing knowledge that leads to a competitive edge. Motorola is recognized for its vigor in developing new products and its adroitness in adapting others' processes, such as benchmarking and Total Quality Management (TQM) procedures.

Although colleges and universities have made gains in technology and quality management, they are not organized to compete with new competitors. Under the protective mantle of accreditation, costs remain high and enrollments remain assured as long as students view courses and degrees as credentials for a job. Competition occurs among like providers with identical organizational structures and delivery systems. Thus, while administrators may think their institutions are competitive when strategic plans and marketing initiatives are carried out, a broader scale of competition exists outside of college walls that could disrupt resources and operations. For example, corporations could team up with telecommunications companies to develop courses, offer them through distance delivery, and provide their own form of "accreditation" by certifying students as prepared for jobs through course completion. A new form of credentialing would come into being and the rules guiding competition would change.

Table 1.1
Common Principles in New Organizational Models

1. Competitive	**7. Information Sharing**
Focus on strategies to increase competitiveness of the organization through adjustment to dynamic changes in markets	Commitment to sharing information about financial and critical success factors as a strategy for getting staff to take ownership of projects and to be accountable for performance
2. Decentralized	**8. Core Competency Focus**
Emphasis on a flattened hierarchy and streamlined staffing to develop nimble organizational strategies	Focus on building excellence in a small number of competencies as a method for cutting costs and limiting investment
3. Empowerment/Owner Mindset	**9. Seamless/Boundaryless**
Considerable effort to delegate decision making power to staff; empowered staff view the organization from the perspective of a stakeholder, not hired help	Close working relationships with suppliers and customers to ensure constant awareness of market needs
4. Teamwork	**10. Customer Service Emphasis**
Preference for the use of teams to solve problems through the interaction of ideas and skills to develop innovative products	Continuous effort to determine customer needs and satisfaction as a strategy for improving service
5. Speed/Flexibility	**11. Visionary Leadership**
Organization-wide emphasis on rapid response to market changes through streamlined structures and flexible staff	Efforts by leaders to articulate vision, engage in its implementation, and interact with staff to turn the vision into reality
6. Continuous Learning	**12. Market Foresight**
Ongoing commitment to gathering information about the organization and its markets at all levels as a strategy for innovation and renewal	Commitment to anticipating market needs and forecasting changes as a strategy to "get to the future first"

Decentralized Organization

Do colleges and universities maintain pyramids or hierarchical organizational structures by choice or by default? Most of the new organizational models eliminate the hierarchical structure found in traditional organizational designs. A flattened hierarchy and streamlined staffing enable organizations to move quickly in anticipating and responding to market changes. Observers have noted that decentralized organizations tend to innovate more readily and do a better job of meeting customer needs. The difference is between many and few layers in the organization and how many approvals are required before a new service can be designed or an existing service reconstituted. All organizations have layers; the issue is the decision-making power staff have to make changes to meet customer needs.

With their continuing investment in hierarchical structures and centralized decision-making, colleges and universities permit few opportunities to change services and delivery systems based on student input. Administrators spend a significant amount of time managing resources and monitoring operations. They pay less attention to "people processes" than to systems, although many of them acknowledge the importance of delegating authority. A growing number of executives are finding that productivity can be improved in institutions experiencing resource decline through organizational models that empower faculty and staff and hold them responsible for resource management. The question is: What events or circumstances will impel administrators to flatten the organization and distribute authority? Must the institution reach a state that to conserve resources it must undergo restructuring, or will it take action before that time?

Empowerment/Ownership

What kinds of decisions do faculty and staff make? Have colleges and universities established an atmosphere that encourages ownership or one in which a more structured, controlled approach prevents staff from taking responsibility for decisions? High-performing organizations believe that decision-making power should be delegated to staff working directly with service markets. Being involved with major decisions makes staff more responsive to internal and external audiences. It also encourages them to assume leadership roles and to become involved in organizational strategy. In the more structured approach of colleges and universities, senior administrators determine strategy and make decisions about programs and resources. They determine what information should be shared and used by others across the organization. Top-down approaches to management prevent faculty and staff from getting involved in decisions that affect the bottom line. To create change, ownership is what seems to make the difference—faculty and staff reaching out to markets and pushing ideas to advance the institution, while simultaneously advancing their own interests.

Teamwork

Do colleges and universities use both individuals and teams to accomplish important goals? Most of the new management models rely on teams to develop innovative services and processes based on the interaction of ideas, skills, and experience among staff in different units. Corporate executives have begun to realize that the challenge goes beyond satisfying their own needs for information and control. They must build a network through which all members of the organization can exchange information, develop ideas, and support one another. To do so, they must create teams and nurture the horizontal information flows that vertically organized institutions generally short circuit.

In colleges and universities, academic departments and service units have long been insulated from each other despite the existence of organizational challenges that require collaborative action for solutions to be effective. Although formal reports and traditional governance systems can identify common problems and opportunities and assess their importance, they cannot so easily communicate their causes and potential solutions. Such subjective information requires personal interaction. For example, when the educational and skill requirements of employers changed in the early 1990s because of global competition and advancing technology, academic departments moved slowly to modify curricula and courses. Their allegiance to existing course structures and delivery systems encouraged them to believe that change was not needed to meet employer requirements. Staff working in corporate services and continuing education departments have always been aware of changing employer needs because their work is conducted off-site and their delivery systems are customer-driven. They can readily identify shifts in employer needs and understand the gap that exists when academic departments fail to respond. Unfortunately, not until enrollments decline do faculty understand the necessity for change.

Such incidents show the limits of formal systems-driven communication in walled organizations. Teamwork across divisions is needed to improve communication and launch changes that keep colleges and universities in touch with their markets.

Speed/Flexibility

Do colleges and universities have a capacity to respond quickly to market changes? In recent years, researchers and corporate leaders have emphasized the importance of organizational flexibility and agreed that bloated staffing and top-down decision making are trouble spots in many organizations. High-performing organizations have worked to strip away layers of staff and support systems to produce a lean, flexible structure that is capable of responding more quickly to new technologies and business environments. Increasing speed—getting to the market first—is the objective of these restructuring efforts. Colleges and universities are not organized around the principle of speed. Numerous environmental scans involving external publics have portrayed colleges as slow-moving organizations ill-equipped to change programs on the basis of need. Budgeting is incremental or decremental based on prevailing numbers; the overriding objective is to maintain the base—the complex of activities and positions that has become "the organization."

Continuous Learning

What investments do colleges and universities make in "learning"? All organizations are learning systems with formal and informal processes and structures for acquiring, sharing, and using knowledge and skills. Investments in learning vary among organizations, however, depending on their culture and approach to management. For example, the entrepreneurial culture of successful corporations such as Motorola and General Electric results in a learning approach in which information is continuously gathered and made available to staff throughout the organization. Learning is derived from interaction with and between cross-functional work groups and from improved communication. Meanwhile, the culture of other organizations is more heavily focused on unit performance; learning is localized as information is made available to managers and specialists and its use is at the manager's discretion. In addition, there is a good deal of leeway in how managers make decisions based on information; some exchange information with other units and make decisions based on multiple information sources, and others use restricted information.

In contrast, although it is certain that organizational learning takes place in colleges and universities, its emphasis on departmental application has resulted in the reinforcement of a "walled" organization. In a culture that heavily rewards individual and unit performance, management processes that require integrated, intergroup interaction lag behind, particularly in strategic decisions that cut across divisions. The difference is in how hard it is for knowledge to be generated and shared across divisions in a hierarchical organization and how committed staff are to pursuing institution-wide goals. Thus, while colleges and universities are organized to pursue specific goals, their approach to management discourages organizational learning and enables departmental goals to take primacy over organizational goals. For example, institutional goals related to serving regional educational needs often turn into departmental efforts aimed at serving specific clients. In the absence of a strong commitment to organizational learning, there is no reason for departments to share information or to work toward organizational goals.

Information Sharing

Are the boundaries around information permeable so staff can actively access and share information? Many decisions in high-performing organizations are a function of daily, often unplanned interactions among staff with common access to information. In addition, the opportunity to meet with other groups and see higher levels of management in operation promotes sharing. Staff need freedom to generate ideas through information access and legitimate discussion and debate. Another critical aspect is the extent to which errors and successes are shared and not hidden (Argyris 1977). Perhaps the most dramatic example of information sharing is in organizations where errors or deviations are openly reported and analyzed throughout the entire organization. The company treats such events as learning experiences and follows up with team-based activities to determine the extent of learning. It then disseminates this knowledge throughout the organization. While this openness may be useful in high-performing organizations as a way to cut costs and increase productivity, we can only speculate as to its usefulness in organizations such as colleges and universities, which are only beginning to share information.

Core Competency Focus

Do colleges and universities invest in core competencies that distinguish them from competitors? A core competency is the sum of learning and skills that enable an organization to deliver important benefits to customers (Hamel and Prahalad 1995). To qualify as a core competence, these benefits must also be competitively unique. Organizations that deploy core competencies constantly ask five basic questions: Does a particular product or service make a significant contribution to "value" perceived by the customer? What are the "value elements" in this product or service? What is the customer actually paying for? Why is the customer willing to pay more or less for one product or service than another? Which value elements are most important to customers and, thus, make the greatest contribution to "customer satisfaction"?

Colleges without well-defined core competencies will experience difficulty in competition with organizations that bring value to customers. Competencies in marketing and enrollment management have been developed to bring students to college, but parallel competencies have not developed to determine value in programs and services. As a result, colleges are not particularly well-equipped to compete with organizations that deploy core competencies in areas valued by students. Likewise, colleges are at a disadvantage when competing with organizations that have moved from *vertical integration* toward *virtual integration*. These organizations have more resources to deploy, in contrast to labor-intensive colleges, because they are part of a network in which a number of organizations specialize in a few core competencies.

Seamless/Boundaryless Organizations

Do colleges and universities think broadly about the interdependency of staff, customers, and beneficiaries? This involves the degree to which organizations break down traditional barriers that divide staff and distance the enterprise from customers. Case-study accounts and anecdotal reports from corporate executives have demonstrated how much leverage organizations can get from the flow of ideas among business units and between business units and customers. Boundaryless organizations become laboratories for ideas and best practices. They give staff a chance to become more involved by giving them organized opportunities to work with individuals and groups in different parts of the business cycle.

Boundarylessness can be achieved in a number of ways, including some that are striking departures from customary ways of organizing and managing staff. One of the more interesting is the use of "design and development teams" to address organizationwide issues related to product development. These teams are typically small and include staff from different divisions who bring a variety of perspectives to problem-solving. They are led by a manager and they draw heavily on information from customers and suppliers to guide decisions about product development. The equivalent in colleges and universities would be to form cross-functional curriculum design teams comprised of members from different parts of the institution who have a stake in educational outcomes—administrators, faculty, student development staff, curriculum specialists, and classified staff. This team would be guided by the expertise of its members and information continuously received from customers (students, families, employers, etc.) and suppliers (technology providers, K-12 schools, state agencies, etc.). It would design new curricula based on multiple inputs, thereby tightening the linkage between institutional units, customers, and suppliers. Are such teams commonplace in colleges and universities today? Clearly, the answer is "no," but the hope is that they will play a more prominent role in the future.

Customer Service Emphasis

Are colleges and universities "close to customers"? Do they anticipate as well as respond to customer needs? It is much in vogue to be customer-focused. Executives in public- and private-sector institutions are telling staff that "everything begins with the customer." Companies claim to be re-engineering their processes from the customer backward. Rewards and incentives are tied to customer satisfaction. And it is almost impossible to complete a transaction with an organization without being asked to rate its customer service.

Organizations approach customer service in many different ways. Some try to lead customers where they don't want to go; some listen to customers and then respond to their articulated needs; and some lead customers where they want to go, but don't know it yet. Superior service comes when staff at every level in the organization are able to empathize with expressed or unexpressed customer needs. For example, to ensure that its product development staff empathize as fully as possible with potential customers, Honda matches the age of its design groups to the age of buyers targeted by a particular model. The youngest designers work on cars intended for young buyers. As designers age, they move along to cars oriented to older buyers. Honda places great emphasis on customer service through hard work to ensure that those charged with product development possess deep insights into the customers they are seeking to serve. Shook (1988), the author of a book on Honda's American success, provides an illustration.

In the late 1960s, shortly after the company began manufacturing automobiles, Soichiro Honda announced that he wanted to make a "world car." To accomplish this, the company sent two teams of engineers to travel around the world to collect data about products and lifestyles of people in other countries. In conjunction with this program, Honda's R&D sent engineers to Europe to spend a full year there doing nothing but observing the relationship between the citizens of those countries and their automobiles. The engineers studied everything from road conditions to driving habits. Then they returned to Japan to report their findings. This information helped Honda to design the first Civic.

One can only wonder how much insight college faculty and administrators have into the educational needs of students and other customers. As much as anything, customer service comes from really wanting to satisfy student needs.

Visionary Leadership

Are leaders at every organizational level in colleges and universities engaged in the development and implementation of vision? This includes eliminating management layers, being visible in the organization, and being an active, early participant in change efforts. Only through direct involvement that focuses on vision can leaders become powerful role models (Nevis, DiBella, and Gould 1995). Truly visionary leaders embrace both continuity and change. They cultivate core ideas reflecting important values of the organization and simultaneously revolutionize the organization. While core ideas provide continuity, stability, and cohesion, the drive for progress promotes change, innovation, and renewal. Continuous improvement is a way of life for these leaders, not a management trend. For them the critical question is not "How can the organization do well?" or "How can we meet the competition?" but "How can we do better tomorrow than we did today?" The challenge is to build for the long-term while doing well today.

Market Foresight

Do college and university leaders have a clear and compelling view of how the market will be different tomorrow? Market foresight is based on deep insights into trends in technology, demographics, regulation, and lifestyles that can be harnessed to rewrite market rules and create new forms of competition (Hamel and Prahalad 1994). The quest for foresight starts with what could be, and then works back to what must happen for that future to come about. It is this type of foresight that has been driving Motorola's commitment to satellite-based personal communicators and Bell Atlantic's view of a complex of entertainment, information, and educational services made available to every home in its service area.

Market foresight grows out of earnest questions about what should be and could be, out of a deep and boundless curiosity of leaders, and out of a willingness to speculate about issues when one is not yet an expert. Colleges and universities experience the same difficulties as profit organizations in anticipating the future. They tend to look at the future through the narrow lens of existing markets. Thus, we often find that the technical imagination of faculty and staff outstrips new program imagination, which, in turn, outstrips new resource imagination. If a college sees itself as only a provider of courses and curricula for traditional learners, its opportunity horizon will be severely limited and its view of the future will be more of what it is already doing. Colleges must learn to search for new opportunities without being constrained by existing markets.

Ultimately, colleges and universities must find ways to free themselves from the past to pursue a future that will demand different approaches to education. Obviously, tinkering with programs and services, identifying new goals, or creating master plans is not the way to prepare for the future. Instead, it is through new organizational designs—through building approaches to leadership and management that use the full resources of the institution. The goal is to challenge leaders to open the institution to change by altering the fundamentals of organizational design. This is the subject of the closing section of this chapter.

CHANGING DESIGNS FOR MANAGEMENT AND LEADERSHIP

In the first part of this chapter, we identified new competitors and some of the strategies—structural and operational—they use to deliver new forms of value. We also identified, by way of contrast, the hierarchical structure and systems aspects of management in colleges and universities that made growth possible in previous decades. The hierarchy enabled leaders and top managers to feel that they were in control by giving them three core responsibilities: to be the institution's chief strategist, its structural architect, and the developer and manager of its information and control systems. However, it is clear that the management model that follows from this doctrine—today's pyramid supported by fragmented departments and service units—cannot change quickly enough to deliver competitive results.

From atop the hierarchy, presidents and deans look down on order and uniformity—a neat configuration of tasks and activities parceled out among academic and administrative divisions. As their label implies, divisions divide. The divisional model fragments institutional resources. It creates vertical communication channels that insulate academic departments and service units and prevents them from sharing their strengths with one another. Consequently, the whole of the institution is often less than the sum of its parts. Furthermore, the divisional structure has little built-in capability for renewal—for discarding old ideas and assumptions as they become obsolete. In other words, for all their growth, colleges and universities have become inflexible, slow to innovate, and resistant to change.

To address these problems, colleges and universities will need to consider new designs for management and leadership. Structural solutions such as "skunk works," strategic alliances, and downsizing are interesting concepts that may deliver early results, but they do not remove cultural impediments to competence building and renewal; they only side-step them. The challenge is: How do colleges and universities reinvent their organization and the postsecondary education market at the same time? Tomorrow's market will be horizontally integrated with institutions competing and collaborating without central coordination. No agency or coordinating board will set rules for competition or tell institutions what to do. And when colleges lose their proprietary advantages, speed—the capacity to change quickly to meet or get ahead of the market—will be what matters most. To succeed, colleges and universities will need to provide value equal to or better than competitors while working faster to maintain market share.

Given the common principles of the organizational models outlined in the previous section, what new designs for management and leadership can we expect to see in the future? It is likely that "adhocracy" will become a dominant theme of leadership and management. Leaders will work to create organizations which are fluid, dynamic, and temporary. Institutions—and units within institutions—will change shape according to the demands of the market. A premium will be placed on decentralized structures that delegate decision-making responsibility to faculty and staff and reward entrepreneurial skills, risk-taking, and a commitment to experimentation and innovation. Streamlined units that stress teamwork and speed will be a centerpiece of the "new" management in colleges and universities. Leadership will be transformational and it will be provided by individuals who enjoy imagining directions and envisioning the future. Tomorrow's college and university leaders will move beyond conventional strategic planning, where endless analysis preceded action. They will focus on the core purposes of the institution and find ways to achieve ambitious goals.

If college and university leaders are to be successful in creating a new kind of organization, they will need to consider some or all of the following strategic actions:

- Identify enduring core values that provide a sense of critical purpose for the college.

- Determine what should and should not change about the college; distinguish between core values that provide *continuity* and operating practices that must *change* to maintain organizational vitality.

- Develop an organizational structure that increases speed by creating a small college "soul" in a big college body:

- flatten and decentralize the organization
- emphasize teamwork
- cultivate an "owner mindset" in faculty and staff.
- Create *stretch* by striving for big gains without an idea of exactly how to achieve them:
    - seek to exceed rather than achieve a goal
    - do not establish a horizon for organizational performance
    - use teams comprised of instructors and staff to develop strategy.
- Break down boundaries and walls to innovation based on organizational structure and function; create a *boundaryless organization* by reconsidering the hierarchical and departmental structure of the college.
- Deepen the commitment of faculty and staff to the values, goals, and operating strategies of the institution by adopting an *open-book approach to management*:
    - all faculty and staff learn and understand the college's "financials," along with all other numbers that are critical for tracking organizational performance
    - faculty and staff learn that part of their job is to move performance indicators in the right direction
    - faculty and staff have a direct stake in the college's success by sharing resources and information.
- Prevent budgets from *minimalizing college and staff performance* by creating goals that: (a) stretch the organization through faculty and staff effort and (b) work outside traditional constraints because they are not attached directly to the operating budget.
- Develop *systems for planning* that maximally involve faculty and staff and use external sources of information to chart the future of the institution.
- Estimate the *organizational will* for change within the institution; a measure of the extent to which faculty and staff at all levels in the organization are interested in and committed to change.
- Determine the capacity for *collective action* in carrying out the process of change.

We conclude with an assignment for college and university leaders: Pick 10 to 15 faculty and administrators in your institution. Ask them one simple question: How will postsecondary education be different in the future? Do not tell them what you mean by "postsecondary education" or by the "future"—let them use their own definitions. Give them a week or a month, but insist on an answer that fits on one page.

When all of the results are in, perform several analyses. First, when they talk about the future, do they mean the next decade or next year? That is, what is their implicit degree of foresight? Institutions cannot create the markets of the future or build leadership in new competencies without a ten-year view. Second, determine whether their concept of postsecondary education is sufficiently broad and encompassing. Have they escaped the myopia of the current market definition so they understand how market boundaries are shifting? Third, do they agree on the most important changes? Without such a consensus, a college or university can pursue a whole range of competing agendas, spend lots of money on competing objectives, and never get to the future first. Fourth, would their answer surprise competitors? Are they competitively unique? Finally, can an action plan be distilled from their answers? Do they know what they will do differently this year, next year, and so on? Many colleges have a vague concept of the long term, and a lot of specifics and budget pressure in the near term-but nothing in between. The linking actions that get institutions from the near to the long term are missing.

Many leaders think of the short and long term as separate agendas, but, in reality, they are closely interwoven. Institutions cannot get to the long term in one big jump. The goal should be to understand what relatively small things they have to do this year that will have enormous implications for the future. Can institutions point to the five or six innovations—such as partnerships, or experiments with beneficiaries—that hold great portent for the future? These innovations should attract a disproportionate amount of leaders' attention. This attention is where leaders can add real value that distinguishes the institution from its competitors.

REFERENCES AND SELECTED READINGS

Alfred, Richard. 1995. *Transforming Community Colleges to Compete for the Future*. Ann Arbor, MI: Unpublished paper.

Argyris, Chris. 1977. Double Loop Learning Organizations. *Harvard Business Review* (September-October): 115–124.

Bartlett, Christopher and Ghoshal, Sumatra. 1995. Changing the Role of Top Management: Beyond Systems to People. *Harvard Business Review* 73(3) (May–June): 132–143.

Case, John. 1995. The Open-Book Revolution. *Inc.* (June): 26–43.

Collis, David and Montgomery, Cynthia. 1995. Competing on Resources: Strategy in the 1990's. *Harvard Business Review* 73(4) (July–August): 118–129.

Galbraith, John. 1994. *Competing with Flexible Lateral Organizations*, 2nd ed. Reading, MA: Addison-Wesley: 108–123.

Hamel, Gary and Prahalad, C. K. 1994. *Competing for the Future*. Boston: Harvard Business School: 220–231.

Nevis, Edwin; DiBella, Anthony; and Gould, Janet. 1995. Understanding Organizations as Learning Systems. *Sloan-Management Review* (Winter): 73–85.

Nonaka, I. 1991. The Knowledge-Creating Company. *Harvard Business Review* 69(6): 96–104.

Peters, Thomas, J. & Waterman, Robert, H., Jr. 1982. *In Search of Excellence: Lessons From America's Best Run Companies*. New York: Harper & Row.

Prahalad, C. K. and Hamel, Gary. 1990. The Core Competence of the Corporation. *Harvard Business Review* (May–June): 79–91.

Ross, Herbert and Kay, Michael. 1994. *Toppling the Pyramids: Redefining the Way Companies are Run*. New York: Times Books.

Schein, E. H. 1993. How Can Organizations Learn Faster? The Challenge of Entering the Green Room. *Sloan Management Review* (Winter): 85–92.

Semler, Ricardo. 1993. *Maverick*. New York: Warner Books.

Semler, Ricardo. 1994. Why My Former Employees Still Work for Me. *Harvard Business Review* (January-February) 94(1): 4–10.

Senge, Peter. 1990. *The Fifth Discipline*. New York: Doubleday.

Shook, Robert. 1988. *Honda: An American Success Story*. Englewood Cliffs, NJ: Prentice-Hall.

Tichy, Noel and Sherman, Strafford. 1993. *Control Your Destiny or Someone Else Will*. New York: Doubleday.

Treacy, Michael and Wiersema, Fred. 1995. *The Discipline of Market Leaders: Choose Your Customers, Narrow Your Focus, Dominate Your Market*. Reading, MA: Addison-Wesley.

Tully, Shawn. 1993. The Modular Corporation. *Fortune* (February 8): 21–22.

2

The Practitioner's Dilemma:
Understanding and Managing Change
in the Academic Institution

John S. Levin

College and university administrators have no easy chore. The pervasive call for planned change in the academic institution is resisted by the culture of the academy, a culture that is weighted heavily toward preservation and maintenance of the status quo, particularly the belief system of faculty and those administrators who moved from faculty ranks (Adams 1976; Dill 1982). Additionally, the very nature of managerial work has entrenched qualities such as decisiveness, action, and control that predispose managers to favor change, indeed to stimulate change and characterize environments as turbulent or dynamic (Crouch, Sinclair, and Hinte 1992; Mintzberg 1989, 1973). Yet the structure and patterns of managing in the modern organization require an approach that is both superficial in its understanding of organizational life and occasionally dysfunctional because of its insistence on control and the acquisition of power to maintain control (Mintzberg 1989).

Among the many views about managing organizational change in the academic institution, two strike the practitioner with experiential realism. The first is that confrontation with change and its companions, contradiction and ambiguity, is endemic to management (Quinn 1991). The second view is that the significance of change is socially constructed, invented, or fabricated by managers and organizational participants and based upon preexisting interpretations and understandings of organization (Crouch et al. 1992; Ferris, Fedor, and King 1994; Morgan 1986). Unfortunately, within organizations there may be no consensual meaning or understanding of organizational behaviors, thus change whether planned or unplanned may be accompanied by diverse and conflicting values, judgments, and interpretations (Bergquist 1992; Morgan 1986).

The dilemma for managers of the academic institution is that they are charged with responsibility for organizational action, yet the meaning and ultimately the values of action and its outcomes are subject to interpretation and dispute. Managing the academic institution in the 1990s is not a journey into the unknown, but it is a struggle not unlike jousting with windmills or opposing a dragon in mortal combat, or even facing demons within.

This chapter is based upon a review of research on managing change in academic organizations, with emphasis on administrative and management science literature and on higher education literature. The purpose here is to clarify concepts of the management of change in higher education and to identify not only forces of change but also approaches to the understanding of and coping with change. What are assumptions about the academic institution that may affect the understanding and management of change? How is organizational change conceived of in the academic institution? What are the forces of change that influence the academic institution? What are organizational responses to forces of change? And, how could the management of organizational change be reconceived and practiced differently in order to enable higher education institutions to survive and even improve in their functioning?

Scholars and practitioners for over a decade now have claimed that a management revolution is under way not only in business and industry but also in higher education. To what extent is this claim compatible or at odds with several important assumptions about higher education institutions? For example, the collegial concept of the academic institution that portrays academic institutions as academic communities, with self-governing scholars, is under attack not only as the role of faculty becomes more entrepreneurial but also as relationships among faculty change as increased competition for scarce resources exacerbates collegial and even civilized relations. On the one hand, the assumption of self-governing scholars suggests that administrators or managers are superfluous; on the other hand, changes in expectations for faculty and consequent behaviors suggest that management has a strategic and critical role to play in the academy, particularly in guiding and managing faculty behaviors.

THE PROBLEMATIC CONDITION OF MANAGING THE ACADEMIC INSTITUTION

While the role of management in higher education is firmly, even complacently, grounded in formal arrangements and normative expectations, the act of managing these institutions is a problematic activity. This conundrum arises from several conditions. First, assumptions about the academic institution are numerous, varied, inconsistent, and sometimes incompatible. Second, concepts of managing the academic institution are in large part contradictory. (Academic institutions refer to postsecondary educational institutions generally known as colleges and universities. This reference applies to four-year colleges and universities and in part to community colleges, but not to two-year technical or vocational institutions.) Third, recent understandings of organization, particularly influenced by postmodernism, have thrown into question not only management practices but also definitions of organization. Finally, in spite of a considerable body of literature on the management and administration of the academy, there are few empirical investigations of managerial behaviors and actions, and thus little real guidance for practitioners.

Assumptions About the Academic Institution

The problematic activity of managing the academic institution has its roots in assumptions about the academic institution. Inconsistency and incompatibility characterize the many assumptions made, held, and articulated about the academic institution. Central to these assumptions are primary values involving institutional purpose, institutional culture, and organizational practices. These values are illustrated as a set of propositions (A):

1. Academic institutions are academic communities, comprised of professionals committed to a set of common beliefs.
2. The primary purposes of the academic institution include research, teaching, and service, with some sectors of higher education more devoted to one component than another.
3. Academic institutions are distinctive organizations, with unique cultures and features.

These propositions assume that the academic institution is populated by self-governing scholars (Keller 1983) and are relatively stable as a result of its routines (Birnbaum 1992). Collective decision making, the autonomy of professors over teaching and research, and standardization of skills and knowledge in the disciplines (Hardy et al. 1984) suggest characteristics of a college (Bergquist 1992) where individual professors maintain control over several domains and where there is considerable continuity, even predictability. Whereas institutional goals may favor teaching, these goals are loosely coupled to actual performance (Weick 1976, 1–19). Ambiguity of purpose, not rationality, characterizes the academic institution, setting it apart from other organizations, such as businesses (Baldridge et al. 1978, 2–25; Riley and Baldridge 1978; Clark 1987).

While these propositions are not the only ones, they are central to the structure of beliefs, or mythology, which surround the academic institution.

Yet, for each of these propositions, there are counterpropositions (B), antithetical views that are either contradictory to or incompatible with, or both, the propositions (A) which reflect academic values and beliefs:

1. The purpose of the academic institution is to:
    a. reproduce social structure;
    b. indoctrinate students in the values of the dominant class;
    c. serve as an instrument of the economy by
        i. providing a trained workforce,
        ii. producing technology and intellectual property for commercial purposes; and,
    d. cool-out college-age students, relieve pressure upon the workforce, and reduce levels of unemployment.
2. Academic institutions are highly political environments, characterized by conflicts in values, purposes, and organizational operations. Individual interest groups compete for the acquisition of resources, for status, for recognition, for control, and for individual and group survival.
3. Organizational research and theory apply to the academic institution; the academic institution is not a unique organization.

These counterpropositions reframe and redefine commonly articulated beliefs about the academic institution, beliefs that may guide organizational behaviors and institutional actions. From a critical theorist perspective, the academic institution is not what its missions claim it to be, but an instrument of larger political and economic forces. They are instruments of domination (Morgan 1986) that have become socially acceptable because they fulfill the purposes of dominant classes or economic elites or political power structures. They are not the collegian of scholars who seek knowledge and truth. Academic institutions are tribal (Hazard 1976) political institutions (Baldridge et al. 1978), where a negotiating culture (Bergquist 1992) prevails. They are not unlike other organizations, and organizational theories, such as the life-cycle theory and the theory of population ecology (Cameron 1984, 122–144), which apply and illuminate organizational behaviors.

These propositions and counterpropositions comprise conflicting assumptions about the academic institution. Their presence suggests that understanding and indeed managing the academic institution is a complex activity.

Managing the Academic Institution

Throughout the 1960s, 1970s, and early 1980s, college and university administrations largely relied upon academic traditions and unobtrusive management practices to guide their institutions. Notwithstanding campus upheavals in the late 1960s and early 1970s, the myth of a community of scholars (Keller 1983; Goodman 1962) outlasted actual behaviors, and the myth was sustained until the 1980s. By the 1980s, there were appeals for and adoption of business and industrial management practices to cope with perceived change, externally (Schuster et al. 1994; Keller 1983). While the impetus for new practices was survival, the underlying motivation suggests a management revolution: the managers of the academy had the opportunity to gain dominance over the institution. The capturing of the academy was achieved through the technology of rationality: policies and procedures, planning, systems, coordinated action by an administrative team, as well as the growth of administrative personnel, including not only administrators but also technical and support staff (Leslie and Rhoades 1995, 187–212; Schuster et al. 1994). The shift from a collegiate culture to a managerial or negotiating culture (Bergquist 1992) marks an alteration in the perceptions and beliefs of campus constituents, a change in the dominant worldview of the collective (Simsek and Louis 1994, 670–695).

The Social Construction of Reality

It is becoming widely acknowledged that organizations exist in part, even in large part, in the minds of their members and to a lesser extent in the perceptions of external stakeholders. That is, interpretations are made of organizational behaviors and actions and meaning is attached to organizational life (Ferris et al. 1994; Morgan 1986). Organizations are social realities, and this applies as well to universities and colleges.

Managing the academic institution is the act of explaining, rationalizing, and legitimizing organizational behaviors and actions (Pfeffer 1981, 1–52). Yale University management explains that graduate students who assist in the instruction of undergraduate education are not employees of the university, but instead students. Thus, because they are not employees they cannot be permitted to form a union, which is a legal entity to represent the interests of employees (*Chronicle of Higher Education*, April 21, 1995). The University of California, Los Angeles (UCLA), adopts an admission practice that attempts to equalize opportunities for applicants. The practice gives preference to minority students over nonminority students in the selection of a small category of 3.5 grade point average (GPA) students admitted from high school (*Chronicle of Higher Education*, April 28, 1995). The rationale is that without preferential treatment, minority students would all but disappear at UCLA, in that with a 4.0 high school GPA as the entrance norm, fewer than 2% of minority applicants could compete with nonminorities. The absence of minorities at a public university in California, a state with a large minority population, is viewed as a travesty by university administration. Finally, the rationale for the growth of administration in public universities is attributed to the increase in accountability and legal requirements (Leslie and Rhoades 1995) such as the Americans with Disabilities Act (ADA). Administrative growth is justified as unavoidable, even at the expense of academic employees. While there are reasons for administrative enlargement, the justifications are impositions of meaning, a substitution of one reality, or system of beliefs, for another. Reality in the 1980s and 1990s has been reconstructed, more along the lines of a managerial culture (Bergquist 1992) than ever before, and managing the institution has become management's problem. The paradox of a managerial culture is that managers are largely alone, in a closed system (Mintzberg 1983) that copes on behalf of the entire institution with survival and growth.

THE MANAGEMENT OF CHANGE

Management theory contains two dichotomous themes. One is that both its history and the history of management are characterized by the theme of control. The second is that the theme of duality pervades management literature. This duality is also focused upon control and pertains to the extent to which managers have the ability to direct, change, lead, and control their organizations (Pfeffer 1981). At one extreme, managers are viewed as directing, leading, and controlling their organizations, using current technology—for example, methods of scientific management, human development, or strategic planning. At the other extreme, managers are more custodial and have little or no influence or control over organizational behaviors and actions (Cameron 1984).

Control

Self-efficacy is believed to be connected to performance: strong belief in one's abilities to exercise control over situations and events enables one to fulfill goals and intentions (Bandura 1988, 275–302). Political perspectives and analysis of management behaviors emphasize control as both a means and an end (Ferris et al. 1994).

Ironically, organizations and organizational behaviors are not fully controllable (Mintzberg 1994), no matter how self-efficacious an organization's managers. Efforts to control organizations, such as strategic planning, which was highly acclaimed in the 1980s (Keller 1983), are futile (Mintzberg 1994, 1989). Instability within the organization and turbulence without have been viewed as characteristics of an organization that is out of control, unmanageable, and therefore in decline (Keller 1983). But the concepts of organizational instability and environmental turbulence are perhaps nothing more than fictions, used to justify control (Mintzberg 1989). Turbulence can be seen as a chimera, the monster of classical myth (Crouch et al. 1992), and managerial behaviors to control turbulence as methods to exert control over organizations. Turbulence in the environment is portrayed by managers, and because turbulence is both unpleasant (Crouch et al. 1992) and a threat to organizational stability (Bolman and Deal 1985; Hardy et al. 1984) managerial action to help stabilize the organization—through control—is justified (Ferris et al. 1994).

Duality of Management

The second theme—the duality of management influence and control—flows logically from the fiction of control. Management literature reflects a conflict between organizations as instruments of internal direction, rational planning, and leadership, and organizations as conditions of a variety of forces, mostly external. While both champions of leadership theories and leadership prescriptions and rational and strategic planners favor the view that organizations can be directed, particularly by managers, recent scholarship on organizational performance and organizational change throws this view into question. The figment of external turbulence and the malevolent drive for organizational control once acknowledged as empirical realities undercut pristine views of transformational leadership and rational planning. If organizations are in fact directed by internal managers, this may be a result of false premises held by organizational members as well as stakeholders about both the purposes of the organization and the relationship of the organization to its environment. Furthermore, in order to control an organization, managers must make it, and make it seem like, a machine (Mintzberg 1994, 1989; Morgan 1986). As a machine, an organization loses its human qualities and is limited in its functioning (Morgan 1986). In other words, managers who direct and control organizations may not be fulfilling the organizational mission and may have altered organizational goals. Indeed, such a narrow approach to an organization, through exercising of control and perceiving the organization as machinelike, may lead to ineffective management and dysfunctional organizations.

This dilemma of control—both the fictions upon which control is based and the outcomes of control—is exaggerated in the academic organization. Like human service organizations (Hasenfield 1983) academic institutions are characterized by loose-coupling (Weick 1976) where goals and actions are not tightly connected. This suggests that control strategies such as rational planning, the use of logic, and formalized procedures are not likely to be effective in the academic institution.

Change in the Academic Institution

The impact of major forces, largely external, constitutes the primary focus of examinations of organizational change for the academic institution. Keller (1983) identifies several of these, including changing student profiles (that is, diminishing 18–24 year olds, greater ethnic diversity), increased competitiveness with the higher education sector, the growth of electronic technology, the grip of external controls and regulations, and internally a "disintegrating" curriculum as a result of specialized training to meet external demands and aging faculty. Vaill (see Schuster et al. 1994) a decade later provides a slightly longer list, but one that is compatible with Keller's. Vaill sees a number of forces pressing in upon higher education, including public resources limitations and rethinking of financing higher education, the assessment movement which demands results in learning, efforts to elevate the importance of undergraduate education, struggles for curriculum reform (that is, greater or lesser inclusivity and greater or less reliance upon European traditions and worldviews), demand for new faculty, expectations for higher education to provide an internationally competitive workforce, the need for rehabilitation for the physical plant, pressure to diversify, escalating specialization of scholarship that affects publishing and libraries, government regulations requiring costly compliance, and the explosion of technology, which promises to transform teaching and learning. Schuster et al. (1994) add to the lists of pressures acting upon higher education the demands from internal organizational constituents to expand employee participation in institutional actions through greater decentralization of decision making. The implications of these forces and pressures are daunting.

Leadership

To cope with forces of organizational change as well as to initiate and direct needed institutional alterations, leadership is called for by numerous scholars and observers. Organizational problems and solutions are consequently framed by concepts of leadership. Simsek and Louis (1994) conclude in their study of organizational change at the University of Minnesota that the worldview of organizational members can be altered by leadership strategies that serve to interpret organizational values and meanings. Schuster et al. (1994) conclude that institutional leaders are constrained by forces acting upon the institution and that new administrative-faculty governance and planning structures need to be adopted to provide institutional leadership. A number of scholars have appealed for institutional leadership that is shared (Birnbaum 1992) symbolic (Bensimon, Neumann, and Birnbaum 1989), cultural (Chaffee and Tierney 1988), and team-oriented (Neumann and Bensimon 1993). Others suggest that more businesslike approaches to leadership are required (Keller 1983).

While there are many appeals for a particular brand of leadership to rescue and steer higher education institutions, few seem to be based upon empirical investigations of observed managerial behaviors. What managers say they do, and even what others will admit to saying what managers do, is not necessarily congruent with actual behaviors. Theory and scholarship seem to lag behind practice (Sergiovanni 1992), and claims of transformational leadership in higher education institutions (Roueche, Baker, and Rose 1989) are quickly juxtaposed to leadership failures (Cooper and Kempner 1991). Acclaimed approaches such as leadership teams (Neumann and Bensimon 1993), while attractive, are not convincing and suggest a repackaging of the single authority figure as a multiple one. Even the proposal to lessen the emphasis of the authority role of the chief executive officer through the use of terms such as steward or facilitator does not alter the reliance upon traditional or modern approaches to organization, upon which conceptions and practices of leadership are based. Whether the organization is conceived of as a machine, an organism, a political system, or collegian, or even a cybernetic system (Birnbaum 1992; Morgan 1986; Bolman and Deal 1985; Baldridge et al. 1978), leadership is a phenomenon assumed to come from the apex of some hierarchy. Organizational theory since its inception has its basis in hierarchical structures with explicit or implicit leadership, formal or informal, combining a relationship between leaders and followers.

In the academic institution, as well, the concept of leadership accompanies a construct of leader and followers, whether formal or informal leadership. This structure is antithetical to many values of the academy. These values, which include scientific and scholarly criticism and even skepticism, while not necessarily practiced, create tensions between concepts and practices of leadership. Authority in academe is not found in personalities or roles, but rather in scholarship, based upon research, evidence, empirical data, and argumentation.

Leadership in the academy cannot be embraced on a professional level. If senior administrators, for example, claim that undergraduate education is in need of revamping, professors will demand palpable evidence of the deteriorated or inadequate condition of undergraduate education before their minds and hearts can embrace the claims. This condition is no doubt explanation for the plethora of task forces and committees on campuses—an effort to legitimize through seemingly scholarly discourse actions. But followership is not a simple transaction, and transformation, especially of the curriculum, the domain of faculty (Hardy et al. 1984), is not common in the academy. Kuhn's (1962) notion of paradigm creation in science—a once or twice in the millennium phenomenon—is an apt characterization of conditions in the academy. Leadership as conceived of in organizational theory and as described in higher educational literature is not part of the paradigm of academics. The call for leadership, then, to rescue the academy from external forces and to give direction to higher education institutions during turbulent times cannot be answered satisfactorily. While the concept of organization as traditionally viewed possesses an inherent imperative for the presence of leaders and followers, the academic institution as a culture or a conglomerate of subcultures embodies a different imperative, which includes the preservation of culture, the pursuit of knowledge, and the maintenance of autonomy.

As Dill (1982) and other scholars have noted, the academy is at least two entities or organizations: one is an academic community, comprised of professionals who share a set of beliefs, including the meaning of authority. The other is an institution managed by rational processes such as personnel and financial management, as well as rationalized decision-making structures and formal approaches to goal-setting. As organizations grow, these two entities become more distinct and organizational actions become isolated and disconnected (Dill, 1984, 69–99). Indeed, in the 1990s, the observation is made for large public universities that the primary change for the academy is the alteration of relations among individuals (Leslie, Rhoades, and Slaughter 1995). This suggests fragmentation and alienation within the academy as academic management is detached from academic life, except perhaps at the department level.

Postmodern Organizations

The disconnected condition of the academic institution—where decisions and actions in one part, or at one level, of the institution are isolated from and unharmonized with decisions and actions in other parts or levels—suggests a breakdown if not in organizational functioning then in shared meanings about the realities of organizational life. It is not so much that reality in the academic institution is not what it used to be (Anderson 1990), but that reality is a challenge to locate beyond its symbols and verbal constructions. While a breakdown of established and accepted practices of the higher education institution was noted in the 1980s (Keller 1983; Dill 1982), not until the 1990s did the theater of postmodern thought play at colleges and universities.

If we step back to observe the academic institution, we can recognize not only a conflict between one faction and another over ownership and authority, but also a struggle about definition and identity. If postmodern implies that the values, assumptions, and workings of the modern are obsolete (Bergquist 1993; Anderson 1990), then even to conceive of colleges and universities as postmodern organizations is to rob them of their identities and to deny them their label "academic." Furthermore, if postmodernism has applicability to higher education, then traditional concepts of change applied to organizations are also obsolete (Anderson 1990).

Within the postmodern framework, organizational change is conceived of as largely definitional: alteration of organizational boundaries, externally, between an organization and its environment and between an organization and other organizations; and internally, by its mission and purpose (Bergquist 1993). Change occurs at the boundaries of definitions involving relationships between entities and within an entity. While the postmodern organization is characterized as having loose, unclear boundaries and clear missions, change in the postmodern organization at the boundaries is frequent and expected; change in mission suggests a transformation, the creation of a new organization. These attributes are the opposite in a modern organization, where boundaries are clear and mission is vague or ambiguous (Bergquist 1993). Higher education institutions, particularly four-year colleges and universities, seem to be making the transition from modern organizations to postmodern organizations as they become less bounded internally as well as externally and more focused in their missions.

THE PRACTITIONER'S DILEMMA

Where does the conception of postmodernism leave the practitioner, especially given the condition of the academic institution as an organization that may be in transition between the modern and postmodern? With authority contested and with reality itself defined as a human or social construction, the nature of managerial work (Mintzberg 1973) has surely altered. Those managers who have failed to acknowledge that what has changed most about the academic institution is how they need to be managed are likely those moving these institutions toward more hierarchical and corporate forms of decision making (Schuster et al. 1994). Coping mechanisms for these managers, include the trying out of approaches borrowed from the corporate sector, such as quality improvement models; others include redefinitions of institutional purpose to meet the expectations of external stakeholders, such as emphasis upon curriculum reform to improve graduation rates or workplace skills. Still others include mechanisms for increasing employee participation in decision making (Schuster et al. 1994).

In spite of improvement initiatives and coping efforts, the management of higher education in the 1980s and 1990s, like that of business organizations, has become more controlling and repressive (Bergquist 1993). The management revolution proclaimed by scholars (Schuster et al. 1994) is more an effort to control the academy. Consequently, there is little management of those conditions that characterize the postmodern organization, such as disconnectedness, alienation, and fragmentation; few efforts to preserve what was modern about the academy—its belief systems, for example; and little guidance or succor for individuals and groups coping with change during the transition from modern to postmodern. In short, managers are not managing change, rather they are creating it.

The dilemma for practitioners is how to manage without causing damage: like the physician's dictum of do no harm. Or, the dilemma is how to use power positively (Fullan 1991). First, the practitioner needs to understand how the organization works, how it becomes dysfunctional, and why conventional approaches to management have affected organizations negatively (Mintzberg 1989). The practitioner needs to accept that organizational behaviors are not controllable and that organizational reality is a social construction. Old methods such as negative, personal politics, monolithic solutions, grand-scale innovations, and managerial isolation (Fullan 1991) are what need to change. Recognition of differences in organizational cultures, in organizational forms, and in situations might indicate that organizations are not only socially constructed but also environments that need to be infused with human spirit (Mintzberg 1989) and managed through intimate, not superficial, knowledge as well in accord with the values and beliefs of its members. The supreme dilemma for the practitioner is how to adjust to changing conditions and yet preserve institutional and individual values.

There are no recipes and no prescriptions that will suffice to aid the practitioner in managing change. But, understanding the institution as a human environment might enable practitioners to be ready to manage change.

REFERENCES

Adams, Hazard. 1976. *The Academic Tribes*. New York: Liveright.

Anderson, Walter. 1990. *Reality Isn't What It Used To Be*. San Francisco: Harper & Row.

Baldridge, J. Victor; Curtis, David; Ecker, George; and Riley, Gary. 1978. Alternative Models of Governance in Higher Education. In Gary Riley and J. Victor Baldridge, eds., *Governing Academic Organizations*, 2–25. Berkeley: McCutchan.

Bandura, A. 1988 Social Cognitive Theory. *Australian Journal of Management* 13, 275–302.

Bensimon, Estella; Neumann, Anna; and Birnbaum, Robert. 1989. *Making Sense of Administrative Leadership*. Washington, DC: George Washington University.

Bergquist, William. 1992. *The Post Modern Organization: Mastering the Art of Irreversible Change*. San Francisco: Jossey-Bass.

Bergquist, William. 1993. *The Four Cultures of the Academy*. San Francisco: Jossey-Bass.

Birnbaum, Robert. 1992. *How Academic Leadership Works*. San Francisco: Jossey-Bass.

Bolman, Lee and Deal, Terrence. 1985. *Modern Approaches to Understanding and Managing Organizations*. San Francisco: Jossey-Bass.

Cameron, Kim. 1984. Organizational Adaptation and Higher Education. *The Journal of Higher Education* 55, 122–144.

Chaffee, Ellen and Tierney, William. 1988. *Collegiate Culture and Leadership Strategies*. New York: American Council on Education and Macmillan.

Chronicle of Higher Education, April 21, 1995; and April 28, 1995.

Clark, Burton. 1987. *The Academic Life: Small Worlds, Different Worlds*. Princeton, NJ: The Carnegie Foundation for the Advancement of Teaching.

Cooper, Joanne and Kempner, Ken. 1991. Lord of the Flies Community College: A Case Study of Organizational Disintegration. Paper Presented at the annual meeting of the Association for the Study of Higher Education, Boston.

Crouch, Andrew; Sinclair, Amanda; and Hintz, Phillip. 1992. Myths of Managing Change. In Dian Marie Hosking and Neil Anderson, eds, *Organizational Change and Innovation: Psychological Perspectives and Practices in Europe*, 23–48. New York: Routledge.

Dill, David. 1982. The Management of Academic Culture: Notes on the Management of Meaning and Social Integration. *Higher Education* (11 May); 303–320.

Dill, David. 1984. The Nature of Administrative Behavior in Higher Education. *Educational Administration Quarterly* 20: 69–99.

Ferris, Gerald; Fedor, Donald; and King, Thomas. 1994. A Political Conceptualization of Managerial Behavior. *Human Resource Management Review* 4: 1–34.

Fullan, Michael. 1991. *The New Meaning of Educational Change*. New York: Teachers College, Columbia University and the Ontario Institute for Studies in Education.

Goodman, Paul. 1962. *The Community of Scholars*. New York: Random House.

Hardy, Cynthia; Langley, A; Mintzberg, H; and Rose, J. 1984. Strategy Formation in the University Setting. In James Bess, ed., *College and University Organization: Insights from the Behavioral Sciences*. New York: New York University Press.

Hasenfield, Yeheskel. 1983. *Human Service Organizations*. Englewood Cliffs, NJ: Prentice-Hall.

Keller, George. 1983. *Academic Strategy: The Management Revolution in American Higher Education*. Baltimore: The Johns Hopkins University Press.

Kuhn, Thomas. 1962. *The Structure of Scientific Revolutions*. Chicago: University of Chicago Press.

Leslie, Larry and Rhoades, Gary; 1995. Rising Administrative Costs: Seeking Explanations. *The Journal of Higher Education* 66 (March/April): 187–212.

Leslie, Larry; Rhoades, Gary; and Slaughter, Sheila. 1995. *The Changing Nature of Academic Labor*. Baltimore: The Johns Hopkins University Press.

Mintzberg, Henry. 1973. *The Nature of Managerial Work*. New York: Harper & Row.

Mintzberg, Henry. 1983. *Power in and Around Organizations*. Englewood Cliffs, NJ: Prentice-Hall.

Mintzberg, Henry. 1989. *Mintzberg on Management: Inside our Strange World of Organizations*. New York: The Free Press.

Mintzberg, Henry. 1994. *The Rise and Fall of Strategic Planning*. New York: The Free Press.

Morgan, Gareth. 1986. *Images of Organization*. Beverly Hills, CA: Sage.

Neumann, Anna and Bensimon, Estela. 1993. *Redesigning Collegiate Leadership*. Baltimore: The Johns Hopkins University Press.

Pfeffer, Jeffrey. 1981. Management as Symbolic Action: The Creation of Maintenance of Organization Paradigms. *Research in Organizational Behavior* 3: 1–52.

Quinn, Robert. 1991. *Beyond Rational Management*. San Francisco: Jossey-Bass.

Riley, Gary and Baldridge, J. Victor. 1978. *Policy Making and Effective Leadership*. San Francisco: Jossey-Bass.

Roueche, John; Baker, George; and Rose, Robert. 1989. *Shared Vision*. Washington, DC: The Community College Press.

Schuster, Jack; Smith, D.; Corak, K.; and Yamada, M. 1994. *Strategic Governance: How to Make Big Decisions Better*. Phoenix: American Council on Education and Oryx Press.

Sergiovanni, Thomas. 1992 *Moral Leadership: Getting to the Heart of School Improvement*. San Francisco: Jossey-Bass.

Simsek, Hasan and Louis, Karen Seashore. 1994. Organizational Change as Paradigm Shift. *The Journal of Higher Education* 65; 670–695.

Weick, Karl. 1976. Educational Organizations as Loosely Coupled Systems. *Administrative Science Quarterly* 21: 1–19.

3

A Memorandum from Machiavelli on the Principled Use of Power in the Academy

Daniel J. Julius, J. Victor Baldridge, and Jeffrey Pfeffer

TO: Presidents, Senior Administrators, and Faculty Leaders Who Would Seek Change

FROM: Niccolo Machiavelli
Former Assistant to Presidents
University of the Medici

Permit me to take a brief moment of your valuable time to introduce myself. I served for years as special assistant to kings, dukes, generals, several popes and, as well, numerous presidents, senior executives, and faculty at the University of the Medici. I have significant domestic and international experience—for in this capacity, I have also worked with governors, state and national legislators, wealthy donors, foundations, public relations firms, religious societies, city and county officials, law enforcement agencies, and community activists. I have also coordinated activities with ministers of education throughout Europe.

I had the distinct pleasure of hearing your recent addresses to your Faculty Senates. You spoke of bold tomorrows, the need for change in your institutions, including the manner in which work is accomplished and evaluated. You discussed technology, distance learning, diversity, student services, the need for alternative criteria to evaluate faculty, new relationships with unions, funding, and student and alumni constituencies. You discussed how the role of the university, with the state, the city, and the federal government, will change. You cited emerging relationships with the business community and argued persuasively, in my opinion, that unless the academic establishment begins to refocus its priorities, the university, as it once existed, will lose the autonomy and freedom to offer sound educational programs.

I am in no position to quarrel with your premises. (I am unemployed at the moment.) I was impressed with your grasp of fundamental issues facing higher education. I am, however, curious as to how you will implement these new ideas. Since I have advised over one hundred senior executives and faculty on change and implementation strategies, I thought you might appreciate my observations. My comments are based on real experiences. They are offered to you as a gift, yours to keep or discard at your pleasure.

Parenthetically, I do not mean to be presumptuous or overbearing in this letter. University executives and faculty leaders are (on occasion) startled at my directness and characterization of the uses of power and influence. I understand you are gifted individuals and would not hold your positions and titles unless you possessed exemplary traits. Most intelligent people with whom I have worked appreciate candor. (Please ignore my biases though!) I do not want to sound as if I am sending you into an armed battle. Neither should we pretend, if you are serious about your ideals and goals, that people will simply adopt "your" new visions.

DECISION PROCESSES IN PROFESSIONAL ORGANIZATIONS: CONTEMPORARY REALITIES

The key to being effective and the ability to make change begin first with an accurate assessment of the type of organization in which you work. Second, you must appreciate how decisions are made and who, if anyone, implements them.

Universities and colleges have a number of unique characteristics. Fundamentally, they are people-processing organizations, and, in order to handle that complex and delicate task, they usually have large staffs of highly trained professionals. Since people cannot be divided into segmentalized tasks in the same way that physical products can, professionals with a high level of expertise are needed to deal holistically with clients' needs. Thus the first characteristic of academic organizations is that they are highly professionalized, client-serving systems.

Second, "people-processing" organizations have extremely ambiguous goals, and a list of legitimate activities for a university is extremely long. Because goals are often unclear, almost any activity that serves a "client" may be considered legitimate. While many activities can be considered legitimate, many are also questioned. This is important for understanding change processes. If a college or university does not know its specific objectives, then an individual with an idea (and the energy) can often bend the institution in his or her direction. Ambiguity and contest over goals pave the way for the skillful politician.

Finally, colleges and universities are extremely vulnerable to outside pressures. Since the clients themselves—students—are relatively powerless, society generally demands accountability from the organization. As a consequence, outsiders demand the right to influence internal decisions. Be assured, however, that the public's success varies considerably: in school systems, outside voices are often influential; in hospitals or legal firms, the organization has generally listened with deaf ears.

CHARACTERISTICS OF THE DECISION-MAKING PROCESS

You operate in an unusual kind of organization. It is one that serves clients, has a highly professionalized staff, has unclear and contested goals, and is subject to much external pressure. The decision-making process can be characterized by the following:

Decision is by committee. Since expertise, not hierarchical office, is the organizing principle, then committees of experts decide many of the critical issues.

Fluid participation. Many of the decision makers are amateurs, engaged in pursuing their professions, not in making decisions. As a consequence, they wander in and out of the decision process, and power belongs to those who stay long enough to exercise it.

An issue carousel. Issues have a way of always coming around again. Decisions do not last long because pressure from outside groups, from clients, and from other professionals push the same or similar issues full circle. Decisions are not made as much as they are pinned down temporarily.

A "subsidiary" process. The longer it takes to make a decision, the greater the number of issues that are piled onto the original subject. People, hoping to accomplish several things at one time, burden simple decisions with countless subsidiary ones.

Conflict is common. Professional groups, clients, and outsiders support divergent interests in setting the ambiguous goals of academic organizations. As a consequence, conflict over goals is common as decision makers cope with the pressures from diverse interest groups.

How can I summarize? The image that captures the spirit of the decision process in an academic organization does not resemble a normal bureaucracy; nor does it look like the "community of peers" that is often associated with the medieval guild. Several images capture the spirit of the decision-making process. First, the structure of the organization is fluid, can be challenged, and is highly political. Second, the decision-making process reflects competing groups who often conflict. Finally, the unsettled character of the decision-making process can be captured by using the term *decision flowing* instead of decision making. Decision making has a finality to it; decision flowing sounds like a never-ending process that must continued in order to make outcomes really work.

CHANGE AND THE ABILITY TO MAKE IT

In the academic organization, seeking change, or accommodation to new trends, ideas, contexts, political or fiscal realities, is not for the faint-hearted. This is so particularly in your schools. At least in your cases, you will have some formal authority over internal constituents—but it is not formal authority in the real sense. As one ascends the organizational hierarchy in academic organizations, one has less and less real authority over anyone needed to get the job accomplished. Put another way, if you ever have to "invoke" your authority, you have, in effect, lost it. Success depends on managerial savvy coupled with moral and political persuasiveness.

Most in higher education believe "change" is laudable, but it remains difficult to manage. Some would say, we are busy reacting to change instead of being proactive. We even ask our search consultants to bring us candidates who can implement "change." In my experience, however, our colleagues in academe do not readily adopt new definitions of what is or is not important, or how work is accomplished or evaluated. (I suspect this may be attributable to the notion that professionals believe that what is good for them is also good for the student.) Everyone will sign on to the platitudes—the real work remains in the details of implementation; persuading; cajoling, and, in reality, making it impossible for others not to follow you; exercising power and influence in nonhierarchical and informal settings. This is the realm (implementation) where the truly successful and effective administrators flourish.

The truth of the matter is that anyone who seeks to transcend the status quo will be met with opposition. Those who can neutralize or overcome opposing constituencies (or individuals) will succeed. Most senior executives and faculty, however, cannot and, for that reason, do not succeed in changing the organization in a positive way (and so they relegate their efforts around the margins of the institution; ignoring or shying away from the difficult structural issues). Of course the worst-case scenario results when change is effectuated without accommodating careers and egos of others. There are numerous examples of "negative" or destructive changes.

RULES AND TACTICS FOR THE "CHANGE ORIENTED"

Rule #1: Integrity, Wisdom, Selflessness

A new vision cannot be successfully implemented unless the individual (you) motivating others to change is perceived to have the highest of values (e.g., integrity, sensitivity, selflessness, striving for the good of the organization). Creative organizational evolution will not occur unless your constituency perceives you to be sincere, honest, fair; one who understands the university, scholarship, and the role of other core constituents as well. (In the case of nontraditional executives or presidents, you will be judged on a different—higher—standard than would a more "traditional" person.) The one absolute I can offer is this: if the perception exists that you do not have integrity, wisdom, or selflessness, or this issue is effectively presented or manipulated in a negative way by an opposing constituency, you will lose your influence and ability to manage change in the organization. There are presidents, for example, who are president in title only. This is fine as long as the organizational goal does not entail implementation of a new vision. Within the context of this first rule, I would offer a word about your personal relationships and the importance of managing external constituencies.

Personal Relationships: Protect those individuals and allies who risk their professional standing and administrative careers for you. Many good efforts flounder because senior executives or faculty (who desire institutional transition and convince others to implement it) do not support these individuals when conflict emerges. If those who articulated change (on your behalf) are abandoned, few will trust you again. Professional administrators and colleagues are a pretty smart lot. They can make or break you! You must guard those individuals (and honor formal lines of authority—e.g., those who report to them). Reward the constituents who give you their support. However, while engaging in this action be very wary of your "open door" policy! Few messengers are without a personal agenda. Reward those who are. Never expel the messenger though. Utilize their services wisely. Cultivate informal channels of communication without undermining the reporting or political relationships of others. Moderate your "reaction" to information gained through informal networks. If those around you feel you overreact to "negative" information, they will funnel only "good" news and, like most leaders who encourage or tolerate only good news, your authority and influence will eventually fracture and vanish, probably while you are busily engaged in what you consider important (and others consider trivial—e.g., designing the alumni magazine or visiting facilities off-site).

External Constituencies: As I noted earlier, colleges and universities usually have strong external constituents who apply pressure to the decision-making process. The wise strategist uses support from these external constituencies to influence the internal process. In building coalitions, it is useful to associate with outside groups as well as inside groups, particularly since major decision makers themselves are often tied to outside groups. Insiders, with their limited view of the outsiders' role, naively overlook the political strategy of cultivating external allies. Legislators, trustees, parents, alumni, and foundations can help change universities. The potential power of external constituencies must never be neglected.

Rule #2: Build a Team

You will need a team. In this respect do not underestimate the value of loyalty as well as competency. New appointments will be important ones, particularly senior nonacademic appointments. Nonacademic administrators are crucial because without them, you cannot maintain your influence and run the institution effectively. Some academic types do not understand this. However, loss of confidence in your regime will come when your primary constituents (faculty, trustees, students, the public, academic administrators) feel: (1) they cannot trust university data; (2) think that student services or student-related issues are out of control; (3) perceive that a crisis (usually fiscal) exists on campus with personnel, auxiliary services, and such; (4) believe "funding" or "political" problems exist; (5) suspect that some senior advisors are out of control or incompetent.

Your agenda cannot be accomplished in the academic division alone. Good politicians know that much of their job is not influencing decisions as much as it is building a political base for influencing decisions. This means that a dedicated cadre of change agents must be formed, a committed group that exchanges ideas and reinforces each other's efforts. In addition, a strong change group needs equally strong links to those in viable political coalitions. In this respect, I should discuss the mechanics of building a team. This may entail making new appointments. Here is where many inexperienced administrators and faculty make fatal mistakes.

I advise that you break out of traditional recruitment and appointment processes. Be wary of a search committee's propensity to find the right people. Search committees often recommend those who are acceptable to the group (or those who may offend the fewest). Assembling a team requires you to resist strong pressures to appoint "traditional" individuals. Traditionalists are not often comfortable with nor do they usually understand how to manage "change" or "conflict." Go outside of the traditional realm. The appointment of excellent and supportive academic administrators will be a task to which you should devote attention. Do not assume a search committee will simply do what you ask. Check the details of "who" serves on the committee, the charge of the committee, and read the position description before the position is advertised. I would offer a word here about the concept of accountability.

Accountability: You must demand it. Unless there are consequences for "behavior," you cannot realize your objectives. Many in academe are not held accountable because much of what we do is not readily measurable (so it is difficult to determine success or failure). People who care more about popularity than being strong managers (or effectuating change) do not hold others accountable. (I have rarely witnessed a situation where a well-liked individual could remain on excellent terms with faculty and staff *and*, initiate change in the school, division, or college.) Nor can you succeed with administrators who are vindictive, territorial, jealous, too lax (classic symptoms of "powerlessness"), or those who sanction inappropriate behavior—for example, when the "wrong" people are promoted. Unfortunately, many in academe often do a less-than-stellar job of evaluating managerial and academic effectiveness. It is not realistic to believe that senior faculty or administrators can be held accountable in an environment where there is little or no agreement on performance objectives. Appoint self-motivated people, set goals, ask for benchmark measures of success, demand more than "acquiescence."

In summary, your senior teams must be provided with a positive emotional atmosphere; reward and encourage them in visible and immediate ways, express confidence, let them do their jobs, promote independence, initiative, and responsibility.

Rule #3: Concentrate Your Efforts

A basic mistake made by people interested in change is that they frequently squander their efforts by chasing too many rainbows. An effective political change agent, realizing that change is really difficult, concentrates efforts on only the important issues. Remember that in academe, most people do not care about all the issues. If you care enough to concentrate, you have enormous power to be effective. The frustration caused by the resistance offered by an immovable system is usually the result of scattered and dispersed efforts. If "fluid participation" is the rule, then most people wander in and out of the issue. If you stick with one or two critical issues, you are more likely to be effective. Make a list of priorities. Select the top three or four. Force yourself to ask the following questions in regard to these priorities:

- Who else is or will be influential as you endeavor to accomplish this priority?
- Whose cooperation and support will be needed?
- Whose opposition could delay or derail this action?
- In regard to those whose support is necessary or those who will oppose you, analyze:
    - What are the sources of their influence and authority?
    - Who will be more influential in the decision-making process?
    - Under what circumstances will (the) opposition coalesce?
    - Who will be affected by what you are trying to accomplish (e.g., effect on "their" power or status)?
- Ask which strategies and tactics will be the most appropriate given faculty and administrative support (or opposition) for the idea or action.
- Ask who will determine success or failure.

In this context, may I offer advice on the notion of *timing?* You must get a core constituency to agree upon priority objectives early in the game, and on measurable criteria for success. Following this, you should ensure that (someone) evaluates the effectiveness of actions against these measures. The sooner the process starts, the better. Academic organizations are tolerant of new presidents for short periods of time. They are, in a real sense, skeptical of anyone in a position of authority. The honeymoon will end quickly. Afterward, a bureaucracy (and your opponents) can destroy creativity. Do not, however, take on the whole community at once! Choose your priorities (your allies and your adversaries) carefully.

Remember also, after one year, your predecessors' problems (largely through "nonaction") become your problems. Be a visionary and a missionary to constituents who object to your goals or who have power to block new initiatives. Understand where those constituencies derive their status and support.

Rule #4: Know When to Engage Conflict

To concentrate is to choose a few issues, and a tactical genius knows which ones to choose. Most of the time, it makes sense to support issues when you know you can be effective. If it is obvious that you will lose, wait. Remember, with the "issue carousel," the situation will probably return, allowing you time to master your resources for the next battle. There are exceptions to the "fight to win" rule. Sometimes it is wise to engage confrontation because the moral issue is great, or because it is possible to make future martyrs. We do not always fight to win today; sometimes we fight today so that we can win tomorrow. Most of the time, however, the rule is to choose issues with high payoff.

The sophisticated and astute observer can usually tell the difference between who is effective and who is not. A word here about conflict in the academic environment. Don't avoid it, manage it. Many presidents and senior executives fail to grasp this. Redirecting the priorities, possibilities, and, if you will, the mission of a university requires organizational tension. Very simply put, you must convince your core constituencies to support (and buy into) new ways of conceiving and evaluating work and, perhaps, new educational or process outcomes (e.g., new relationships with unions or other core constituencies). This will require those who are "secure" with the current mission, or comfortable with present priorities and outcomes, to change. Change can evolve peacefully to be sure. However, when it is necessary to "redirect" institutional priorities, change is more often associated with conflict primarily because folks have a vested interest in the way work is accomplished now.

Remember that your institutions are places wedded to their "traditions." This cultural trait will manifest itself, cloaked in the argument that "we never did it that way here," or those who oppose you will hear in your words, "he (or she) doesn't value my (our) work." Managing this kind of conflict successfully requires that you:

- Encourage opposing constituencies to choose a course of action early in the game.
- Offer real alternatives for those who oppose you.
- Advance the notion of "mutual interests" rather than focusing on the positions of those who disagree.
- Act decisively, act soon, and act in a determined manner.
- If you feel senior administrators will not be supportive, find another place for them soon. You are probably not going to win them over and you will not succeed as long as they hold their positions.
- Have a strategic plan and stay to it. Pay attention to detail. Develop measurable criteria for success. Remember that most academic folks are trained to make a critical analysis but are not trained to implement decisions. People need guidance and supervision.
- You must love the academic soul. But remember, faculty, as a group, will complain. Offer them some cheese with their whine.
- Find the right incentives. Do not assume others will follow you simply because you are right. People will embrace your vision when your ideas provide them with (intrinsic/extrinsic) rewards.
- How you go about managing conflicting interests and personalities may be almost as important as what you actually do. Be very humane and civil.
- Once a constituency (or an individual) is neutralized or won over, allow for face saving; but do not be obsequious to those who opposed you.
- Declare your program a success; find small successes to celebrate along the way.
- Utilize (rely) on external pressures to encourage internal change. Redirect and manage those pressures. Force convergence of internal and external policy.
- Be wary of showing weakness. Do not readily admit you do not know something. Few are sanguine about following a person who has never "been there" before.
- Colleges and universities are organizations with low tolerance for conflict. Use this resource wisely.

Rule #5: Learn the History

Every issue has roots deep in the past. The issue carousel has trotted it past several times before. Consequently, the wise tactician searches for the historical bases of an issue. When was it around before? Who took what position? Who won? Who lost? Knowing the history can reveal which coalitions fight together and which tactics prove useful—information that helps in planning strategy. Under most circumstances, the person who is historically naive about the issue is not effective.

A word here about two issues related to "history." The first concerns the use of data and research and the second involves policy convergence.

Data/Research: Many ideas go awry because the data and/or research underpinning these issues can be criticized or, worse, are faulty. Just as there is nothing so good as good theory, there is no substitute for well-conceived and adequately presented institutional research. Be sure your opinions and ideas are based on solid assumptions and that they are defensible. Once anyone demolishes the basis of your (informational or research) objectives, you will lose your influence. In the academic milieu, if people cannot trust your data, they will not trust you.

Policy Convergence: Unless institutional policies and procedures reflect new visions and priorities, you cannot succeed. Policies and procedures form the basis upon which others act and, through implementation of policy, how others are evaluated. Once you articulate a new direction, institutional policies must conform to them. A "vision" cannot overcome policy, which in itself may serve as a disincentive. Take the example of "fiscal prudence." A seemingly harmless policy, which requires returning unused funds to a central account, may undermine this idea. Policies such as these sometimes work as an incentive for an administrator or faculty member to spend funds unwisely or "hide" accounts in an effort to circumvent the policy. (Of course, those who hide moneys will do so for the best of academic reasons!)

The policy criteria upon which people are evaluated will determine, to a large extent, their behavior and priorities. For example, you must endeavor to modify standards for promotion and tenure if you want to redirect the academic priorities of faculty. (No mean feat!) Making even small changes in this realm will require agreement and assistance of deans and department chairpersons. Redirection will come, ultimately, only if new criteria are related to outcomes that the "academic establishment" can support. In this respect, new priorities can be engineered if they are not seen as "imposed" but come as a product of mutual agreement. I am not suggesting this be done in all disciplines, but it must be attempted for some, as I understood your goals.

Rule #6: Strategic Planning

Your goals cannot be realized without strategic plans. Everyone knows this. However, what many do not do is demand answers to the "right questions" in their plans. Review key priorities and concomitant strategic planning issues with your senior teams. Next, force the teams to address the following:

• Have you defined short-term and long-term objectives?
• Is a strategy adequately developed?

- Identify the key assumptions underlying your strategy. What evidence are you relying on to ensure assumptions are valid?
- Is the action plan feasible given the constraints and opportunities inherent in the situation?
- Is the action plan realistic given your sources of power?
- Has the impact of the action plan been assessed? (Is the plan ethical, will it benefit the institution?)
  - Are you cognizant of trade-offs, or who will be directly and indirectly affected by your plan?
  - Were the risks of the plan analyzed?
- Were all contingencies planned for?
- Are mechanisms in place to ensure the plan is periodically evaluated?
  - Can the plan be modified?
- Have you assessed the timing and sequence of decisions?
  - Differentiate between urgent and less important matters.
  - Does the plan contain incremental steps?
  - Do early steps preclude future alternatives?
- Will you be able to reflect on and communicate successes or failures with overarching plan objectives?

I have known of administrators who manage the development of elaborate plans (or "mission" statements) but fail to understand that unless these statements revolutionize the nature in which work is accomplished, or the actual behavior of individuals responsible for merging fiscal and academic priorities, these documents will remain abstract concepts. Implementing a strategic plan requires closure on the following issues and actions (basic, yet essential):

- Assuming the identification of participants, accountability matters, institutional goals and objectives, and the timing and sequence of implementation,
  - How will new initiatives or programs be introduced in different functional units?
  - How will you approach the management of organizational resistance?
  - What resources will be required?
  - Who will coordinate the plan?
  - How will everyone know when the plan becomes an integral part of the values and mission of the organization?
  - What steps must be taken in each organizational unit to reflect integration in the way decisions are made, relationships are maintained, and services are provided?

- How will the organization (you) respond to any decrease in the will to sustain implementation of the plan? What is the appropriate response to loss of motivation and support? What is the minimum support needed in order to proceed?

- Assuming the plan will enhance the function, efficiency, and productivity of others,

  - What actions need to be taken to inform the organization of the plan and its purpose?

  - What will be the actual impact of the plan on people, functions, and the like? How will you know when everyone have possessed requisite knowledge and skills?

  - How will the consequences of the plan be identified and assessed?

  - What behavioral and process changes are expected of employees?

- Assuming the plan will result in development of new standards of productivity, compensation, performance, or evaluation (to reflect desired changes or mitigate unacceptable actions or reactions),

  - How will the organization demonstrate the value of the plan? Will it connect to performance and productivity?

  - At what point in the process are individuals and units expected to adopt new behaviors?

  - What behaviors and achievements should be acknowledged and rewarded?

  - How will formal and informal rewards be managed? Care should be taken to prevent the process of acknowledging and rewarding from being misinterpreted by others in the organization. (Always one of the challenges posed by compensation systems which purport to reward—competence and merit.)

- Assuming the plan will measure the quality and quantity of change,

  - What information is needed? How will this information be acquired to determine the quality of changes?

  - How will "change" be reviewed and quantified to insure continual movement toward desired goals?

  - What are the agreed upon elements, functions, and services considered most important to the success of the plan? How will they be measured?

  - Will it be known that benchmarks have been met?

  - Will alternate strategies or assessments of benchmarks be developed?

As you can see, simply writing a plan is only a small first step. Small wonder then that most plans are eventually relegated to a storeroom in the library.

Rule #7: Use Committees Effectively

Most major decisions in academic organizations are made by committees of experts who combine their specialized knowledge to solve organizational problems. Therefore, organizational politics often center around committee politics. Having influence on a committee is frequently equal to having influence over the decision.

How can a committee be used to effect organizational change? First, appoint the right people to the right committee or get appointed by simply asking for an appointment from an incumbent official. If the organization has a "committee on committees," it is wise either to know someone on it or to be on it yourself. Such rule-making appointive committees wield power in all academic organizations, and this can be exploited to the best advantage. In addition, after acquiring membership, it is critical simply to *be there*. Remember, fluid participation is a characteristic of colleges and universities. The first tactic, then, is to get on the committee, be there with great regularity, stick it out even when others drop off.

The second tactic of committee success is to do your homework. Expertise is vital in a professional organization. If you observe the earlier rule of concentrating your efforts, you have more time to accumulate the knowledge that will put you ahead of others. In addition, it is always useful to make part of your homework the job of being secretary or chairperson of a group. The chairperson can set the agenda and often has the power to call committee meetings, while the secretary controls the memory of the committee. Committees are blessed with short memories, since most members do not recall or care what is recorded in the minutes. Controlling the memory of a committee means reiterating the issues that you consider important, a definite advantage for political bargaining. Doing your homework—whether it is gathering knowledge, learning the history, being the chairperson, or doing the secretarial chores—puts you in a strategically advantageous position.

A third tactical procedure in effective committee management is to keep ideas flowing. Since decision issues, like garbage dumps, attract various irrelevant material, they can be used to the change agent's advantage. Dump new ideas into the discussion and then compromise readily on the unimportant issues. Helping to load the garbage can leave plenty to bargain over when the deadlines are close and allows you the chance to insist stubbornly about retaining key issues.

A fourth tactical consideration concerns structuring the decision-making process. Decisions do not, in themselves, result in action. More often, we spend a negligible amount of time making a decision and a great deal of time (sometimes a lifetime) managing the consequences of our decisions! Decisions are effectuated through people. It is a well-known premise that more efficient and concrete outcomes of the decision-making process will result if the human processes used to implement decisions are structured; for example, committees are appointed, tasks are defined, priorities are set, deadlines are met, and, perhaps most important, as decisions are prioritized and legitimized, core constituencies (who are represented on committees) are given a vested interest in decisional outcomes. Task forces, committees, group consultation, all are essential components of governance in higher education. I advocate a decision-making structure which blends ad hoc and permanent constituent members, legitimized through formal appointment. However, unless the consultative process is directed with a firm hand, endless debate may result.

A formalized approach permits administrators to effectuate decisions, when they lack the "status" of president. Used correctly it precludes the "end run" and it mandates that everyone in the room, after discussion, "agrees." As decisions are legitimized by sources (groups) holding increased status, it becomes difficult for your opponents to undermine, ridicule or sabotage (through inaction) decisions arrived at using this model. The structure is especially effective when implementation, discussion, review, and analysis must cross jurisdictional divisions. It will permit input from the best minds in the organization. Too often do we preclude ourselves from obtaining the benefit of the brightest and most intelligent in the organization because there is no formal mechanism to accommodate their views in decision-making processes, and academic and administrative leaders rarely reach out beyond their division or school (or their trusted friends) when studying a critical issue. It remains your job to insure that the best opinions, even those voiced by organizational pariahs, are resourced. This normally does not occur in informal consultative systems or when institutional concerns cross organizational lines of authority.

Rule #8: Use the Formal System

Colleges and universities, like other bureaucracies, have complex formal systems to carry out their activities. Often naive change agents are not aware that they can achieve a desired outcome simply by asking the appropriate official for it. This requires savvy. It requires experience within the organization. It requires knowing where the levers are, and which ones to push.

Inexperienced change agents may fail to realize that most organization officials are eager to please. Success is difficult to judge in most professional organizations because the tasks are too ambiguous to be assessed. As a consequence, most officials depend on "social validation" for judgments of success. That is, they are successful if people are pleased and think they have done a good job. The ambiguity of the task, the lack of hard evaluation criteria, and the psychological need of most faculty and administrators for approval give tremendous advantage to partisans who want to get something done. Do not forget a basic idea: ask for what you want and you will be surprised how many times you get it.

Rule #9: Follow Through to Push the Decision Flow

I have said that the concept of "decision making" is a delusion. Decisions are not really made; instead, they come unstuck, are reversed, get unmade during the execution, or lose their impact as powerful political groups fight them. In real life, decisions go round and round in circles, and the best one can hope for in the political battle is a temporary win.

As a consequence, effective individuals know that they must follow important decisions even after they have supposedly been made. What do most people do after the committee has reached its decision? They evaporate. The person who traces the decision flow on through to execution, and who fights when issues are distorted, is the person who really has power. The truly dedicated partisan who wants to implement change is a tenacious watchdog, monitoring the steps of the decision, and calling public attention to lapses in implementation.

Permit a final word on tactics associated with this rule. Set deadlines in the process of making decisions. Delay is the enemy of change; deadlines are flags that help call attention to stalling. Second, give ideas "sheltered starts." If placed back into the regular routine of the organization, a new change will be smothered by powerful old routines. As a consequence, the shrewd individual builds a shelter around the change in its infancy. This often means giving the program or idea a home under the wing of a strong, hospitable executive or faculty member in the college. Only later, after the new idea has established roots, should it be placed into the regular structure of the organization.

Several follow-through techniques involve managing people. It is always useful to place your allies in the vanguard of those responsible for executing the decision. If allies embodying your ideas are influential, the change is more likely to succeed. Reward systems are also very important. Do you want things to change? Then reward people whose behavior helps promote the change. Rewards can be straightforward in the form of money, or they can take the equally valuable form of prestige, status, and public acclaim.

Rule #10: Glance Backward

Let us assume you have followed my advice and have been effective. The last admonition is the hardest to make: be skeptical about your own accomplishments. Few good changes have eternal lives. A deep ego-investment can be made in a project that does not work. In this sense, following through means evaluating, judging, and deciding whether performance lives up to expectations. If it does not, you must start again.

Evaluating your own idea as objectively as possible and listening carefully to the evaluations of others are valuable and necessary skills for true change agents.

Any organization's vitality and creativity depend heavily on the constant influx of new ideas and people. Even the new ideas that you worked so hard to establish will, in time, be dull and old. The conservatives of the present era championed ideas that, at one time, were considered radical. The last step, then, is the most ruthless of all: kill your own projects when they have outlived their usefulness. This is where most fail. After building their investments they fight like Phoenicians to hang on to ideas long since grown old. Cycles must continue, and the change agent must once more struggle to infuse creativity and excitement into the academic organization.

A FINAL WORD TO ACADEMIC LEADERS

A final word to would-be leaders. There are many books and mountains of articles which concern themselves with leadership. Much of what is written is valuable but it is written, by and large, by those who study the topic as opposed to those who implement solutions. As you are no doubt aware, there is a big difference. My concept of leadership is simple and direct— leaders identify an issue that is perceived by a larger community as an important dilemma or a critical problem. The true leader offers (and implements) a solution. For example, Moses conceived of freedom and a vision of the promised land—and led a group of former slaves through the desert. (And even Moses was allowed only to see Israel, never to set foot there!) Leaders are those who identify and articulate a vision and successfully manage a solution. Implementation demands a "buy-in" and sacrifice from key constituents/community members.

It is my hope you will find a few valuable ideas hidden within my rhetoric. Were it your pleasure, I would be honored to follow up and discuss your reactions to the enclosed. I am, at the moment, planting tomatoes in my garden and would welcome a return to the challenges of advising esteemed individuals such as yourself.

ACKNOWLEDGMENTS

"A memorandum from Machiavelli" by Daniel J. Julius, J. Victor Baldridge, and Jeffrey Pfeffer, *The Journal of Higher Education*, Vol. 70, No. 2 (March/April 1999) is reprinted by permission. Copyright 1999 by the Ohio State University Press. All rights reserved.

Also, a grant from TIAA-CREF Research Foundation was utilized for this study.

SELECTED READINGS

Adams, H. 1976. *The Academic Tribes*. New York: Liveright.

Alinsky, S. 1969. *Reveille for Radicals*. New York: Random House.

Argyris, C. 1957. *Personality and Organization: The Conflict Between System and the Individual*. New York: Harper & Row.

Baker, W. E. 1994. *Networking Smart: How to Build Relationships for Personal and Organizational Success*. New York: McGraw Hill.

Barry, J. M. 1989. *The Ambition and the Power: The Fall of Jim Wright: A True Story of Washington*. New York: Viking

Baldridge, J. V. 1971. *Academic Governance in the University*. Berkeley: McCutchan.

Baldridge, J. V. 1983. Rules for a Machiavellian Change Agent: Transforming the Entrenched Organization. In J. V. Baldridge and T. Deal, eds., *Managing Change in Educational Organizations*. Berkeley: McCutchan.

Bazerman, M. H. and Lewicki, R. J. 1983. *Negotiating in Organizations*. Beverly Hills, CA: Sage.

Ben-David, J. 1972. *American Higher Education*. New York: McGraw-Hill.

Bennis, W. 1989. *Why Leaders Can't Lead: The Unconscious Conspiracy Continues*. San Francisco: Jossey-Bass.

Bennis, W. G. and Nanus, B. 1985. *Leaders: The Strategies for Taking Charge*. New York: Harper & Row.

Bergquist, W. H. 1992. *The Four Cultures of the Academy*. San Francisco: Jossey-Bass.

Bergquist, W. H. and Armstrong, J. L. 1986. *Planning Effectively for Educational Quality: An Outcomes-Based Approach for Colleges Committed to Excellence*. San Francisco: Jossey-Bass.

Birnbaum, R. 1988. *How Colleges Work: The Cybernetics of Academic Organization and Leadership*. San Francisco: Jossey-Bass.

Blake, R., Mouton, J. S., and Williams, M. S. 1981. *The Academic Administrator Grid*. San Francisco: Jossey-Bass.

Blau, P. M. 1964. *Exchange and Power in Social Life*. New York: John Wiley.

Bolman, L. G. and Deal, T. E. 1991. *Reframing Organizations: Artistry, Choice, and Leadership*. San Francisco: Jossey-Bass.

Brubacher, J. S. and Rudy, W. 1958. *Higher Education in Transition*. New York: HarperCollins.

Caro, R. A. 1974. *The Power Broker: Robert Moses and the Fall of New York*. New York: Alfred A. Knopf.

Caro, R. A. 1982. *The Years of Lyndon Johnson: The Path to Power*. New York: Alfred A. Knopf.

Charan, R. 1991 How Networks Reshape Organizations for Results, *Harvard Business Review* (September-October): 104–115.

Cohen, A. R. and Bradford, D. L. 1990. *Influence Without Authority*. New York: John Wiley.

Conger, J. A. 1989. Leadership: The Art of Empowering Others. *Academy of Management Executive* 3(1) (February): 45–53.

Davis-Blake, A.; Pfeffer, J.; and Julius, D. J. 1995. The Effect of Affirmative Action

Officer Salary on Changes in Managerial Diversity: Efficiency Wages or Power. *Industrial Relations* 34(1) (January): 73–95.

Deal, T. E. and Kennedy, A. A. 1982. *Corporate Cultures: The Rites and Rituals of Corporate Life.* Reading, MA: Addison-Wesley.

Drucker, P. F. 1988. The Coming of the New Organization. *Harvard Business Review* (January–February): 45–53.

Fulbright, J. W. 1966. *The Arrogance of Power.* New York: Vintage Books.

Gabarro, J. J. 1986. The Development of Working Relationships: 172–189. In J. Lorsch, ed. *Handbook of Organizational Behavior.* Englewood Cliffs, NJ: Prentice-Hall.

Gabarro, J. J. 1987. *The Dynamics of Taking Charge.* Boston: Harvard Business School Press.

Gabarro, J. J. and Kotter, J. P. 1980. Managing Your Boss. *Harvard Business Review* (January–February): 92–100.

Gillam, R. 1971. *Power in Postwar America: Interdisciplinary Perspectives on a Historical Problem.* Boston: Little, Brown.

Halberstam, D. 1979. *The Powers That Be.* New York: Alfred A. Knopf.

Heifetz, R. A. 1994. *Leadership Without Easy Answers.* Cambridge, MA: The Belknap Press of Harvard University Press.

Hill, L. 1992. *Becoming a Manager: Mastery of a New Identity.* Boston: Harvard Business School Press.

Hirschhorn, L. and Gilmore, T. 1992. The New Boundaries of the "Boundaryless" Company. *Harvard Business Review* (May–June): 108–115.

Jencks, C. and Riesman, D. 1968. *The Academic Revolution.* Chicago: University of Chicago Press.

Julius, D. J. 1993. *Managing the Industrial Labor Relations Process in Higher Education.* Washington, DC: College and University Personnel Association.

Julius, D. J. 1998. Applying Machiavellian Principles to University Management. *University Manager* 6(2) (Spring).

Kanter, R. M. 1977. *Men and Women of the Corporation.* New York: Basic Books.

Kanter, R. M. 1979. Power Failure in Management Circuits. *Harvard Business Review* (July–August): 65–75.

Kanter, R. M. 1983. *The Change Masters: Innovation for Productivity in the American Corporation.* New York: Simon and Schuster.

Kanter, R. M. 1989. The New Managerial Work. *Harvard Business Review* (November–December): 85–92.

Kaplan, R. E. 1994. Trade Routes: The Manager's Network of Relationships. *Organizational Dynamics* (Spring): 37–52.

Katz, R. L. 1974. Skills of an Effective Administrator. *Harvard Business Review* (September–October): 90–102.

Kemerer, F. R. and Baldridge, J. V. 1975. *Unions on Campus.* San Francisco: Jossey-Bass.

Kerr, C. 1963. *The Uses of the University.* Cambridge, MA: Harvard University Press.

Keys, B. and Case, T. 1990. How to Become an Influential Manager. *Academy of Management Executive* 4: 38–49.

Konrad, Alison M. & Pfeffer, Jeffrey, 1990. Do You Get What You Deserve? Factors Affecting the Relationship Between Productivity and Pay. *Administrative Science Quarterly 35* (June): 2, 258–286.

Kotter, J. P. 1977. Dependence, and Effective Management. *Harvard Business Review* (July–August): 125–136.

Kotter, J. P. 1982. *The General Managers.* New York: Free Press.

Kotter, J. P. 1985. *Power and Influence: Beyond Formal Authority.* New York: Free Press.

Kotter, J. P. 1988. *The Leadership Factor.* New York: Free Press.

Krackhardt, D. and Hanson, J. R. 1993. Informal Networks: The Company Behind the Chart. *Harvard Business Review* (July–August): 104–111.

Lawler, E. E., III. 1986. *High-Involvement Management: Participative Strategies for Improving Organization Performance.* San Francisco: Jossey-Bass.

Lawler, E. E., III. 1992. *The Ultimate Advantage: Creating the High-Involvement Organization.* San Francisco: Jossey-Bass.

Lax, D. A. and Sebenius, J. K. 1986. *The Manager as Negotiator: Bargaining for Cooperation and Competitive Gain.* New York: Free Press.

Lenski, G. E. 1966. *Power and Privilege: A Theory of Social Stratification.* New York: McGraw-Hill.

Lewicki, R. J. and Litterer, J. A. 1985. *Negotiation.* Boston: Irwin.

Luthans, F. 1988. Successful versus Effective Real Managers. *Academy of Management Executive* (May): 127–132.

Luthans, F., Hogdetts, R. M., and Rosenkrantz, S. A. 1988. *Real Managers.* Cambridge, MA: Ballinger.

Maccoby, M. 1981. The Leader: *A New Face for American Management.* New York: Simon and Schuster.

Manz, C. C. and Sims, H. P. 1989. *Superleadership: Leading Others to Lead Themselves.* Englewood Cliffs, NJ: Prentice-Hall.

McCall, M.; Lombardo, M.; and Morrison, A. 1988. *The Lessons of Experience.* Lexington, MA: Lexington Books.

Mills, C. W. 1959. *The Power Elite.* New York: Oxford University Press.

Mintzberg, H. 1973. *Nature of the Managerial Work.* New York: Harper & Row.

Mintzberg, H. 1975. The Manager's Job: Folklore and Fact. *Harvard Business Review* (July–August): 49–71.

Mintzberg, H. 1983. *Power in and Around Organizations.* Englewood Cliffs, NJ: Prentice-Hall.

Pfeffer, J. 1981. *Power in Organizations.* Marshfield, MA: Pitman.

Pfeffer, J. 1992. *Managing with Power: Politics and Influence in Organizations.* Boston: Harvard Business School Press.

Pfeffer, J. 1994. *Competitive Advantage Through People.* Boston: Harvard Business School Press.

Pfeffer, J. 1997. *The Human Equation.* Boston: Harvard Business School Press.

Pfeffer, J. and Davis-Blake, A. 1987. Understanding Organizational Wage Structures: A Resource Dependence Approach. *Academy of Management Journal* 30: 437–455.

Pfeffer, J. and Moore, W. L. 1980a. Average Tenure of Academic Department Heads: The Effects of Paradigm, Size, and Departmental Demography. *Administrative Science Quarterly* 25: 387–406.

Pfeffer, J. and Moore, W. L. 1980b. Power in University Budgeting: A Replication and Extension. *Administrative Science Quarterly* 25: 637–653.

Pfeffer, J. and Salancik, G. R. 1974. Organizational Decision Making as a Political Process: The Case of a University Budget. *Administrative Science Quarterly* 19: 135–151.

Pfeffer, J. and Salancik, G. R. 1977. Administrator Effectiveness: The Effects of Advocacy and Information on Resource Allocations. *Human Relations* 30: 641–656.

Pfeffer, J. and Salancik, G. R. 1978. *The External Control of Organizations: A Resource Dependence Perspective.* New York: Harper & Row.

Posner, B. Z. and Kouzes, J. R. 1993. *Credibility: How Leaders Gain and Lose It, Why People Demand It.* San Francisco: Jossey-Bass.

Raymond, J. 1964. *Power at the Pentagon.* New York: Harper & Row.

Reynolds, M. O. 1984. *Power and Privilege: Labor Unions in America.* New York: Universe Books.

Russell, B. 1938. *Power: A New Social Analysis.* New York: W. W. Norton.

Sayles, L. R. 1980. *Managerial Behavior: Administration in Complex Organizations.* Huntington, NY: Robert E. Krieger Publishing Company.

Schien, E. J. 1981. Improving Face-to-Face Relationships. *Sloan Management Review* (Winter): 43–52.

Smith, H. 1988. *The Power Game: How Washington Works.* New York: Random House.

Snow, C. C.; Miles, R. E.; and Coleman, J. J., Jr. 1992. Managing 21st Century Network Organizations. *Organizational Dynamics* (Winter): 5–20.

Summerfield, H. L. 1974. *Power and Process: The Formulation and Limits of Federal Educational Policy.* Berkeley: McCutchan.

Tuchman, B. W. 1984. *The March of Folly: From Troy to Vietnam.* New York: Alfred A. Knopf.

Ury, W. 1993. Getting Past No: *Negotiating Your Way from Confrontation to Cooperation.* New York: Bantam Books.

Walton, R. E. 1985. From Control to Commitment in the Workplace. *Harvard Business Review* (March–April): 76–84.

Whetten, D. A. and Cameron, K. S. 1993. *Developing Management Skills: Gaining Power and Influence.* New York: HarperCollins College Publishers.

Zaleznik, A. 1970. Power and Politics in Organizational Life. *Harvard Business Review* (May–June): 47–48.

4

Higher Education Management in Theory and Practice

Jana Nidiffer

What should professional preparation graduate programs teach about management in higher education? It is an easy and necessary question to ask; it is not so easy to answer. This chapter will examine some prominent theories of management and their implications for practice from the point of view of senior management people in higher education. It also will look at various approaches to the teaching of management; who thinks what is good to teach and why.

Over the years a corpus of literature has developed within the academy that amounts to a canon or at least a widely accepted set of texts that are the basis for many of the courses taught under the rubric of higher education management. Yet there is no unanimity among either academics or practitioners of what constitutes good preparation. Such differences of opinion can be illustrated by any casual survey of the field. Examining several syllabi from various institutions (in an admittedly nonscientific sample); we learned that there was nothing approaching a "core" experience or "core" text for such courses, with the possible exception of Robert Birnbaum's *How Colleges Work* (1989), which appeared more often than not. But there were other texts regularly mentioned. Besides Birnbaum, the works of Keller (1983), Cohen and March (1986), Cohen, March, and Olsen (1972), recur with some frequency.

Not surprisingly, there is also no corresponding consensus on what constitutes good practice. Interestingly, there are a few senior management people on the academic side of colleges and universities who are themselves scholars of higher education or, more particularly, higher education management. As background for this chapter two people were interviewed who have taught management, published research on administration and management issues, and hold top positions in major institutions.

Day-to-day workplace issues rarely get resolved by overt recourse to theory. The press of time does not permit such luxury. This does not mean that there is no theory at work as decisions are being made. It does mean that by the time one reaches senior-level decision making one has developed a management identity—a sense of self as decision maker—which is rooted in a variety of identities, only some of which have been developed in a management arena.

It is out of this sense of identity that preferences for particular theoretical orientations emerge. Just as a sophisticated palate guides one's choice of wine, so does one's education guide one's choice of theory. But it is not training alone, any more than it is palate alone, that determines one's choices. There is a dialectical interaction between one's sense of self and the cultural expectations of the institution that condition the specific choice made in a given instance.

There are other limiting factors, however. Prime among these is the repertoire of possible theories a person may choose among. One can't make a Freudian analysis without knowing Freud anymore than someone can adapt Blanchard's 60 second approach to management without having read Blanchard. Thus, there is a necessary correlation between academic training and one's choice of theory, but academic background alone is not sufficient to explain the preference for a particular theory or the reason for the choice.

THEORY OF ACTION

In 1974 Chris Argyris and Donald Schön wrote an influential book, *Theory in Practice: Increasing Professional Effectiveness*. The cornerstone of Argyris and Schön's argument is that an individual's behavior (both professional and personal) is controlled by a private "theory of action." Such theories of action guide all deliberate human behavior, the authors argued, because such theories are actually assumptions about the nature of what is effective to *do* in any given situation in life or on the job. Put more succinctly, such theories are personal prescriptions for procedure, or mental guideposts that inform behavior.

Argyris and Schön identify two distinct types of theories that influence one's theory in action. The first is *espoused theory*. When asked what we might do in any given situation, most of us will champion a particular response. Many managers, for example, when asked how they make decisions, will report that they are democratic and even altruistic: they solicit opinions from many sources, carefully consider all of them, and then act on the decision that is best for the organization. As we all know, practice often falls far short of this espoused ideal. So, espoused theories are what people say they will do; these are the theories that individuals can articulate.

In terms of professional practice, however, the more important of the two theories which inform someone's course of action is *theory-in-use*. An individual's theory-in-use is actually what he or she does do. It is a person's sense of identity as a manager. Theories-in-use are the internal or implicit rules that people apply in any given situation. If they want consequence C, they will do action A. Most of the time managers cannot fully articulate their theory-in-use for a given situation. In fact, most people are even reluctant to apply the word "theory" in such circumstances, with its connotation of formality and academic pretensions. Ask most managers and they would probably call their "theory-in-use" instinct, intuition, hunches, or even good guessing.

People cannot articulate their theories-in-use in large part because of the enormous number of sources that inform them—including formal training but relying most heavily on the full array of life experiences that a manager brings to the job. Based on all that people know or have experienced, they are able to make assumptions about a set of circumstances (which makes a general situation quite specific), and act accordingly. In this way, professionals can categorize events, recognize assumptions in new situations that were germane on previous occasions, and respond effectively to a new set of circumstances. Because of the vast complexity of human learning and the limitless number of potential situations possible in any work situation, the linear formulation "if they want consequence C, they will do action A" is much too simplistic. In fact, Argyris and Schön suggest that the appropriate representation or model of how theories-in-use effect behavior is, "in situation S, if you want to achieve consequence C, under assumptions a_1 ... a_n, do action A" (1987, p. 6).

At times an espoused theory and theory-in-use will have congruence—people do exactly what they say. However, individuals are not always aware that their theory-in-use is in conflict with their espoused theory. Anyone who has worked for someone who says one thing and does another, has experienced the discrepancy described by Argyris and Schön between espoused theory and theory-in-use.

But, back to how the theories-in-use or management identities are formed in senior administrators. It is likely that the most fundamental reason for choosing (or preferring) one theory over another comes from one's experience, even taking formal ideological preferences into consideration. Clearly judgments about the experiential success or nonsuccess of an applied theoretical frame will be closely tied to one's ideological stance in the world: a Marxist is not likely to choose supply-side economic theory as a satisfactory basis for explanation, regardless of how convenient it may be. Still, few ideologues become senior administrators in colleges and universities, at least not in the political sense. There are days when we wish more were. Then, at least we would know where our "leaders" were coming from rather than having to guess at motive and speculate about intent. It is probable that most administrators are eclectic and pragmatic, which is to say that they make the best decisions they can under the circumstances and hope for the best. As simplistic as this sounds, a strong case can be made for the absence of coherent theory in most decision making, planning, and policy formation (Cohen and March 1986). It is probably closest to the truth to say that managers pick and choose among the bits and pieces of management theory they remember, combined with their experience of successful practice in the past, combined again with "gut feeling" to form the basis of a decision. Yet we somehow muddle along, on the whole doing rather better than not.

MANAGERIAL METAMORPHOSIS

A full analysis of managerial identity formation is beyond the scope of this chapter. But, in the discussion that follows, one should bear in mind how critically important personal and institutional culture can be in determining preference. An interesting case in point is the career of Charles Young, Chancellor of the University of California–Los Angeles (UCLA), who began as the defiant whiz kid who defended Angela Davis against the California regents only months after being appointed. Recently Chancellor Young moved into a million-dollar house in a gated community and switched his party affiliation from Democrat to Republican. Once a highly visible, student-oriented activist, he is now being criticized for remoteness and passivity. Regardless, he is an effective spokesperson for the campus and a promoter of good for UCLA. Much depends, however, on how one construes "good." Not only have the times changed, it would seem that the man has changed in that he now espouses theories other than those with which he started and as a consequence his practice has altered. One infers that this has been a dialectical process; adjustments to differently perceived "realities" have led to new practices, which in turn shape how one understands the situation and appropriate responses to it. Charles Young may not be the most complete example of this interactive adjustment, but he is a dramatic embodiment of managerial metamorphosis. He went from being on kind of "effective" administrator to seeming to be quite another, but it may be that "effectiveness," perhaps now more than ever, lies in the eye of the beholder (or the regents and their surrogates) and the bottom line rests firmly on shifting sand blown about by political winds.

In spite of this possibly idiosyncratic exemplum, there are ways of thinking about management that allow for generalizations. Most crushing to those who would contend that organizations are rational systems, is the premise that theories of management built upon rational decision-making models do not work, period. This is part of the reason Cohen, March, and

Olsen's "garbage can theory" was so refreshing (1972). But classical theory was not so easily dislodged and we would warn against the continuing tacit assumption that organizations are repositories of reason-in-practice.

THEORIES AND MODELS

Both scholar/practitioners interviewed for this book predicate their daily work on the notion that rational decision-making models may provide a basis for post hoc analysis that is helpful but rarely is there time or inclination to work through or even invoke such models in their workaday life. Closely allied with that position is the equally basic premise that linear models of the sort that lead to a step-by-step sequential checklist not only do not work, they tend to be reductionist, or at least overly simplistic.

The implications of these two observations for theory building and for the teaching of management practice are profound. Strategic planning is a rational choice model much embraced in higher education management circles in these waning years of the 20th century. There is a certain elegance and attractiveness to the notion that one can identify most if not all of the important variables that affect an institution and then design a rational plan of action that takes their influence into account. Yet it is not at all clear that any of the planning that has been done under the rubric of strategic planning follows the model closely (i.e., is rational in its terms), or has been successful (i.e., demonstrates that a rational model reasonably applied can produce predictable results). Too many unpredictable, unexpected, uncontrollable factors such as history, whim, personal prejudice, or coincidence come into play. Sometimes these can be "rationalized" in terms of the model, but experienced hands tend to wink at such exertions and go on playing the hand dealt them as they would have before the model was adopted. Yet the model offers hope and for many shines a light where there had been none—primarily, we would argue, because it seems to produce reason. Consequently, it affords managers rationalized grounds for fulfilling their agenda while being faithful to the values of objective process so beloved by the academy.

A cynic might argue that strategic planning is a sham engaged in by manipulative administrators to gain their own ends. That's an extreme and probably unfair argument. However, it may not be going too far to suggest that the process itself is so full of choice points for which there is no rationale other than preference that the appearance of sequential decision making is tainted by intellectual dishonesty. Planning processes which involve the whole community are feel-good activities draped by a gossamer cloak of academic respectability because they have been named "theory." This is not to argue that one should not plan. It is to argue that intellectual honesty requires full disclosure. Unexamined assumptions cannot warrant viable conclusions.

Similarly, theories of budgeting often depend upon linear rational choice models that rarely, if ever, take into consideration enough of the naturally occurring variables to be other than an approximation of what is. There may be some place in the world where planned expenditures exactly meet actual outgo, but this is doubtful. It probably isn't even possible in colleges and universities. This is not because colleges and universities are necessarily anymore chaotic and less susceptible to order than other organizations, so much as it is because things don't work in an orderly and predictable manner. Positivism long held that there were rules and laws out there waiting to be discovered. As soon as the right technologies and appropriate methods were developed, and enough time passed, order would be found—and named. Once order is named it is captured and then controllable; its behaviors are then predictable and whole industries develop to package and market the named order.

Perhaps academic organizations were created to challenge such a linear view of the universe, perhaps not. But somehow there are too many things going on at once, even in the most simple, homogeneous, and tightly managed colleges, to be contained in one philosophy. Albert Einstein said "God does not play dice with the universe," or something to that effect. Stephen Hawking (1988), whose work on black holes continues to challenge accepted thinking, has retorted "Not only does God play dice with the universe, He hides the dice". So it is also with institutions of higher education. Seldom can one know enough about what is going on at any one time to have full confidence that any predicted outcome will closely approximate what actually happens. One can hope, gamble, make educated guesses, perhaps even pray, but one can not be certain.

Possibly certainty is too great a burden to put on any theory. Perhaps theory isn't intended to produce certainty; only acceptable uncertainty. But theory is intended to provide explanation. Sometimes the explanation is post hoc and then is broadened to include similar (preferably identical) eases. Alternatively, theory sweeps so broadly (e.g., academic behavior is fundamentally political) that it may point in a useful direction but having pointed it takes a little lie down because it has exhausted its capacities.

TEACHING MANAGEMENT THEORY

What, then, is the use of teaching management theory to neophyte administrators? To return to Argyris and Schön's terms, practice is informed by one's theory-in-use, which is developed over time as a result of some mixture of formal training (espoused theory) and life experience. A good preparation program will help students develop in both areas or, as we stated earlier, help students hone or refine their managerial identity. It is in the classroom, however, where students typically acquire the espoused theory of the profession.

A typical higher education curriculum exposes students to the classic texts and ideas of the field, introduces them to history, philosophy, and ethics, and asks them to be aware of the most current thinking on particular issues by offering specifically targeted courses such as budgeting, the role of the president, Total Quality Management, adult education, the problems and contributions of the community college, the role of student affairs, and so on. Good case method teaching can even simulate learning from experience. The full extent of the graduate school experience—readings; individual research; informal conversations with peers, supervisors, and faculty members; internships; observations—should help students acquire a solid foundation in the theory and practice of higher education administration— one hopes.

But faculty members continue to speculate on how students actually perform in their jobs as professional administrators after graduation and what role the curriculum played, if any, in influencing future job performance. While it is highly probable that theories-in-use cannot change without learning the espoused theories, the antithesis is a dubious assertion. It does not automatically follow that simply learning the espoused theory will, in fact, substantially change someone's theory in use. To say this in a different way using an example we alluded to earlier, if faculty actually thought that students ought to bring Freudian analysis to bear on administrative decisions, then we must at least expose them to Freud's ideas. Such exposure is not a guarantee that practice will improve or that they will use Freud, but unless they learn Freud or Cohen and March or Birnbaum or Keller or Weber or whomever, they certainly will not have the option of employing their theories.

The challenge for faculty, therefore, is to consider what content and, especially important, what pedagogy can increase the likelihood that students will alter their theories-in-use based on what we teach as established theory and best practice. As the old pedagogue said, "it is not what you pour on a student that matters, it is what you plant." One can pour management theory on students, but it is more effective to plant certain habits of mind that encourage students to move away from a narrow and monolinear viewpoint (closely held theory) and instead to consider multiple ways of approaching a problem before action is taken. When we surveyed one of our scholar/senior practitioners about teaching management she replied, "the hardest thing to do is to get students to realize that not absolutely everything about running a university is political."

REFRAMING ORGANIZATIONS

Lee Bolman and Terry Deal's book, *Reframing Organizations: Artistry, Choice, and Leadership* (1991) is a powerful exemplar of judiciously applied multiple perspectives that students emulate with ease and understanding. At one level, *Reframing Organizations* is primarily synthetic. Bolman and Deal have sorted through an enormous body of literature (they have a 27-page bibliography), principally on organizational behavior, management theory, and leadership theory. They assert that all the theories regarding organizations can be grouped into four frames: structural, human resource, political, and symbolic (pp. 3–42).

The structural frame comes largely from the work of sociologists and addresses "fit" for any organization. The human resources frame comes from organizational social psychology, and assumes that organizations are inhabited by people with needs, feelings, skills, values, desires, and so on. Human resource theorists look at people and organizations, endeavoring to find solutions that meet the needs of both. As one might expect, the political frame originated in political science. Conflict and power are central themes, as are bargaining and negotiating. Political theorists concentrate on enmity among employees and the distribution of resources. The symbolic frame draws upon cultural anthropology and abandons the assumptions of rationality implicit in the other three frames. Symbolic theorists focus on meaning.

Even if the book was only synthesis, it would still be a useful tool. It exposes students to immense amounts of theoretical material in an organized and coherent manner. The bibliography is also an important resource, because it allows students to select readings on topics and subjects that interest them. But two additional aspects of the book make it especially useful.

The first is the accessibility of the material. The writing is clear and lively and engages students who invariably find it easy to understand. For a higher education course, Bolman and Deal should be considered domain independent—that is, it teaches theories and concepts applicable to college and university management but is not about higher education per se. On the other hand, Birnbaum's, *How Colleges Work*, a frequently required text in management courses, is domain specific—the principles of the book have been applied directly to the field of higher education. But because Birnbaum organizes his book in a way that compliments the four-frame analysis of Bolman and Deal, and the presentation of ideas is so clear in *Reframing Organizations*, students find understanding Birnbaum an easier task after reading Bolman and Deal.

The second reason Bolman and Deal is so beneficial as a text in the course, is because the book is dedicated to increasing a manager's theory-in-use so that performance is enhanced. The authors stress that the need in management is to match the right idea to the right problem and the book is intended to provide an increased awareness of options:

The ability to reframe experience enriches and broadens a leader's repertoire. . . . Expanded choice enables a manger to generate creative responses to the broad range of problems that they encounter. . . . We cannot count the number of times that mangers have told us that they handled a particular problem the "only way" it could be done. Such statements betray a failure of both imagination and courage. . . . [I]t can be enormously liberating for managers to realize that there is *always* more than one way to respond to *any* organization problem or dilemma. Managers are imprisoned only to the degree that their palette of ideas is impoverished. (p. 4)

Bolman and Deal remind students that organizations are complex and surprising. They are run by people who are complex, their interactions are complex, and the outcomes of policies and decisions are hard to predict, much like hitting a cue ball into the racked triangle of balls. Organizations are also deceptive and quite ambiguous. Members of organizations will camouflage surprise and fail to communicate in open and candid ways. In addition, information in organizations may be incomplete, it may be interpreted differently by different people, and ambiguity may be deliberately created to hide a problem. Sometimes the reality is so complex that the "truth" is not easily comprehended. To cope with ambiguity, managers must first ask "what is going on here?" and then go deeper to ask, "what is really going on here?" (pp. 24–29). To do so requires a new way of thinking on the part of managers. Bolman and Deal state that their goal is not to "produce specific kinds of behavior but to cultivate habits of mind. . . . In particular, we want to reduce the gap between how managers, consultants, and policy makers typically think and how they might think" (p. 16).

Bolman and Deal also provide interesting case studies from a wide variety of organizational settings, including higher education, which are helpful teaching tools. Although case study teaching is typically used to enhance or exercise particular managerial skills, it is also an effective device for problem analysis according to the frames proposed by Bolman and Deal. As mentioned above, the point of Bolman and Deal is to get students to look at organizations through different lenses so that an analysis of the problem is complete and richly textured. Case studies are an effective device for promoting such learning. Students can then solve the problems by offering prescriptions based on theoretical knowledge and thereby illustrating a successful blending of theory and practice.

Clearly, *Reframing Organizations* adheres to the philosophy that students should approach problems from different perspectives. It provides the knowledge base that facilitates such a goal, and presents the information in a way that is both understandable and challenging. Looking at management from multiple perspectives is not only good advice for students, but also for college presidents as well. Richard Chait and his colleagues (1993) give the same advice to members of boards of trustees. In their prescriptive book, *The Effective Board of Trustees*, Chait et al. recommend that board members, in order to be more effective, learn from Bolman and Deal:

These theories, termed "frames" by Bolman and Deal, provide lenses or perspectives that managers use to gather information, reach decisions, and take actions. . . . To quibble about the number or description of these frames would be to miss the central point: where and how we look determines what we see. If a trustee were to view a college (or an executive to view a corporation) through only one of these frames, some facets of a problem would be sharply illuminated, while other aspects would be blurred or even invisible. (p. 60)

CONCLUSION

Unanswered in this argument for classroom-based learning is the question, "Why not just put people to work and then trust on the job training to supply all that's needed to perform well as a manager?" In some cases that is all that is needed. But most of us need contexts within which to think about things we observe and experience. All of us who do academic administration are little theory makers. We constantly check this experience against that experience or current practice against past practice, in order to find patterns to guide our next decision or to help us out of the next crisis. Rarely is large theory invoked, although pieces of theory abound and are bouncing around in our heads. These, like platelets, attach themselves to our thoughts and guide our thinking in unexamined (perhaps unknowable) ways, but in ways that would not be possible were it not for the already encountered theories. The platelets coagulate into a critical mass that combines enough pieces of theory with enough experience to produce insights adequate to the task. Built into this thought pattern are sensibilities about what is right and what will work that are so inchoate as to defy description. But, like talent, you know it when you see it even if you cannot account for it. These sensibilities act like alarms that go off when something is not working. With good luck and good experience the alarms go off more often at the right time than as a consequence of short circuits or over heating or anxiety attacks.

We can't really teach talent—though we can burnish it. What we can do, through exposure to case studies and intelligent compatriots with whom to share good conversation, is provide safe forums. Whether these are called seminars or workshops or courses doesn't matter. What matters is that inexperienced practitioners get to test their thinking in a cauldron of shared intensity where fully formulated theory comes into contact with workaday theory making. Here we begin to arrive at possible understandings without risking fortunes or the welfare of others. Here we elaborate and formalize the on-going process of filtration that we began as youngsters and refined as we grew; filtration that begets appropriate discrimination, that lets in the right data and keeps out the wrong, that allows the mixing of theory with theory and experience and observation. This is rigorous filtration, where disciplined minds can interact and reflect with a suspension of disbelief that is almost never possible on the job. These encounters provide a reservoir of unpracticed knowledge that can be invoked or, more likely, that come bubbling up when needed, to inform a decision or to guide a choice. With luck and some talent good management may result.

REFERENCES

Argyris, C. and Schön, D. 1987 (originally published, 1974). *Theory in Practice: Increasing Professional Effectiveness*. San Francisco: Jossey-Bass.

Birnbaum, R. 1989. *How Colleges Work: The Cybernetics of Academic Organization and Leadership*. San Francisco: Jossey-Bass.

Bolman, L. and Deal, T. 1991. *Reframing Organizations: Artistry, Choice, and Leadership*. San Francisco: Jossey-Bass.

Chait, Richard P.; Holland, Thomas P. and Taylor, Barbara E. 1993. *The Effective Board of Trustees*. Washington, DC: American Council on Education.

Cohen, M. D. and March, J. G. 1986. *Leadership and Ambiguity*, 2nd ed. Cambridge, MA: Harvard Business School Press.

Cohen, M. D.; March, J. G.; and Olsen, J. P. 1972. A Garbage Can Model of Organization Choice: *Administrative Science Quarterly* 17(1) (March): 1–25.

Hawking, S. W. 1988. *A Brief History of Time: From the Big Bang to Black Holes*. New York: Bantam Books.

Keller, G. 1983. *Academic Strategy: The Management Revolution in American Higher Education*. Baltimore: The Johns Hopkins University Press.

Successfully Managing Higher Education Consortia/Partnerships

Albert B. Smith, Ronald D. Opp,
Randy L. Armstrong, Gloria A. Stewart, and
Randall J. Isaacson

INTRODUCTION

The phenomenal proliferation of interinstitutional cooperation and consortia within the American system of higher education has for many years been a topic of intense interest for managers of all aspects of higher education. A review of the literature reveals a wide range of theories and opinions concerning all of the various components and elements of contemporary educational partnerships. Whereas structured and unstructured institutional linkages within the American higher education system have been a recognized entity for many decades, modern consortia are in and of themselves a relatively new phenomenon (Neal 1988). There is an ample body of evidence to support the oft-stated contention that the age of substantial interinstitutional cooperation in American higher education is less than 40 years old. According to Neal (1988), the contemporary concept of consortia and interinstitutional cooperation lumbered forth from the primordial ooze of academe during the "golden years" of the 1960s and early 1970s when higher education was operating in an expansionist mode. Whereas these cooperative programs and agreements were the avenues of growth and expansion during the 1960s, today they are becoming vehicles for consolidation, focus, and self-preservation (Pritzen 1988). Historically, the intent and purpose of American academic cooperation fostered by consortial arrangements has run the gamut from government-mandated collaboration to interinstitutional altruism. A common thread appears to be the notion of strength in numbers and common purpose. In other words, as a member of a consortial arrangement each member institution is assumed to be better able to plan for and cope with the change inherent with the operation of a modern institution of higher learning rather than if it were acting as a unilateral agent.

A veritable plethora of interinstitutional cooperation currently exists in a variety of forms throughout the American system of higher education. However, Swerdlow (1981) suggests these are infinite possibilities for cooperative arrangements. They can be categorized as bilateral, multilateral, legislative, and voluntary. The bilateral approach involves the cooperative linking of just two institutions. Multilateral involvement constitutes three or more institutions. Legislative cooperation is the result of state decree. A fourth type is the voluntary arrangement which may also include the bilateral and multilateral categories.

DEFINITIONS AND FORMULATORS

Although the *1991 Consortium Directory* lists over 120 examples of consortial arrangements spread out over 41 states and involving some 1,000 institutions of higher learning under 62 taxonomically arranged categories, they fundamentally all share the common denominator of cooperation and coordination (Love 1991).

A review of the literature on consortial and interinstitutional cooperation reveals an abundance of denotative and connotative meanings for terms essential to managerial understanding of these partnerships. A prime example of this semantic proliferation is the numerous and varied meanings assigned to the term "consortium." According to Johnson (1971), the word consortium became a permanent addition to the lexicon used by those in higher education because other previously accepted terminology (center, union, association, federation, council, group, committee) proved inadequate when used to denote a variety of shared endeavors. His delineation of the term as found in the *Encyclopedia of Education* offers a view of this now widely recognized educational phenomenon:

a voluntary combination of three or more higher educational institutions for the joint attainment of one or more mutually desired objectives through formal machinery, usually characterized by special officers, a policy-making body, a separate budget, authority to sustain and extend itself as a new corporate entity, and common programs distinct from those of the constituent members. (Johnson 1971, p. 425)

A perhaps more all-inclusive definition of consortium may be found in the *Facts on File Dictionary of Education*. Shafritz, Koeppe, and Soper (1988) describe a contemporary educational consortium as:

a combination of people, groups, associations, or organizations that have joined for a particular purpose. A consortium may be assembled to accomplish a single, short-term purpose, or as a semi-permanent alliance to pursue a number of ongoing purposes. Schools at all levels frequently utilize consortia arrangements for a variety of purposes.

It should be noted that in spite of the preponderance of readily available specific definitions relating to some aspect of educational linkages, a review of the entries under "consortia" and "interinstitutional cooperation" by Educational Resources Information Centers (ERIC) suggests that members of the American educational system use these terms interchangeably to describe any formal or informal educational venture entered into by post-secondary institutions in the spirit of resource pooling.

Although dozens of articles and studies were completed during the 1970s on some aspect of interinstitutional cooperation, three of the more prolific contributors of the period dominated the literature with their scholarly and informative presentations. These formulators of consortial thought emerged during the first half of the 1970s and continued to influence the literature well into the following decades. These three individuals were Franklin Patterson, Lewis D. Patterson, and Fritz H. Grupe. Their names are synonymous with the research and commentary on early collaborative efforts in American higher education.

Franklin Patterson's (1974) *Colleges in Consort* is one of the most widely read studies of academic consortia in the United States. Findings from this study, funded in part by the Ford Foundation, led Patterson to conclude that "the principal impediment to effective interinstitutional cooperation is the traditional commitment of colleges and universities to institutional autonomy" (p. 119).

Patterson called the development of consortia a notable phenomenon in American higher education:

It flies directly in the face of the historic pattern of institutional isolationism and independence which has dominated higher education until the present time. This movement constitutes something new in education: at the very least, a rhetorical and nominal commitment to cooperation, where before had existed a kind of friendly anarchy among colleges and universities. (p. 4).

In addition, Franklin Patterson compiled a list of seven principles that, in his opinion, should be agreed upon and assumed before an institution enters into a cooperative agreement:

1. That the new consortium should improve the quality and range of education available to students in each of its constituent institutions.

2. That, within the consortium, each institution should preserve its identity and maintain as much autonomy as the constraints of serious cooperation permit.

3. That the consortium should minimize duplication of education programs and redundancy of facilities and should aim at complementarity of academic programs and facilities among its constituent institutions.

4. That the consortium should seek to reduce or control institutional operating costs by collective means wherever possible.

5. That the consortium should give central assistance in financial development of member institutions and in financial development of member institutions and have a fund-raising capacity for collective needs.

6. That the consortium should provide planning, development, and coordination for new collective educational programs responsive to changing needs and new clientele in the area.

7. That the governance and executive part of the consortium should have authority equivalent to its responsibility for leadership (pp. 108–109).

Lewis D. Patterson (1970) began a study of consortia in 1967 while a member of the Kansas City Regional Council for Higher Education. Based upon the findings of his study, Lewis Patterson classified interinstitutional arrangements as formal consortia when they had exhibited five specific criteria: (1) a voluntary organization; (2) three or more member institutions; (3) multiacademic programs; (4) at least one full-time professional to administer the programs of the consortium; and (5) a required annual contribution or other evidence of a long-term commitment by member institutions.

Fritz Grupe published no fewer than ten articles on the subject between 1969 and 1975. One of the most significant examples of Grupe's writings, however, appeared in an address he made at Loyola University in Chicago. During the presentation of his paper, Grupe (1970) outlined six areas of possible difficulty encountered by some beginning consortia:

1. There is often a significant difference between "cooperation" as an abstraction and "cooperation" as a reality.

2. Institutional autonomy remains an overriding concern within all consortia.

3. Unrealistic and idealistic expectation for the cooperative effort can lead to frustration.

4. The search for an identity can lead to difficulty.

5. There is a tendency for member institutions to expect the consortium's central office to develop rational long-range plans and suitable programs.

6. The establishment of a consortium does not automatically lead to financial support.

With the rapid proliferation of interinstitutional cooperation it is not surprising that certain cooperative arrangements have been hastily constructed, ill-planned, inadequately financed, and poorly administered. Grupe provides a list of ten particularly significant features that distinguish the quality of some consortium operations: (1) they are creative, (2) they are programmatic, (3) they are expert, (4) they are academic, (5) they are high risk, (6) they are of importance to the institutions, (7) they are open-ended, (8) they have tangible impact, (9) they permit broad access by faculty and students, (10) they reinforce and strengthen existing programs (Grupe n.d., pp. 17–21).

Just as the trio of Franklin Patterson, Lewis D. Patterson, and Fritz Grupe greatly influenced the consortial-related literature of the 1970s, Donn C. Neal became a primary source of astute observations and prophecy for interinstitutional cooperation during the 1980s. In 1984, Neal suggested that consortia, through "imaginative cooperative relationships," can provide college and university leaders with flexibility, resources, and efficiency in a time of retrenchment. He also promoted his concept of a consortium serving its membership while displaying sensitivity to professed needs and desires. In 1985, Neal elaborated on interinstitutional cooperation in continuing education. Three years later he and 13 of his fellow collaboration experts identified the ways in which such interinstitutional cooperation can be vital and effective in helping campus leaders and consortium directors to find new ways in which they can work together (Neal 1988, 1994).

The 1980s and 1990s have been a time for revival, renewal, and redirection for American interinstitutional cooperation and consortia. The consortium concept is no longer looked upon as "wildly innovative," but rather as a logical and feasible mainstay in the shrinking arsenal of administrative weapons used to combat rising costs, reduced revenues, falling student enrollments, and the ever-present need to keep pace with constantly changing technologies.

TWO-YEAR/FOUR-YEAR COLLEGE CONSORTIA AND PARTNERSHIPS

One of the major problems facing higher education institutions in the 1990s, which will continue into the 21st century, is a declining pool of financial resources from traditional sources of funds (*The Chronicle of Higher Education Almanac* 1994). If two-year and four-year colleges are to improve their programs in a time of expanding enrollments and declining resources, then it will be necessary to find new ways of raising money and sharing resources across institutions. This approach of sharing resources via cooperative programs, consortia, and partnerships with other educational institutions, government agencies, and business and industry offers an excellent way for colleges and universities to achieve more, do something better, or reduce the cost of their activities (Neal 1988).

There is a rapidly growing body of literature on cooperative programs in community colleges and universities and between these institutions (Smith and May 1992). One of the major areas of cooperation has been the development of programs to improve articulation between two-year colleges and four-year universities and colleges at both the state and local levels.

In addition to many cooperative programs between two-year and four-year colleges to improve student transfer rates, an equally significant development has been the formation of partnerships between public schools and community colleges. The purpose of many of these partnerships or consortia has been the development of Tech-Prep or 4 + 2 programs that combine the four years of high school with the first two years of college to form a six-year degree program in an occupational field of study (Hull and Parnell 1991; Opp 1995).

Listed below is a summary of some of the other types of cooperative programs that are expanding rapidly in U.S. community colleges and universities:

1. Voluntary consortia are being formed for the purpose of conducting institutional research (Doucette and Seybert 1990).

2. The preparation of minority teachers for the 21st century is another area where community colleges and universities are forming partnerships (Anglin 1989).

3. Cooperation among community college and university libraries or learning resource centers (LRCs) is another major trend in postsecondary education. The major benefits of these consortia are: the cooperative purchase of supplies, equipment, and educational materials; resource sharing; staff development; and information sharing (Weiss and Steike 1986).

4. Many two-year and four-year college consortia have also been established to promote the use of telecourses.

Other types of cooperative programs in universities and community colleges focus on faculty development, customized and contract training projects with business and industry, and faculty exchange programs (Anglin, Mooradian, and Hoyt 1992; Hawthorne and Ninke 1991).

SUCCESSFUL MANAGEMENT PRACTICES IN TWO-YEAR/FOUR-YEAR COLLEGE CONSORTIA/PARTNERSHIPS

Recently a national study was conducted with two-year college presidents to: (1) determine the extent to which two-year colleges were involved in partnerships with other two-year and four-year colleges; (2) determine which types of two-year or four-year partnerships two-year college presidents felt were most important to the current success of their colleges; (3) determine what community colleges presidents felt were the most important elements for successful partnerships/consortia with two-year and/or four-year colleges; and (4) make recommendations as to how two-year colleges could expand and improve their two-year and four-year college partnerships (Smith et al. 1995).

The research questions employed in this study were:

1. How many two-year and/or four-year college/university partnerships/consortia have two-year colleges joined at each of the following levels: (a) local (service area), (b) regional partnerships/consortia (in-state), (c) state level, (d) regional partnerships/consortia (out of state), (e) national partnerships/consortia, and (f) international partnerships/consortia?

2. Of 21 different types of partnerships/consortia, what types do two-year college presidents consider to be the most important to the "current success" of their colleges?

3. Of 31 different elements, what elements do two-year college presidents consider to be the most important in creating successful two-year and/or four-year college partnerships?

4. How much are community colleges spending from their operating budgets on two-year and/or four-year college/university partnerships/consortia fees, costs, and so on?

RESEARCH DESIGN

Definitions

For purposes of this study "partnership" was defined as "close cooperation between parties having specified and joint rights and responsibilities (as in a common enterprise)." (*Webster's* 1981) With this definition in mind, a questionnaire was developed to send to all of the two-year college presidents in the United States.

Sampling

Community college presidents were used as the unit of analysis. Within each two-year institution, the president was surveyed to obtain information about the college's two-year/four-year college partnerships/consortia. Given the responsibility for approving all cooperative programs with other institutions or agencies that this administrator typically has, it was assumed that this individual would be knowledgeable about both the types of cooperative programs at his or her institution and the success of these programs.

The president at each two-year college was identified by using the *Who's*

Table 5.1
Number of Two-Year and/or Four-Year College/University Partnerships/
Consortia Reported at the Local (Service Area) Level (N = 617)

Number	Frequency	Percentage
0	139	22
1	94	15
2	90	15
3 or more	294	48
Total	617	100

Who in Community Colleges (1993). This particular reference guide was chosen because it is an authoritative source of recent information about administrative leaders at virtually every two-year institution in the country. A total of 1,172 presidents at individual two-year college campuses was identified through the use of this reference guide. Of these 1,172 administrators, 617 responded to the survey, for an overall response rate of 53%. Data collection took place in July and August of 1994.

RESULTS AND DISCUSSION

Characteristics of the Sample

The presidents who responded to the survey tended to be white (87%) males about 54 years of age, with either an Ed.D. (41%) or Ph.D. (43%), and roughly 18 years of community college administrative experience; 15% of the respondents were female. The average number of years that the 617 responding presidents had been in office was 8 years. This profile of respondents to this research investigation had backgrounds similar to community college administrators nationally.

Number and Nature of Partnerships/Consortia

The first research question related to the number and nature of two-year/four-year college/university partnerships/consortia at the (a) local (service area), (b) regional (in state), (c) state, (d) regional (out-of-state), (e) national, and (f) international levels. Table 5.1 summarizes some of our findings and shows that 139 or 22% of the presidents either did not respond or reported having "no" local partnerships with either another two-year college or a four-year college in their service area. On the other hand, 294 of the presidents (48%) reported having three or more local partnerships with two-year and/or four-year colleges. This does not mean that the presidents reporting "no" partnerships at the local level are not involved in partnership arrangements. One needs to keep in mind that this study only looked at partnerships between two-year and four-year colleges. These same presidents may be involved in a number of other partnerships at the local level with public school districts, business and industry, governmental agencies, and the like. Although this study only looked at one type of partnership in the community college field, future investigations now under way at Texas Tech University will look at partnerships with these other agencies as well.

In summary, this part of our study and data analysis showed that 617 presidents reported being involved with 9,990 two-year and/or four-year college or university partnerships at six different geographical levels: local (2,565), regional in-state (2,460), state (2,962), regional out-of-state (767), national (704), and international (532). One begins to feel that this is only the tip of the iceberg with respect to the number of partnerships that community colleges have formed with universities and other public and private agencies in our country.

MOST IMPORTANT PARTNERSHIPS/CONSORTIA

The second research question in this study related to what types of two-year/two-year or two-year/four-year partnerships or consortia did community college presidents believe were most important to the "current success" of their colleges. Here the presidents were asked in Part II of our questionnaire to evaluate the importance of 21 different partnership activities, assigning each of the 21 activities a rating of 1 to 4. (1 = very important, 2 = somewhat important, 3 = not important, 4 = not applicable). Table 5.2 summarizes some of the findings from this phase of our research.

Table 5.2 shows the 9 most highly rated partnership activities in this study. This table shows that 582 of the 617 (94.4%) two-year college presidents who responded to this study rated "Articulation Agreements with Universities" as "very important" or "somewhat important" to the current success of their college. This item received the greatest number of combined "very important" and "somewhat important" ratings of the 21 activities that were rated. This list of the 9 most highly rated partnership activities should give both two-year and four-year college presidents an idea of the types of partnerships and consortia they should try to develop in the remaining years of this decade and into the 21st century.

Most Important Elements for Successful Consortia

The third research question in this 1994 study related to what elements did community college presidents believe were the most important in creating successful partnerships/consortia with other two-year or four-year

Table 5.2
Nine Most Important Types of Two-Year or Four-Year College Partnerships
According to Two-Year College President' Ratings (N = 617)

Type of Partnership	No. Indicating Very Important or somewhat Important	Percentage
Articulation Agreements with Universities	582	94.4
2 + 2 Programs with Universities	503	81.5
Participating in Computer Networks with 4-Year Colleges	462	74.9
Participating in Computer Networks with 2-Year Colleges	455	73.7
Teleconferencing Networks with 2-Year Colleges	445	72.2
Conducting Institutional Research with 2-Year Colleges	438	70.5
Articulation Agreements with other 2-Year Colleges	426	69.1
Teleconferencing Networks with 4-Year Colleges	422	68.4
Distance Education Projects with other 4-Year Colleges	411	66.6

colleges. Here the presidents, based on their experiences with these types of partnerships, were asked to rate the importance of 31 elements for creating a successful partnership. The presidents' assigned a rating of 1 to 4 for each of the 31 elements (1 = very important, 2 = somewhat important, 3 = not important, and 4 = not applicable). Table 5.3 summarizes some of the findings from this phase of our research.

Table 5.3 shows the ten most highly rated elements by the 617 responding two-year college presidents. This table shows that 517 of the 617 (83.8%) responding presidents rated "Shared Objectives" as being either "very important" or "somewhat important" in creating successful partnership. This item received the greatest number of "very important" or "somewhat important" ratings of the 31 elements that were rated. The second

Table 5.3
Ten Most Important Elements for Successful Two-Year or Four-Year College
Partnerships According to Two-Year College Presidents (N = 617)

Elements	No. Indicating Very Important or Somewhat Important	%
shared Objectives	517	83.8
Capability of Partners	514	83.3
Benefits for all Involved	512	83.0
Cost Effective Programs	498	80.7
Financial Resources	493	79.9
Adequate Staffing	491	79.6
Reputation of Partners	490	79.4
Programs Based on Needs Assessment	486	78.8
Start Small and Buil	474	76.9
Formal Contractual Agreements	473	76.6

most highly rated element was "Capability of Partners" with 514 (83.3%)
of the responding presidents indicating that this item was either "very important" or "somewhat important" in creating successful partnerships. The
ten items in Table 5.3 are the criteria college and university presidents
should use to establish successful higher education consortia in the future.
These are the criteria recommended by college presidents who have developed successful college and university partnerships.

Expenditures for Partnerships

With respect to one last research question, 315 of the 617 two-year
college presidents (51.1%) reported spending money from their campus
operating budgets for partnership fees, costs, and such. The range of reported expenditures was $300–$1,400,000 with the average reported expenditure amounting to $86,084 in the 1993–94 academic year. Some 163
of the presidents (26.4%) reported spending between $300 and $25,000
for partnerships at their colleges, another 43 presidents (7.0%) reported
spending between $30,000 and $50,000 per year, and another 109 presidents (17.7%) reported spending between $60,000 and $1,400,000. Depending on the type of consortium, great sums of money may not be needed
for colleges and universities to establish successful consortia; however, college and university administrators must be willing to invest some funds in
consortia if they hope to succeed in this type of activity.

RECOMMENDATIONS FOR EXPANDING AND
IMPROVING CONSORTIA/PARTNERSHIPS

When asked if their colleges were involved in more formal two-year and/or four-year college partnerships/consortia than they were five years ago, 73.6% of the two-year presidents (454) in the above-mentioned study indicated they were. With more colleges and universities becoming involved in two-year/four-year college partnerships and other forms of partnerships with business, industry, schools, and public agencies, it will be important for higher education administrators to give more attention to these new developments. Based on this study we recommend the following for college and university presidents, administrators, and faculty members considera-tion:

1. Concentrate on partnerships with other two-year and four-year colleges primarily at the local, in-state, and state levels. These are the part-nerships that are likely to provide the greatest benefits to the college, par-ticularly at the local (service-area) level.

2. Concentrate first on developing articulation agreements and then on 2 + 2 programs with universities. These are the two programs that re-spondents to our study felt were the most important types of postsecondary partnerships.

3. In forming new partnerships, try to make sure that all ten of the most important elements for successful two-year and four-year college partner-ships are part of your partnership development plan. The presence of such elements should insure initial success.

4. Finally, and perhaps most important, consider developing a new po-sition in your college or university with the title of Assistant to the President for Partnership Agreements. With the need for more partnerships in colleges and universities, this position should more than pay for itself in the future. This full-time person, with a minimum of a master's degree, should be responsible for coordinating the development, implementation, and evalu-ation of all formal and informal consortia/partnerships with colleges and universities, business and industry, public schools, and other public and private agencies.

SUMMARY

At the present time there is a general lack of knowledge as to the nature and types of consortia and partnerships that colleges and universities have formed in our country among themselves and with other public and private agencies and individuals. We hope that this chapter has shed some light on the historical development of consortia, the nature of consortia in post-secondary institutions, and how college and university administrators can be successful in creating consortia and partnerships in the future that will benefit their students.

REFERENCES

Anglin, L. W. 1989. Preparing Minority Teachers for the 21st Century: University Community College Model. *Action in Teacher Education* 11(2): 47–50.

Anglin, L. W.; Mooradian, P. W.; and Hoyt, O. L. 1992. Institutional Renewal Through Professional Development Partnerships. *Community College Review* 19(4): 52–56.

The Chronicle of Higher Education. 1984. What a College Should Expect When It Joins a Consortium (20 February): 23–31.

The Chronicle of Higher Education Almanac. 1994. (1 September) 41(1): 44.

Consortium and Interinstitutional Cooperation. 1988. New York: American Council on Education/Macmillan.

Doucette, D. and Seybert, J. A. 1990. Research by Voluntary Consortium. *Models for Conducting Institutional Research, New Directions for Community Colleges* 72: 59–71. San Francisco: Jossey-Bass.

Grupe, F. 1970. Toward Realism in Initiating Collegiate Cooperative Centers. A paper presented at the Academic Consortium Seminar, Loyola University, Chicago, March 1.

Grupe, F. H. n.d. Major Difficulties to be Confronted. *Inter-college Cooperation at the Department Level.* Postdam, NY: Associated Colleges of the Saint Lawrence Valley, 17–21.

Hawthorne, E. M. and Ninke, D. 1991. A Focus on University Faculty Service to Community Colleges. *Community College Review* 19(1): 30–35.

Hull, D. and Parnell, D. 1991. *Tech-Prep Associate Degree.* Waco, TX: CORD.

Johnson, E. L. 1971. Consortiums in Higher Education: 425. In L. C. Deighton, ed., *Encyclopedia of Education* 2, (New York: Macmillan).

The Journal of Continuing Higher Education. 1985. Interinstitutional Cooperation in Continuing Education. (Spring) 33(2): 11–14.

Love, S. and Barnett, J. 1991. *1991 Consortium Directory.* Leawood, KS: Council for Interinstitutional Leadership.

Neal, D. C. 1988. *Consortia and Interinstitutional Cooperation.* New York: American Council on Education and Macmillan.

Neal, D. C. 1994. New Roles for Consortia. *Planning for Higher Education* 12(2): 23–31.

Opp, R. D. 1995. Tech Prep Consortia in Texas. A paper presented at the International Conference on Teaching Excellence and Conference of Administrators, NISOD (May 23), Austin, Texas.

Patterson, F. 1974. *Colleges in Consort.* San Francisco: Jossey-Bass.

Patterson, L. D. 1970. *Consortia in American Higher Education.* Washington, DC: Clearinghouse on Higher Education, Document Reproduction Service, ED 043 800.

Pritzen, J. M. 1988. Academic Programs. *Consortia and Institutional Cooperation,* ed. D. C. Neal (New York: American Council on Education).

Shafritz, J. M.; Koeppe, R. P. and Soper, E. W. 1988. *Facts on File Dictionary of Education.* New York: Oxford.

Smith, A. and G. May. 1992. Gaining Stature through Community College/
    University Consortia: 63–75. In G. May and A. Smith, eds., *Prisoners of
    Elitism: The Community College's Struggle for Stature, New Directions for
    Community Colleges* 78, (Summer). San Francisco: Jossey-Bass.
Smith, A. B.; Opp, R. D.; Stewart, G. S.; and Isaacson, R. J. 1995. A National
    Study of Partnerships/Consortia with Two-Year and Four-Year Institutions
    of Higher Learning. A paper presented at the Annual Meeting of the Council
    of Universities and Colleges (CUC), American Association of Community
    Colleges (April 22). Minneapolis.
Swerdlow, K. G. 1981. Selected Voluntary Academic Consortia in Higher Educa-
    tion. Dissertation: 3–4. Bloomington: Indiana University.
Webster's Third New International Dictionary. 1981. Springfield, MA: G. & C.
    Merriam Co.
Weiss, J. A. and Steike, R. G. 1986. Change through Cooperation: The NILRC
    Model: 21–28. In G. H. Voegel, ed., *Advances in Instructional Technology,
    New Directions for Community Colleges.* (Fall). San Francisco, Jossey-Bass.
Who's Who in Community Colleges. 1993. Washington, DC: American Association
    of Community Colleges.

The Financing of Higher Education

David S. Honeyman

INTRODUCTION

Higher education is a costly enterprise. In 1993 the National Center for Education Statistics (NCES) reported that the total revenues for higher education in the United States exceeded $170 billion: a 6% increase over the previous year. These revenues supported programs that educated almost 15 million students in undergraduate, graduate, and professional programs.

Higher education is also a complex operation that is funded by a delicate balance of revenue sources, which are diverse and differ in each state. In 1993, public, tax-supported revenue accounted for almost 40% of all revenues and were derived from a combination of federal, state, and local sources. Additional revenues were generated by tuition and fee payments (26.5%), gifts and grants (5.7%), sales and services (23.3%).

One of the primary sources of funding for higher education has been the federal government. Federal funds expended on all education exceeded $18 billion in 1990 and grew to approximately $21 billion in 1993. However, this was a 14.3% reduction in federal support when measured in current (1980) dollars. As a result of the reduced support of the federal government, almost every institution of higher education is struggling to operate effectively with diminished resources. One of the key factors in the current fiscal crisis is the decrease in federal support to college students in higher education. Since 1990, federal funds to higher education have increased slightly (15%) but there has been a reduction in assistance to college students (8.3%). In addition, most federal funds for education have flowed as block grants to the individual states, with no guarantee that the funds were spent on higher education. These funds to "state agencies" increased almost 98% from 1980 to 1994.

Coupled with an understanding of the costs of higher education, attention continues to be focused on the economic and social outcomes of higher education. During the decades of the 1980s and early 1990s this interest was driven by institutional survival needs and by the public expectation that colleges and universities contribute to the economic well-being of our nation by producing a highly trained and skilled workforce. Projections concerning the composition of the student body in the future were daunting for higher education leaders. Research conducted in the early 1990s indicated that by the turn of the century, students were likely to be older, non-Anglo, poorer both financially and educationally, and limited in numbers. Changes in the composition of students on campus signified many challenges for college and university leaders. Student enrollment forecasts in several southern and western states were formidable. Issues of resource constraint, accountability, and outcomes all emerged as important when predicting the financial stability of the institution. Both student and institutional factors interacted to create an evolving dynamic which has resulted in the diminished support of postsecondary education in the mid-1990s.

DEMOGRAPHIC PROJECTIONS

The student body attending higher education institutions across the country experienced dramatic changes heading for the turn of the twentieth century. Garcia (1994) contended that the changing composition of student bodies may be responsible for lengthening the actual time necessary to complete a baccalaureate degree program and commensurably increase the cost of education.

The percentage of the population classified as white declined relative to the percentage comprised of people of color due to low birth rates among whites and changing immigration patterns (Renner 1993). Population projections indicated that in the period from 1985 to 2000 the nation's youth population would rise by 2.4 million Hispanics, 1.7 million blacks, 483,000 other ethnic children, and only 60,000 Caucasians (Hodgkinson 1990). By the year 2000, whites were projected to compose a little more than 33% of the pool of college applicants, blacks 17%, Hispanics 12%, and Asians about 4% (Levine 1990).

The early 1990s saw the socioeconomic status and family backgrounds of students entering higher education also shifting. More and more children were being born into poverty. Hodgkinson (1990) reported almost 15 million children were growing up in single-parent homes. Hispanics and blacks, the largest of the nonwhite groups, had the highest rates of poverty and the lowest rates of educational attainment (Levine 1990).

By the mid-1990s, the number of traditional-age students entering post-secondary education, those in the 18–24 year-old cohort, had declined while the population of students over the age of 25 was growing significantly. In 1994 O'Connor reported that about 43% of all college students were age 25 or older. The number of students over the age of 30 more than doubled in the period from 1974 to 1994 and growth of 16% was projected by the year 2000, while growth in the traditional student group was projected to remain constant. Primarily women and minorities comprised the adult learner population.

The lower socioeconomic status of students coupled with changes in financial aid policies and a shift from grants to loans made it necessary for many student to work, either full- or part time, often interrupting or delaying degree attainment. The proportion of students in four-year institutions attending part-time increased from 26.7% in 1970 to 31.4% in 1989 (Tinto 1993).

However, this trend is expected to decline into the year 2000. At the start of the 1990s, demographic information indicated changes in racial and ethnic composition, socioeconomic status and family background, age, and gender of the student body.

While the demographics of the student body attending higher education will continue to change, total enrollment is expected to increase through the year 2005. High-end projections for enrollment growth in all institutions of higher education expect the student population to exceed 16 million by the year 2005. The largest growth in public-supported higher education is anticipated in the four-year institutions (8.8% growth for 1994 to 2005) while two-year schools will grow at approximately 7.6% for the same period. Private undergraduate education will grow at 10.9%.

THE ECONOMIC EFFECTS ON EDUCATION

In addition to demographic projections, the changing economics of higher education have had a strong effect on students' decisions to attend college and the financing of higher education. The late 1980s and 1990s were a difficult time for higher education and its relationship with the public. Colleges and universities experienced significant tuition increases, but higher education did not see a commensurate growth in financial aid. Colleges and universities charged higher prices with no noticeable change in the services provided, causing the American public to become skeptical of higher education's objectives and the efficiency with which institutions fulfilled these objectives. Two themes received increased attention in American higher education: institutional accountability and educational quality. State legislatures challenged public institutions with new performance-based accountability demands. Heavy competition with other government agencies for state funding made it necessary for colleges and universities across the country to demonstrate to lawmakers the value of an education to both the individual and to society. With high tuition charges and decreased financial aid, students and parents needed information on both the economic value of an education and how colleges and universities spent the funds allocated to them.

Recent discussion of the value of an education have focused on costs and benefits. The individual and the public have a clear understanding of the financial investments and sacrifices committed to higher education. Indeed, the cost side of the equation has gained a great deal of attention from the early 1990s. During this time period, as the job market became increasingly competitive and employment prospects for college graduates were bleak, both the individual and society questioned their investment in education and pressure mounted for the benefits of this investment to be better articulated. Productivity demands by policy makers and the public meant the higher education institutions had to make adjustments to increase financial and educational yields on taxpayers' investments.

Alexander (1993) stated that the benefits of education

may be broadly categorized as anything which (a) increases production through income in the capacity of the labor force, (b) increases efficiency by reducing unnecessary costs, thereby reserving resources for the enhancement of human productivity—for example the release of public resources from law enforcement to more productive pursuits—and (c) increases the social consciousness of the community so living conditions are enhanced.

In general the explanations of a value of an education can be divided into four basic categories: (1) economic value expressed as monetary value to the individual; (2) economic value expressed as monetary value to society; (3) social value expressed as skills, sensitivities, and knowledge provided to the individual; and (4) social value as a contribution to the efficient functioning of society. These four explanations frequently overlap, as do the benefits associated with education, and they often drive decisions concerning attendance made by students and their parents.

MONETARY VALUE OF HIGHER EDUCATION TO THE INDIVIDUAL

There are three ways to estimate the monetary yield of a college education to the individual: earnings differentials, the net present value of a college education (the present value of a college education after costs are subtracted and corrections are made to adjust for the changing value of money over time), and traditionally calculated private rates of return (Becker and Lewis 1992; Leslie and Brinkman 1988).

The earnings differentials concept has been identified as the most rudimentary approach for estimating the pecuniary value of a college education. The earnings measure indicates how much more, on average, a college graduate earned than other individuals with less education. This measure has been used because it is easy to calculate and generally less contentious than more complex measures. A drawback to the earnings differential is that the measure identified only benefits and omitted costs. Because of this, earnings differentials were of little value when comparing the yield on an investment in education with other investment alternatives. The measure also failed to account for preexisting differences between college attendees and nonattendees.

Despite the weaknesses of this measure, it was widely used as a method for quantifying the value of a college education to the individual. In 1972, the income per year of male high school graduates averaged $10,433 in comparison with $16,201 for male college graduates (Alexander 1993). Comparative data revealed that the mean annual income for male high school graduates in 1939 was about 60% of that for male college graduates—a percentage that had not changed significantly by 1972. In 1983, the median income of college graduates was more than $6,000 greater than that of high school graduates for males aged 25–34 (Leslie and Brinkman 1988.) Further, it was noted that while education did not pay as well for black males or for women, all groups realized a substantial rise in income with progressive education. The ratio of median college to high school graduate earnings stood at 1.47 for white males, 1.94 for white females, 1.76 for black males, and 2.04 for black females in 1990 (Becker and Lewis 1992).

Net present value (NPV) was a second measure for quantifying the economic value of an education to the individual. NPV estimated the present value of an education by subtracting costs from benefits adjusted to reflect the changing value of a dollar over time. For example, based on 1979 data, it was reported that the benefits of education for male college graduates relative to high school graduates were $60,000, net of foregone earnings. This research also revealed that for males, the present value of benefits exceeds the present value of costs by $23,000; for females the difference was only $7,000. A dollar investment in four years of college yields, on average, $1.62 for men and $1.19 for women in benefits (Cohn and Geske 1990).

A drawback to NPV analysis was the sensitivity of the measure to discount rate selection. Questions often arose as to the determination of the discount rate and whether the real or nominal interest rate was a better measure. A slight change in the magnitude of the discount rate produced large changes in the size of the net present value. Higher lifetime earnings were indicated when a person completed more years of schooling and a lower discount rate was chosen.

By the mid-1990s, the internal rate of return was the most broadly used measure for estimating the value of an education. This measure related total resource costs of education to income benefits and was derived by projecting a lifetime stream of earnings and the costs of attendance. Costs were corrected to current dollars and the analyst calculated the interest or discount rate that set the earnings value equal to the cost value. The internal rate of return was the discount rate at which the net present value calculation equaled zero. The net present value analysis was heavily influenced by discount rate selection, while this measure was not. Additionally, the internal rate of return was more widely understood by the general public. Rate of return measures are highly sensitive to cost fluctuations. Because of this, private rates of return to elementary and secondary education were much higher than those to postsecondary education, due to the relatively low costs to the individual associated with K-12 schooling and the reduced foregone earnings resulting from the earlier return to the workforce. In 1990, it was reported that the private rate of return for four-year higher education to be between 10 and 15%. The private rate of return was somewhat higher for white males than it was for females and African Americans (Cohn and Geske 1990).

MONETARY BENEFITS OF HIGHER EDUCATION TO SOCIETY

Three methods are commonly used in the calculation of the economic benefits of education to society. Historically, these measures were the social rate of return, growth accounting studies (which assess the percentages of national income growth derived from education), and economic impact studies.

Social rates of return were calculated in the same way as private rates of return. This measure differed from the private rate of return in that it used costs to society for supplying educational services in the calculation. These costs, in most cases, were specified as the Educational and General (E&G) expenditures of institutions plus all or part of the student's foregone earnings. Education and General expenditures have grown consistently over the past 15 years. In 1980 E&G expenditures were $44 billion or approximately $10,993 per full-time-equivalent student. Recent projections indicate that E&G expenditures will exceed $92 billion or $17,234 per full-time student by the year 2004. Since benefits were assessed by the pretax wages and earnings a student accrued over their lifetime, the rate of increase of E&G expenditures would have a negative effect on the rate of return calculation.

Social rates of return were often used to guide policy makers as they made decisions concerning fiscal allocations. Over time, social rates of return have typically been a few percentage points below private rates of return because of the manner in which higher education is subsidized; students pay only a fraction of the total costs of educating themselves and the remainder is borne by society.

A variety of studies found social rates of return to range from 11% to 15% during the period 1965 to 1990. The drawback to social rate of return analysis was that the measure excluded both monetary benefits that spill over to others and all nonmonetary benefits of education. The interpretation of social rates of return presented similar limitations to private rates of return and was also highly sensitive to costs.

One approach to overcoming the benefits omissions of social rate of return studies was to analyze the proportion of economic gain attributable to higher education and related activities. National income growth was used as the dependent variable and classic measures of production—land, labor, and capital—as the independent variable. Educational outlays were treated as influencing a portion of labor's contribution to the national economy's growth. Again various studies revealed estimates generally in the 15–20% range with approximately one-fourth of this economic growth assigned to education. In 1992 it was reported that although higher education directly connected to only 4–5% of the national income growth, it was probably indirectly linked to another 20–40% of this growth (Becker and Lewis 1991).

Economic impact studies were designed to measure the increase in a region's economic activity attributable to the presence of a college or university. Economic impact studies were viewed as studies of externalities because they drew attention to the value added by colleges to their communities to prove the social benefits to education. Economic impact studies traditionally examined short-term benefits of higher education and did not study the long-term quantifiable investment benefits of education.

The traditional method of economic impact assessment was developed by Caffrey and Isaacs in 1971 and rests on the economic base approach. Studies that modeled the Caffrey and Isaacs framework isolated economic gains attributable to the presence of a college or university. These analyses attempted to factor out consumption activities that merely recycled community funds and focused on economic gains represented by the export of goods and services in exchange for outside revenues.

Utilizing the Caffrey and Isaacs framework, economic impact studies assessed the impact of postsecondary institutions by measuring the following regional components: the impact on local business, the impact on local government, and the impact on local individuals. The major analytical task of these studies was distinguishing between expenditures representing actual gains to the local economy from those that were recycled funds. Economic impact studies of this nature ignored long-range economic impacts such as the enhancement of workers' skills and the relationship between research and local industry.

Despite these shortcomings, economic impact studies were widely used to highlight higher education's economic contributions to society. For community colleges, the type of institution most frequently considered in an economic impact assessment, studies revealed that the mean business volume to college budget ratio was 1.6 and the jobs created to budget ratio, in millions of dollars, was about 55, expressed in 1988–89 dollars for the period 1985–86. This meant that a community college annual budget of $10 million generated $16 million in business volume and created 550 jobs in 1988–89. For four-year institutions in the same time period, the business volume to budget ratio was 1.8 and the jobs to budget ratio, in millions of dollars, was 53% (Becker and Lewis 1992; Leslie and Brinkman 1988).

An alternative approach to economic impact studies focused on input-output analysis and utilized information about transactions with local industries. A regional input-output model was "designed to estimate the indirect impact of properly and carefully specified direct or initial impact experienced in one or more industry sectors within a region" (Goldstein 1990, 53). For example, this method was used to estimate the impact of the University of North Carolina–Chapel Hill's sponsored research budget on the state. It was concluded that for fiscal year 1983, the university's total sponsored research funds of $52.5 million resulted in $26.6 million in direct in-state expenditures and in $26.8 million of indirect and induced expenditure in the state economy, yielding a total output impact of $53.4 million. The drawbacks to this type of economic impact analysis were the time and costs associated because of the enormous data requirements and the failure to account for the nonmonetary stimulus colleges and universities provided to local economies.

CURRENT INSTITUTIONAL REVENUE AND
EXPENDITURE PATTERNS

In the 1980s, American higher education enjoyed a substantial increase in its revenues from each of the major sources of revenue: state and local funding, tuition and fees, annual gifts and endowment income, and federal funds. The increase in revenue resulted in increased expenditures for all higher education from $104.5 billion in 1980 to an estimated $151 billion in 1990 (in constant 1992 dollars). The seeming intent of colleges and universities to maximize revenues in the 1980s from any and all sources contributed to the erosion of public trust and confidence in American higher education and set the stage for the push on accountability and the careful scrutiny of resource allocation that occurred in the 1990s. Postsecondary education leaders focused on increasing quality by spending more instead of spending differently, creating the public perception that program quality and student learning had not kept pace with resource increases. The increase in expenditures were most notable in the public four-year sector which experienced a 35% ($14,019–$18,011) growth in per student expenditure from 1980 to 1994, while two-year institutions experienced a 12.7% growth ($5,345–$6,028) for the same period.

Hauptman (1993) suggested that the financial issues facing postsecondary institutions in the 1990s be divided into two basic questions: (1) How do colleges and universities finance themselves? (2) How is the money spent?

From a financing perspective, the most pressing challenge facing public institutions during this era was what to do about state cutbacks brought about by the recession and increased competition for state resources from prisons, healthcare providers, K–12 education, and other state agencies.

For private institutions, the most prominent issue was the question of the limits of the high tuition/high aid strategy that worked so well in the 1980s. Students in private four-year and two-year schools depended on financial assistance to offset the high tuition charged by these institutions. Private institutions had seen the greatest increase in expenditures during the 1980s, which increased approximately 49% ($17,009–$25,451) per full-time student from 1980 to 1994. In addition, almost 70% of private-school students received some form of financial assistance by 1993. The projected decrease in tuition/student assistance from federal sources would greatly influence the ability of students to attend these schools.

The environment of limited resources and public accountability pressures on colleges and universities that surrounded higher education institutions in the early 1990s led to considerable concern over how colleges and universities spent the funds they received. While higher education consumers were still interested in the monetary and nonmonetary returns of a college degree, more interest focused on spending patterns and how these spending patterns affected student learning and degree completion. Cost pressures impacting colleges and universities were students going into higher-cost majors, the need for new technology, socially mandated programs, and the cost of borrowing to purchase land, buildings, and equipment. Colleges and universities responded to these cost pressures in an environment of limited resources by freezing the number of faculty members, allowing the faculty to shrink through attrition, imposing tighter budget controls at all levels of the institution, delaying or deferring renovations of facilities and capital maintenance projects, eliminating marginal programs, and adjusting course offerings each semester.

Odden and Massy (1992) identified four categories of the cost/productivity/resource allocation debate:

1. The "cost disease" was associated with any activity that was labor intensive. As costs or salaries rise, the cost of the activity also rises. This assumed that faculty salaries must increase to keep education competitive. The "cost disease" also assumed that the way institutions provided services was fixed and did not take advantage of new technology to increase productivity.

2. The "growth force" was the idea that quality costs money and that any activity, such as education, has to grow over time in order to increase quality.

3. The "administrative lattice" was the phenomenon of middle managers and staff increasing at a rate faster than front line service providers—in this case, faculty.

4. The "academic ratchet" was the evolution of teaching norms that, over time, produced lower class sizes and teaching loads and more support staff for functions professors performed in the past, changes which require more resources.

Applying these concepts to higher education provided insight into re-source allocation decisions made by colleges and universities in the early 1990s.

Application of the "cost disease" to higher education was simple. When wages rise in the economy as a whole, it is usually a combination of both inflation and increases in general productivity. Since higher education is labor intensive it is common sense that teaching costs will rise. This assumes that that teaching is done by professors, the student-faculty ratio remains constant, and there are no internal efficiency improvements. Therefore, if higher education is to remain competitive, according to the cost disease concept, professors' salaries would have to rise in accordance with the in-flation rate plus the increase in productivity.

This was the exact behavior colleges and universities engaged in during the 1980s. Higher education institutions continually tried to expose stu-dents to new ideas. Eventually, new knowledge, coupled in some cases with the quest for increased academic prestige and stature, led to a need for increased technology, more classes, and the addition of new fields of study, while at the same time maintaining traditional paths of study. In an attempt to continually improve quality, the "growth force" caused a "constant lay-ering of new ideas, methods and programs on top of old ones resulting in a constant pressure to add courses, faculty, technology, and facilities to keep pace with expanding knowledge (Odden and Massy 1992, 13). The construction or renovation of recreational, cultural, and housing facilities on many campuses contributed to criticism that colleges spend too much money on frivolous items not central to the institution's educational mis-sion. Much of this activity took place, however, to maintain a "quality" edge (Hauptman 1993; Waggaman 1991).

Growth in revenues in the 1980s led to an increase in administrative staffs on many campuses, referred to as the administrative lattice. Haupt-man (1993, 19) noted, "in the 1970s and throughout the 1980s, admin-istrative costs were one of the fastest growing components of higher education expenditures, and administrative staffs grew much faster than the number of faculty." Administrative staffs grew an average of 60% be-tween 1975 and 1985, while faculty increased by an average of less than

6% in the same period (Odden and Massy 1992). Higher education leaders defended this growth in administrative staffs by arguing that regulatory burdens resulting from the enactment of environmental, healthcare, disability, campus crime, and other legislation created a greater demand for staff. Higher administrative costs were also associated with greater staff professionalism and the delivery of better services to students.

Faculty salaries overall increased in real terms in the 1980s, attributed to the catch-up from the 1970s when faculty salaries lagged behind the rate of inflation. Faculty priorities over the last several decades have changed, a phenomenon known as output creep and the academic ratchet. By the early 1990s, faculty no longer devoted the majority of their time to teaching and related activities such as academic advising and mentoring; instead, their primary focus increasingly was research, scholarship, and professional service. Faculty spent more time on research and scholarship because curriculum changes and increases in support staff or faculty/student ratios allowed this flexibility. Colleges and universities paid additional staff to provide advising and counseling services, once the responsibility of faculty. Institutions attempted to improve productivity by substituting lower paid individuals for those with higher levels of expertise. Odden and Massy (1992, 13) stated:

In academic departments, this means hiring graduate teaching and research assistants, administrative assistants, secretaries, and technicians to take over certain faculty functions. Using less costly individuals frees up faculty to devote more time to research and other professional activities. But even less costly individuals require more resources. In most cases, therefore, leveraging faculty time drives up the overall costs of higher education.

"Enacted norms," shared beliefs about the faculty relationship with the environment, as well as curriculum restructuring also had resource allocation implications for colleges and universities. Faculty developed certain "property rights" they felt were inherent in their position such as student/faculty ratios, number of courses taught per term, the division of teaching between upper and lower division courses, and ideal class size. Property rights had implications for students in terms of when classes were taught, the number of sections taught, and class size. Additionally, colleges and universities moved away from a more structured curriculum to one that provided a large menu of courses, unconstrained by traditional sequence requirements. For students, this lack of structure often meant taking courses unnecessary for degree requirements.

By the early 1990s, competition for declining numbers of postundergraduate students had resource allocation implications for colleges and universities. Institutions began spending more money on recruitment activities and expanding facilities and services such as recreational and cultural facilities, student unions, and grounds to make their campuses more attractive to prospective students. Institutions that experienced rising enrollments did not experience a concurrent growth in resources for faculty and facilities. The number and size of course sections taught did not meet student demand and was often restricted by limited classroom space and the number of faculty available to teach.

Resource limitations in the 1990s meant that colleges and universities could not do as much as they did in the past. Where institutions chose to spend these limited funds had implication for time-to-degree rates.

SUMMARY

The higher education environment in the 1990s differed significantly from the environment of previous decades. Continued growth, changing student demographics, diminished revenue sources, coupled with increased concern over accountability for monitoring the relationship between performance and finance presented new challenges for postsecondary education. Outcome measurements assumed a new importance with the growing public demand for accountability. Traditional outcome measurements such as graduation rates, student employability upon graduation, persistence and retention rates, and economic and social returns of the education process gained greater importance in assessing the effectiveness of colleges and universities.

ACKNOWLEDGMENT

This chapter was prepared with the assistance of Karen Sayles.

REFERENCES

Alexander, K. 1993. The Value of Education: 86. In David W. Breneman, Larry L. Leslie, and Richard E. Anderson, eds., *ASHE Reader on Finance in Higher Education*, Washington, DC: Association for the Study of Higher Education.

Becker, W. E. and Lewis, D. R. eds. 1992. *The Economics of American Higher Education*. Boston: Cluwer Academic Publishers.

Caffrey, J. and Isaacs, H. H. 1971. *Estimating the Economic Impact of a College or University on the Local Economy*. Washington, DC: American Council on Education.

Cohn, E. and Geske, T. G. 1990. *The Economics of Education*, 3rd ed. New York: Pergamon Press.

Garcia, P. May. 1994. *Graduation and Time to Degree: A Research Note from the California State University*. Eric Document Reproduction Services, No. 373 643.

Goldstein, H. A. 1990. Estimating the Regional Economic Impact of Universities: An Application of Input-Output Analysis. *Planning for Higher Education* 18: 53.

Hauptman, A. M. 1993. *Higher Education Finance Issues in the Early 1990s.* New Brunswick, NJ: Consortium for Policy Research in Education: 19.

Hodgkinson, H. L. 1990. Hard Numbers, Tough Choices. In *AGB Reports* (November/December): 12.

Leslie, L. L. and Brinkman, P. T. 1988. *The Economic Value of Higher Education.* New York: American Council on Education and Macmillan.

Levine, A. 1990. Defying Demographics. *CASE Currents* 16:26.

O'Connor, P. J. 1994. The Needs of Adult University Students: A Case Study. *College and University* 69:84.

Odden, A. and W. Massy. 1992. *Funding Schools and Universities: Improving Productivity and Equity.* New Brunswick, NJ: Consortium for Policy Research in Education (November): 13.

Renner, K. E. 1993. On Race and Gender in Higher Education: Illusions of Change. *Educational Record* 74:12.

Tinto, V. 1993. *Leaving College: Rethinking the Causes and Cures of Student Attrition.* Chicago: University of Chicago Press.

The Process of Setting Tuition in Public University Systems: A Case Study of Interaction Between Governing Board and Campus Management

Robert H. Fenske, Frank H. Besnette, and Stephen M. Jordan

This chapter provides a descriptive case study of the complex relationship and shared responsibility of a public university governing board and campus management. Few activities reveal the character of this relationship better than the process of setting tuition in the climate of shrinking state appropriations for institutional budgets and rapid changes in student financial aid.

The governing board must set the tuition level based on projected revenue from a number of sources, but the optimal level is a compromise affected by external factors beyond the control of the board (such as political climate and governmental appropriations) and by campus administrative decisions, most particularly those relating to student aid. Adding to the complexity is the influence of the state government (executive and legislative branches) on one hand and students as organized consumers on the other.

In the past, tuition levels at public universities were mainly determined by state financial resources and information provided by campus administrators. But that was before the era of an adequate number of competent board staff enabling trustees to make informed decisions that are less dependent on data provided by campus presidents. It was also before the participation of student organizations capable of sophisticated data analysis and effective lobbying. In addition, executive and legislative branches of state government now have specialized staff capable of effective analysis of university budgets. Furthermore, federal government decisions on funding of student aid greatly affect total institutional finances.

We use as the basis for our discussion the actual process of tuition setting in the public university system of two states, Arizona and Kansas. In both states a single board has governing responsibility for all state-supported universities, and each board determines tuition and fee levels for the set of institutions it governs. As will be shown, the tuition-setting process is a complex and sometimes tension-filled annual activity that spans most of the year.

The following two sections provide background information and an overview of the many interacting issues and forces affecting tuition levels. Both state university systems have a unique set of variables peculiar to the history and political climate of the state, yet both are profoundly influenced by national trends such as tuition levels in similar institutions used for peer comparisons, the actions of the federal government in funding student financial aid, and, by the attempts by other states to manage the relationship between tuition and state-funded student aid.

Both Arizona and Kansas are proud of their universities. This pride causes many of the players in the tuition-setting process in each state to regard their system as both unique and self-sufficient, yet these boards, legislative and gubernatorial staffs, campus administrators, and student organizations will not hesitate to use regional and national yardsticks to support their particular perspectives.

After the discussion of national and regional trends, we identify the major players in each university system's setting and then describe the interactions of these players in the tuition-setting process. The chapter concludes by highlighting how events and interactions in the process can inform campus administrators about the importance of the interplay and influence of these external forces on the welfare of the campus. Tuition setting is a good example of the continuing loss of insularity by today's public universities.

BACKGROUND

Historically, costs to attend public institutions levied on students and their families were low, comprising a very small portion of the total cost of educating each student. Low or no tuition appealed to the populist instinct through the 19th century, and carried on through to the middle of the 20th century. However, the Veteran's Readjustment Act of 1944 (the so-called GI Bill) rapidly increased enrollments, and that spurt, along with the jump in the percentage of 18-year-olds completing high school and planning for college, created a higher level of enrollment demand that has not abated to the present time. Despite the enrollment pressure, tuition in public universities remained relatively low well into the 1970s.

By the late 1950s over half of the states provided student financial aid both to ensure access by students from lower-income families and, in many states, to protect the competitiveness of the private higher education sector by making the grants and scholarships available for use at private colleges as well as public ones. The massive student programs initiated by Title IV of the 1965 Higher Education Act (HEA) were modeled after the state programs, but were intended to pursue a national agenda of ensuring equal opportunity for higher education to disadvantaged youth. The entrance by the federal government into the financing equation caused a reexamination of the issue of how the states should finance higher education (Bowen 1974).

The 1972 Amendments to the HEA brought the concept of access to higher education as a near entitlement through the Basic Educational Opportunity Grant (later renamed Pell Grants) program. The intent of Congress was to ensure that every high school graduate admissible to an accredited postsecondary institution was provided a "floor" of basic financial support keyed to cost of attendance at a college selected by the student. Need for the grant and other types of aid such as work-study programs was determined by a formula responsive both to the ability of the students and their families to pay and to the cost of college, either public or private. As the Carnegie Council on Policy Studies in Higher Education (1975) observed, the era of low or no tuition in public colleges was over by the mid-1970s. The tradition held on through the decade in the western and southwestern states, but tuition moved higher in all other regions. Beginning in the early 1980s, however, tuition in the private sector increased rapidly and the public sector largely followed suit. In both sectors, tuition increases exceeded both the rate of inflation and the modest increase in family income through the decade and into the 1990s.

Gold (1975), in a thorough analysis of state fiscal policies and problems in the decade of the 1980s and the first half of the 1990s, characterizes this period as one of "crisis." He labels higher education a "weak" contender for its share of state finances in an era that saw demands for expenditures far outstrip the slower growth in revenues. In the case of four-year colleges and universities, the state can simply curtail appropriations and assume that the institutions can meet the shortfall by finding new sources—for example, raising funds from private sources such as individual and corporate donations, or by entrepreneurial means including establishment of research parks or provision of expert services like survey research. Most pointedly, however, the state in a fiscal crisis can in effect tell the institutions to increase user fees in the form of tuition and charges for academic services like laboratory and computer usage and field trips that were formerly free to the student. This approach assumes that increases in net price to students and their families can be met without forcing the students to disenroll or never matriculate in the first place because of inadequate resources. In the case of middle- or high-income families of traditional age (18–24) students, this is generally a valid assumption. But access and retention become crucial issues for students with low ability to pay.

In 1987, Allan Ostar (p. 133), in writing about state tuition policies and public higher education, asked, "Who should assume the major share of the costs of public higher education? Individual students and their families? Or society as a whole?" He concluded that "no single issue is more vexing to relationships between state governments and public colleges and universities." Recent increases in tension between legislatures and public universities over funding underscore the validity of an observation made over sixty years ago: "Legislatures are interested (or should be) in education from the point of view of state welfare and economy, and are not interested greatly in institutional welfare" (Kelly and McNeely 1933).

ISSUES

Tuition charges to students at public institutions have become a perennial issue in the financing of public higher education. . . . The context within which tuition decisions are made also has become much more financially and politically complex. Today, tuition policies are pulled in different directions by competing ideas about the most "efficient" pricing and allocation of higher education, about the best way to deal with escalating costs in providing education, and about the relation of tuition to the availability of need-based student assistance, to mention just a few of the related economic and policy considerations. (Lenth 1993, 1)

Public universities in Arizona and Kansas share in the problems and issues besetting public higher education across the country. The Western Interstate Commission for Higher Education (1994) identified the interplay among the factors of access, quality, and student costs (especially tuition) as the major dilemma of higher education in the 1990s. The dilemma has its roots in the fiscal crisis of the states as discussed above. But tuition in many states began to increase faster than inflation or the cost of living as early as the mid-1970s. Some observers trace the increase to the 1973 report of the influential Carnegie Commission on Higher Education entitled *Higher Education: Who Pays? Who Benefits? Who Should Pay?* Essentially, the Commission pointed out that while society in general benefits from a highly educated workforce, the individual who attains a college baccalaureate personally benefits greatly through a relatively high lifetime income. Furthermore, the earnings advantage is gained at the expense of the taxpayer when the graduate earns the degree at a low-tuition public college or university. A basic question of fairness is raised when citizens with less than a college degree provide a relative advantage to the graduate through involuntary taxation.

Access

The Carnegie Commission recommended in 1973 that public colleges and universities abandon the strategy of low or no tuition and allow tuition to rise to about one-third the cost of education to the student (p. 109). In regard to concern that higher tuition might unduly restrict access to low-income students, the Commission pointed out that "a policy of low tuition by itself does no good for a student who cannot afford to go to college even at low tuition" (p. 7). As Fischer (1990) and Wallace (1992) pointed out more recently, low tuition mainly benefits students from middle- and upper-income families who would have gone to college anyway, since they could afford to pay more if necessary. Little research has been done to directly examine the relationship between tuition increases and enrollment of low-income students. However, Savoca (1990) found that "tuition hikes cause a substantial shift in the composition of the applicant pool away from low-income students" (p. 129).

The major factor in buffering the effects of increased tuition on low-income students was the rise of modest state programs of need-based aid in the 1950s, and then the advent of the massive federal need-based aid programs in the 1965 Higher Education Act. The Washington Office of the College Board recently calculated that federal student aid expenditures from 1965 through the 1995 fiscal year totaled $410 billion. Have these massive expenditures maintained wide access to higher education? Unquestionably, need-based aid has allowed many low-income youth to attend college who otherwise could not have gone. Yet socioeconomic status remains the major determinant of college-going within all ability levels (Fenske and Gregory 1994).

Many reasons have been advanced to account for the persistent under-enrollment of students from low-income families despite the massive expenditures of need-based student aid. The pronounced shift from "gift aid" (grants and scholarships) to "self-help" (loans and employment) is often cited as a primary reason. Low-income families usually borrow only in emergency situations and consequently have difficulty repaying loans because they have low or nonexistent net worth to use if one or more payments are missed. In contrast, middle- or upper-income families often borrow for strategic reasons—for example, refinancing a house mortgage to take advantage of lower interest rates or to consolidate other loans, or borrowing to leverage an income opportunity such as investing in a business. In any case, the prospect of incurring a large debt burden as the opportunity cost of obtaining an educational credential is more palatable for students from families with a high level of financial capacity.

Cost

Over the past decade, attention has increasingly turned to what Hearn, Griswold, and Marine (1995) have termed the "rationalization" of tuition policy through the "high tuition/high student aid" model. Vermont is the leading example, but a few other states also have deliberately moved toward this model. Essentially, the model calls for raising tuition at public four-year institutions to a level equal to at least half of the actual cost of education and, in those states where there is a significant nonprofit private sector, to a level that would come close enough to private colleges that they would become competitive on the basis of cost alone. The additional institutional revenue generated by public institutions through tuition would be made available to needy students in the form of institutional grants to preserve access for low-income students. This model is the antithesis of the populist low or no tuition philosophy. The latter is seen as basically inequitable because, by overestimating societal benefit compared to individual benefit, it amounts to an unneeded subsidy to students who could afford to attend anyway, while at the same time denying access to low income students who cannot afford the "threshold" costs of attendance regardless of tuition.

Despite the rational arguments of these and other advocates, the high tuition/high aid model has not been adopted by many states. Apparently, there is a reluctance to discard the populist basis on which most public universities were founded. The view of higher education as of general societal benefit especially appealed to developing states west of the Mississippi in the 19th century. Arizona and Kansas, like California and other western states, maintained this "frontier" populist philosophy until very recent times. There is also the recognition that the "set-aside" funds for need-based aid generated by increased tuition revenues would be too tempting a source of funds to use in a fiscal emergency (Johnstone 1993). Another consideration is that middle- and upper-income families accustomed to low tuition regard it as a subsidy derived from their own taxes paid to the state to support higher education. Such families include, much more often than low-income families, registered voters who are willing and able to influence state government policies in the voting booth. Finally, campus administrators would be wary of too obvious a process of "robbing Peter to pay Paul," which is how some students would view paying high tuition to directly subsidize the attendance of fellow students (Greer 1994).

Of major interest in recent years is the possibility of obtaining sufficient budgetary savings through cost containment measures to reduce or eliminate the need to continually increase tuition. Cost containment has been advocated in many forms, most of which involve streamlining various university operations and even "downsizing" by eliminating outmoded or low-enrollment academic programs. Often, the specific rationale for such measures is the need to keep tuition costs down. Student leaders contesting tuition increases will often point out that such increases would not be necessary if the institution could become more cost-efficient.

Despite the persistent evidence that student aid has only partially removed financial barriers to college attendance, college costs continue to rise faster than inflation and the modest increase in net family income. Thus, the dilemma has produced a situation wherein rising costs continue to restrict access to public universities of low-income students despite massive expenditures of student aid. At the same time, political pressure to keep tuition as low as possible combined with the declining rate of state higher education appropriations have generated questions about the effect of such pressures on quality in higher education.

Quality

The challenge of balancing access and rising costs takes on a new and more complex dimension when the factor of quality is added to the mix. Can a public university maintain wide access, especially to low-income and educationally disadvantaged students, and at the same time maintain and even increase quality of its educational programs? And how can this be done within the constraints of rising costs and shrinking resources?

The question of quality is increasingly raised along with higher tuition because students and their parents begin to perceive that they are no longer primarily recipients of public largesse as was true in the low or no tuition era. Then, the university could, and did, have the attitude that students must prove themselves educationally worthy of admission, retention, and graduation. Even in those states like Ohio and Kansas that had the tradition or legal requirement of admitting all graduates of the state's high schools, the qualitative imperative was imposed after matriculation. "Weeding out" courses were many and the "flunk-out" rate was high. State appropriations were more often in the form of block grants rather than tied to an enrollment-driven formula, so the university had every incentive to maintain high standards and little incentive to inflate enrollment to capture appropriations.

The attitude vis-à-vis the student and university has now reversed. Since every student enrolled not only brings a state subsidy for the educational budget, but also pays an increasingly significant proportion of that budget, the attitude reverses to the institution proving itself worthy as the students' choice of college as well as a recipient of state largesse. Consequently, direct bargains are sometimes struck in the tuition-setting process wherein student leaders will accede to a hefty tuition increase if the governing board and the universities under its control will agree to a specified qualitative improvement. One of the problems, is that the board, the institution, and students often have divergent views of what constitutes quality. The university president may give highest priority to faculty salary increases in order to avoid losing the best faculty to competitors, the board may want to replace the tenure system with periodic evaluations, and the students may demand expanded course offerings taught by ranked faculty.

TUITION SETTING IN ARIZONA PUBLIC UNIVERSITIES

Major Players

Arizona Board of Regents

According to the Report of the Commission on Student Costs and Financial Assistance (1994), the Arizona Board of Regents (ABOR) is the governing board of Arizona's three public universities: Arizona State University, the University of Arizona, and Northern Arizona University. There are nine members appointed by the governor and confirmed by the senate. The governor and the state superintendent for public instruction serve as voting ex-officio members. Each appointed regent serves an eight-year term with the exception of the student regent, who serves a one-year term. Appointments are staggered, so that two regents are replaced every two years. Regents meet nine to eleven times per year, including one retreat session during the summer to devote focused study on selected important issues.

Members of the ABOR guide policy development for the three state universities. The board monitors development of financial policies and procedures and administers state and federal student financial aid programs.

Board Staff

Perhaps one of the most significant responsibilities of the board entails the setting of tuition. Five members of board staff at this point in time are involved in the tuition-setting process: the executive director, the associate executive director for financial affairs, two financial affairs assistants, and an administrative assistant. The executive director coordinates central office staff for the tuition-setting process. The associate executive director for financial affairs works directly with senior officers for financial and business affairs at each university, and provides leadership in developing financial policies and procedures. In addition, the associate executive director for financial affairs provides support to the board's resources committee, chairs the tuition work group, and reviews all financial and capital activities of each university. The financial affairs staff provide support to the associate executive director in the tuition-setting process. Some of their responsibilities include reviewing and analyzing university budgets/requests, calculating the cost of education per student used to determine certain financial relationships in the process, determining ability of universities to incur debt for capital projects, presenting the annual financial ratio analyses, providing analysis of tuition options, compiling data on tuition and fees in all 50 states for comparison purposes, and formulating the initial proposal for the amount of tuition and fee revenue to be "set aside" for need-based student aid.

Legislative/Governor's Staff

Another dimension of the tuition setting process involves the legislative staff and governor's staff. These staff members indirectly work with ABOR's central office during the tuition-setting process. Arizona's legislative staff in relation to tuition setting consists of an associate director for research, a research fiscal analyst, and staff from the budget committee. The budget manager from the Office of Strategic Planning and Budgeting is the representative from the governor's office. The legislative staff and the budget manager primarily monitor ABOR staff work in conjunction with university presidents, vice-presidents for student affairs, financial aid directors, and directors for fiscal planning and analysis.

Campus Management and Staff

Each of the three Arizona university presidents acts as the nexus between governmental and governance entities on the one hand, and the campus and its constituencies on the other. However, in the tuition-setting process, the student constituency is, as often as not, in an adversarial position to the campus administration. This relationship is increasingly true due to the perception by students that, as their share of institutional revenue grows, so should their influence in decisions about the level of tuition and fees and the expenditure of those funds. For example, if student leaders are told that higher tuition is needed to maintain adequate growth in faculty salaries, then they are likely to respond that they expect better quality of teaching and more ranked faculty in the classroom instead of teaching assistants.

The president must rely on many staff members to develop data and an effective strategy to achieve institutional budget goals in the tuition-setting process. The director of budgets and fiscal analysis, the director of the office of institutional research, the student financial aid office, the vice-presidents for student affairs and for external relations, and many others comprise the administrative team in the process. Issues of access, retention, program completion, and excessive student loan burden often surface; and as tuition increased rapidly beginning in the early 1980s, the controversies often were played out in the public media in an uncontrolled fashion. Beginning in 1993–94, the board acceded to student requests and provided a regularly scheduled public forum through interactive closed circuit television across the state. These annual events take place a short time before the board must make its final decision on tuition and fee levels.

Student Leaders

Student leaders play a significant role in the setting of tuition through an organized group called the Arizona Students Association (ASA). Each university has three voting representatives that include the student body president and two ASA directors. In addition, the student body president from the newly emerging components of the Arizona university system (Northern Arizona University–Yuma, The University of Arizona–Sierra Vista, and Arizona State University West) each have one vote. Through the organization of information and presentations, ASA provides the student perspective in the setting of tuition. ASA focuses on tuition and fees and the extent to which they are offset by student aid to produce a reasonable "net cost" to students.

The Tuition-Setting Process in Arizona

The Arizona Constitution states that education "shall be as nearly free as possible." The board of regents has operationalized this requirement by limiting the total mandatory resident student fees to an amount within the lower one-third of rates set by all other states for resident fees. Each year, a survey of tuition and mandatory fees at institutions throughout the 50 states is completed as part of the board process for setting tuition and fees. When comparing Arizona institutions to similar public universities, Arizona's resident rates have been well below the average rate.

Board policy establishes tuition and fee rates based in part upon a review of: (1) availability of student financial aid, (2) number of students receiving aid, (3) amount of aid by type of aid, and (4) ratio of gift aid to self-help aid. These data are categorized as need-based and non-need-based aid. Furthermore, reports are provided on the cost of education per student as well as on the demographic characteristics of Arizona students, including ethnic and economic status profiles.

In setting tuition and fees, the students and the presidents of the universities often disagree on two issues: the timeline for setting tuition and fees, and the amount that tuition and fees increase each year. Students are continually concerned about tuition being set too late in the spring semester. They advocate the setting of tuition and fees during the fall semester, which would allow them to plan their educational expenses for the following year. However, the university presidents encourage tuition setting after the legislature has decided on its annual appropriation, to allow the university to keep tuition and fee increases low as possible and to recognize that student fees should be a last resort in finding the universities in view of the Arizona Constitution provision that education "shall be as nearly free as possible." Generally, the presidents support higher tuition levels if sufficient increases in state appropriations are not forthcoming. This position is somewhat awkward and risky for the presidents because it puts them at odds with their students. Although students have attempted on a number of occasions to enlist and marshal the faculty and other staff in their tuition battle, the other segments have remained silent.

Students' Role

Students play a role in the setting of tuition by participating in tuition hearings and the tuition and fee work group that works directly with the associate executive director for financial affairs of the board of regents. The work group is composed of budget directors, financial aid directors, central office staff, ASA, and other student representatives. It gathers information and develops recommendations that are presented to the board in a formal report. Regents consider information heard from the group at the tuition hearings in their deliberations. Students in the work group participate in the same manner as university staff, providing information and making recommendations. The students have been instrumental in providing research information and position papers such as *Crafting a Managed Plan for Setting Tuition and Fees* (Arizona Students Association 1994) that presents recommendations for tuition, fees, and financial aid.

Tuition and fees fund additional student financial aid, multiple program needs (academic, academic support, and student services), federal and state mandates, and possibly additional academic bonds (debt). Students claim tuition and fee increases are driven significantly by institutional debt. Universities argue that increased debt has little, if any, effect upon tuition and fees and that one cannot establish such a relationship from the data.

TUITION SETTING IN KANSAS PUBLIC UNIVERSITIES

Major Players

The Kansas Board of Regents

The Kansas Board of Regents (KBOR) is the governing board for the six state public universities in Kansas, comprising four regional institutions (Wichita State University, Emporia State University, Pittsburg State University, and Fort Hope State University) and two research-oriented institutions (the University of Kansas and Kansas State University). The board is made up of nine members appointed by the governor and confirmed by the State Senate. An appointment to the Board of Regents is considered to be the most prestigious nonjudicial appointment in the state. By statute, there must be at least one regent from each congressional district, and there may be no more than one regent from any county. In addition, there may not be more than five regents from any major political party. Each regent serves a four-year term and appointments are staggered, typically with two appointments each year. Regents meet nine to ten times per year and have recently added a retreat session in August to discuss two or three policy issues jointly identified in consultation with the council of presidents (the six chief executive officers).

The Kansas Board of Regents is a policy-making body with broad responsibility in the areas of: (1) administration, (2) fiscal management, (3) facilities management, (4) academic affairs, (5) student affairs, and (6) legal affairs. The board reviews and approves the legislative budget requests of each university and establishes funding priorities for the regents system. The board also fixes tuition, fees, and charges collected by the institutions; reviews and approves land transactions; and has ultimate responsibility for university budgets totaling $1.2 billion.

Board Staff

The board is assisted in its six areas of responsibility by twelve professional staff and six support staff. There are four professional staff and one support staff participating in the evaluation and setting of tuition. In addition, one professional and two support staff are involved in evaluating and recommending state-supported financial aid programs. However, in Kansas, the setting of tuition and the evaluation of financial aid needs have proceeded along separate, and not necessarily parallel, tracks.

Lead responsibility for preparing information and analysis on tuition rates falls to the director of planning and budget. The director acts as the chief staff officer to the Regents Tuition and Fees Committee. He is assisted by the associate budget director and the research associate who have the principal responsibility for the preparation of an annual report entitled "The Value of Tuition in Kansas." The report has four major components: a comprehensive examination of current tuition rates in Kansas for all postsecondary institutions, public and independent; a comparison of Kansas Regents institutions' tuition rates compared to peer and national averages; an examination of the influence of tuition and fees upon Kansas relative to the consumer price index, per capita income, and family income; and an examination of the influence of tuition and fees upon the annual operating budgets. Staff also prepare various tuition-rate scenarios as requested by the committee.

Financial aid staff do not participate in preparation of materials for the Regents Tuition and Fees Committee nor in the discussions of the committee. Information about Kansas financial aid programs is provided by the staff during discussions of the regents budget which includes the state funded financial aid programs. Board staff are responsible for communicating the board's position on tuition and fees and on financial aid to the governor and the legislature. This is accomplished through written communication, testimony and one-on-one meetings.

Legislative/Governor Staff

Kansas is a strong executive state. Consequently, the governor plays an important role in the setting of tuition through the state budget director and his or her professional staff assigned to university budgets. While the setting of tuition is clearly a statutory authority of the Board of Regents, the revenues generated by tuition are a significant component of the budget process. The budget director is kept apprised of the alternatives the board is considering and provides input into the process through the board staff. The budget director is primarily concerned with two issues: What are the estimated revenues projected to be raised by the tuition rates? and What specific uses does the board propose to make with the incremental revenues resulting from tuition increases?

Legislative staff typically play a more passive role in the tuition-setting process. First, they act as observers of the process so that they can report to legislative leaders and committees on the actions of the board relative to tuition rates and their implications for the budget. Second, as the legislature makes adjustments to the governor's budget, legislative staff adjust revenue sources, including tuition, accordingly.

Campus Management and Staff

The six university chief executive officers play an important role in balancing institutional interests in assuring sufficient revenues to maintain institutional quality and student interests in maintaining low tuition. As state support to the universities as a percent of the total budget declined, the institutions have turned to tuition revenues to help maintain, if not enhance, academic quality. Specific tuition differentials for professional programs and tuition increases—dedicated to systemwide initiatives, such as faculty salary raises—have become increasingly popular within the campus administrative structures.

The chief executive officers frequently find themselves, along with their student affairs officers, meeting with student leaders to obtain student support for these tuition and expenditure proposals. They share with the student leaders in the student concern that the ratio of tuition revenues to total expenditures has grown significantly and, as university officials, are genuinely interested in constraining tuition increases to preserve student affordability. Their interests in maintaining quality while preserving affordability often lead to compromise with students on these proposals, giving students greater influence or proposals for spending the tuition revenues. Since this process is carried out on all six campuses independently, it often leads to competing proposals that must eventually be reconciled through the Regents Tuition and Fees Committee and ultimately by the board's actions.

Student leaders play a limited role in the setting of tuition, principally through a statutorily created committee called the Student Advisory Committee (SAC). SAC consists of the student body president of each university and, among other responsibilities, is charged with advising the board in the "formulation of policy decisions on student affairs." In reality, SAC, as a formal group, has not been particularly active in advising the board about tuition issues.

The Tuition-Setting Process in Kansas

Kansas has always been a populist state. Its tradition of populism manifests itself most directly in postsecondary education through its long history of open enrollment at each of the six regents universities. Any Kansas resident who is a graduate of an accredited Kansas State school must be admitted to the regents university of her or his choice. The underlying premise is that every Kansas should have the opportunity to succeed or fail.

To make this populist view a reality, Kansas has maintained a low tuition policy. This policy is neither constitutional (as in Arizona) nor statutory; rather, it has been acted out over a long period of time through the tuition-setting process. Tuition rates for regents universities are consistently below their peers and a comparison with national data would show Kansas tuition rates to be well below the average rates for comparable institutions. At the same time, Kansas has very little state-funded financial aid for its state institutions. State appropriations for need-based financial aid totaled $3.8 million in fiscal year 1994–95, and of that amount $560,000 was financed from the federal State Student Incentive Grant program.

The tuition process typically begins in February with the appointment of the Regents Tuition and Fees Committee. Membership on the committee includes four regents, two university presidents (one from a research university and one from a regional university), and two members of SAC (one from a research university and one from a regional university). The committee is charged with presenting the board with recommendations on tuition rate increases and with reviewing and commenting upon any specific proposals referred to the committee that may affect either tuition or fees at one or more of the universities. At the first meeting of the committee, board staff review with the committee "The Value of Tuition in Kansas" annual report. Board staff is then given initial direction in the preparation of alternative tuition scenarios.

The role of the Tuition and Fees Committee has evolved over the past ten years. The evolutionary change that has occurred can, in large measure, be attributed to the changing fiscal environment within which the institutions operate. Like many systems around the country, the Kansas regents system has seen diminishing state support caused by constrained state resources coupled with increased competition for public funds. The percentage share of state general fund appropriations to the regents universities declined from 18.4 in fiscal year 1984–85 to 13.2 in fiscal year 1994–95. The share of all other education during the same period increased from 44.3 percent of the state general fund budget to 52.2%.

As state funding began to diminish over the last decade, both presidents and board members began to see tuition as a potential revenue source to fund specific needs of the universities. Consequently, by the early 1990s, both the presidents and the board members on the Tuition and Fees Committee initiated proposals to increase tuition by amounts sufficient to fund specific expenditure proposals. This culminated with a three-year proposal to begin in fiscal year 1994–95 known as the "Partnership for Excellence," in which the board and presidents proposed raising tuition rates to the average of the peer comparison institutions in exchange for increasing ranked faculty salaries to the average of the peer institutions. While the proposal was not successful as a three-year initiative, it was successful in raising salaries for the first year, and meeting its budgetary needs.

Student Role

As discussed earlier, students have not played a strong role in the setting of tuition. Student leaders tend to identify more with their counterparts within either the research or regional university sector in the regents system than they do with a collective student interest across all six universities in the system. As a consequence, students have not significantly affected the deliberations of either the Tuition and Fees Committee or the final tuition and fee decisions of the Board of Regents.

Students have attempted to lobby the legislature to effect some change in the tuition and fee decisions, but that also has not been very successful because of the tendency for the students to divide their efforts along research versus regional mission divisions. For example, in the 1994 legislative session, students became so divided they created two separate student organizations, one supporting the board's "Partnership for Excellence" proposal, and the other opposing it. The split in student organization neutralized the students' ability to effectively lobby the board's proposal.

SUMMARY

From the perspective of public university management, the annual tuition-setting process is particularly challenging because it creates adversarial relations specific to the process that would otherwise not exist, and is consequently a perennial public relations problem for the president and his or her staff. The president on the one hand must publicly favor the smallest possible tuition increase to maintain wide access and ease the net cost and loan debt burden on students. On the other hand, the president knows that under continuing conditions of constrained state funding, large tuition increases will be necessary for the foreseeable future to maintain educational quality and support faculty salary increases. Student financial aid buffers the impact of high tuition on low-income students. However, except for a portion of tuition "set aside" for needy students, it is largely controlled by federal or state policies and is increasingly available as loans, a form unpalatable to most students.

As Lenth (1993, 1) pointed out, "Tuition policies raise questions for which there are no simple or permanent answers . . . tuition-setting is a process more than a product, a negotiation more often than a technical formula, and a search for the best balance among objectives more often than a permanent solution." Illustrative of the continuing search for the "best balance among objectives" is the recurring interest in tuition indexing and differential tuition charges.

In 1987–88 the Arizona Board of Regents appointed a task force to examine tuition setting and student financial aid. Student leaders on the task force pressed the group to recommend a method that would index future tuition changes to annual fluctuations in family income.

The task force was interested in indexing to make future tuition increases more predictable and less susceptible to wide variations from year to year. The presidents had objected to indexing on exactly the opposite grounds. They contended that wide variations are sometimes necessary to cope with unforeseen changes in circumstances, such as a drastic downturn in state revenues that would prevent the legislature from meeting minimal needs for appropriations to the university system budget.

The question of indexing to some measure of student and family ability to pay or to some alternative comparison such as tuition levels at peer institutions has surfaced in every annual tuition-setting process in the Arizona university system since the mid-1980s. In 1995–96 the issue heated up again, and at the board's April meeting in which tuition was set for the following year, the board agreed to appoint a group that would study various indexing schemes and make a recommendation to the board early in the next academic year.

As described earlier, the Kansas board in 1994–95 accepted a proposal for a three-year program in which tuition rates would be indexed to the average of peer institutions, and the resulting increases would then also be indexed to the goal of increasing faculty salaries to the average of peer institutions. However, the proposal failed as a three-year initiative and the board abandoned the specific indexes in the proposal. It is safe to predict, however, that the issue of indexing will continue to surface in the Kansas tuition-setting process just as it has in the Arizona process. Once the concept of increasing both tuition rates and expenditures in relationship to peers was presented, it put on the public policy agenda the question of whether Kansas should move away from the long-standing populist tradition of low tuition with high access in order to fund faculty salaries. The regents argued that there was an absolute need to preserve quality in the universities and if the state was unable to accomplish that through higher state general fund appropriations, then the regents felt compelled to accomplish it through higher tuition rates. The discussion became focused on only two alternatives: there could either be higher tuition and higher quality or lower tuition and higher access. At no time was there a meaningful discussion of balancing quality, cost, and access through the use of financial aid.

Differential tuition has a long history of acceptance in certain forms—for example, when public universities differentiate tuition charges between state residents and nonresidents or for medical school students (or other relatively costly professional or graduate programs). However, consensual support or at least acceptance often breaks down when attempts are made to differentiate tuition on a highly detailed programmatic basis, even when the differentiation is made on relatively broad distinctions such as upper and lower divisions in undergraduate programs or between laboratory or intensive, field-oriented programs and those involving mostly large lecture courses.

A number of scholars have concluded that the more complex and detailed the cost of instruction tuition differentiation, the more likely it is that the system will be inequitable and outdated (Simpson 1991). Actual cost of instruction is always difficult to compute and allocate down to the specific academic program level because of the difficulty of disentangling generalized overhead costs from those for specific programs. And such program costs can change too rapidly to be captured accurately for annual tuition purposes. High- or low-salaried faculty can come or go annually, equipment and supply costs can vary monthly, and so forth.

Both Arizona and Kansas have moved cautiously beyond the basic differentiation of tuition between residents and nonresidents. In both states, higher tuition is charged for higher cost professional programs such as medicine, and Kansas has become interested in extending such differentiation to more professional programs.

The impact of differential tuition on student curricular and major choices is also questioned. For example, would low-income students be reluctant to select a high-cost major when they have unmet need remaining after all available student aid is awarded? The probability that this would be the case along with the cost of establishing and updating a complex system has dissuaded many states from implementing such a system for their universities. Nonetheless, interest in exploring differential tuition continues in many states, although some have shifted their attention to a closely related system of charging specific fees to students for instruction-related costs. This process is sometimes called "unbundling of user fees" (Simpson 1991) and can evolve into very complex and specific charges—for example, per field trip or per hour or even per minute of computer usage. Again, all of the objections raised for differential tuition have been raised for user fees, including those of complexity, equity, and the actual costs of developing and maintaining a complex system that must be paid for by either the institution or the student.

Arizona and Kansas, as discussed, have shared in the various strategies used by many other states, yet they have developed and pursued tuition-setting processes unique to the history and circumstances of their own university systems. The two states are similar in the structure of governance of their universities, in a history of relatively low tuition and modest state-funded direct student aid appropriations. But they differ in important ways that impact on campus management in the tuition-setting process. For example, the Arizona university system has, since the mid-1980s, dealt with a strong and feisty state student organization that has presented a common front to all three universities and to the Board of Regents. The organization has an effective policy research capability and a strong lobbying presence with the legislature. The Arizona universities also have a program of tuition and fee waivers that may be the largest on a per student basis of any system in the country. Each annual tuition setting invariably includes intense discussion of how the waivers interact with tuition increases via "set-aside" and in other ways. The student financial aid and institutional analysis offices on each campus work closely with the president as well as the student affairs vice-president and the budget office to make sure that the campus student aid component interacts effectively with tuition and waivers in the annual process.

Student financial aid on the Kansas university campuses is less closely coupled with the tuition-setting process compared to Arizona. Also, the linkages between state government and the university are different due to the more active role of the governor and his or her staff and the correspondingly less active role of the legislature and its staff. In Kansas, the executive director of the board staff is an active liaison between state government and campus management. Also, as noted earlier, student involvement takes place mainly on each of the campuses, student organization interaction with the board, and state government is sometimes split between the four regional universities and the two research universities. Finally, tuition increases in Kansas are more likely to be earmarked for specific campus purposes such as faculty salary increases, and lacking a large-scale waiver program there is correspondingly less attention to the linkage between tuition set aside for campus student aid. Challenges to campus management in the Kansas universities are no less difficult than in Arizona, but are configured differently, with more interaction with board staff as intermediary with state governments.

Tuition setting in public universities probably involves more major players than any other process. In contrast, for example, to educational program development or the operating budget process, tuition setting involves nearly the complete array of internal and external constituents. The only exceptions are faculty (internal) and alumni (external). As described above, different players get involved to somewhat different degrees in different states. Arizona and Kansas vary in the centrality of, for example, the governor and student organizations. But in both states the process involves strong interplay between campus and state. Probably no other process includes, to a similar extent, involvement of such an extensive campus management team from all three administrative domains (academic, business, and student affairs) as well as external relations staff. All of these interact to varying degrees with, on the one hand, students and their organizations (and their families who have a strong vested interest in the process) and governing board as well as legislative and gubernatorial staff, on the other.

In few states does tuition setting occur within an established, formal policy framework. In most states the process is strongly affected by annual changes in such important elements as state revenue, legislative leadership, the political stance of elected officials (which can vary markedly between election year and nonelection year), and the ideological agenda of leadership on the governing board. In most years, the process largely follows tradition, but lacking a set policy framework, sudden and radical shifts can occur due to changed circumstances, especially when disastrous changes occur in the state revenue picture or in the political and economic ideology of state government.

University presidents and their supporting teams drawn from all areas of administration are in a continual state of assessing the impact of tuition changes from previous years, managing the current results of the last change, and are somewhere in the ongoing process of setting next year's tuition. And each succeeding year the campus management is likely to interact with yet another task force or commission comprised of many players charged with exploring yet another possible solution to what many observers have called "the tuition dilemma."

ACKNOWLEDGMENTS

The authors would like to express their gratitude for assistance throughout the development of this chapter to James H. Bley, Jon E. Keller, Cristie L. Norwood, and Elizabeth A. Sias. Bley and Keller are policy analysts with the Arizona Board of Regents staff; Norwood and Sias are graduate students in the Higher Education program at Arizona State University.

REFERENCES AND SELECTED READINGS

Arizona Board of Regents. 1994. *Report of the Commission on Student Costs and Financial Assistance*. Phoenix.

Arizona Students Association. 1994. *Crafting a Managed Plan for Setting Tuition and Fees*. Tempe.

Bowen, Howard E. 1974. Financing Her Education. The Current State of the Debate: 11–31. In Kenneth E. Jones, ed., *Exploring the Case for Low Tuition in Public Higher Education.* Iowa City: The American College Testing Program.

Carnegie Commission on Higher Education. 1973. *Higher Education: Who Pays? Who Benefits? Who Should Pay?* New York: McGraw-Hill.

Carnegie Council on Policy Studies in Higher Education. 1975. *Low or No Tuition: The Feasibility of a National Policy for the First Two Years of College.* San Francisco: Jossey-Bass.

Fenske, Robert H. and Gregory, Brian D. 1994. The Dream Denied? Evaluating the Impact of Student Financial Aid on Low-Income/Minority Students: 141–160. In Henry J. Frierson, ed., *Advances in Program Evaluation.* Boston: JAI Press.

Fischer, Frederick J. 1990. State Financing of Higher Education: A New Look at an Old Problem. *Change* (January/February): 42–56.

Gold, Steven D. 1995. *The Fiscal Crisis of the States: Lessons for the Future.* Washington, DC: Georgetown University Press.

Gose, Ben. 1995. *The High Cost of College, Chronicle of Higher Education* 6(A) (October): 37.

Greer, Daryl G. 1994. Not An Aid To Education. In *Tuition and Finance Issues for Public Institutions.* Occasional paper no. 15. Washington, DC: Association of Governing Boards.

Hearn, James C.; Griswold, Carolyn P: and Marine, Ginger M. 1996. Region Resources and Reason: A Contextual Analysis of State Tuition and Student Aid Policies. *Journal of Research in Higher Education* 37(3): 241–278.

Hill, David S. 1934. *Control of Tax-supported Higher Education in the United States.* New York: The Carnegie Foundation for the Advancement of Teaching.

Johnstone, D. Bruce. 1993. The "High Tuition–High Aid" Model of Public Higher Education Finance: The Case Against. *Issues and Answers for Public Multi-Campus Systems* 1(1): 1–10.

Kelly, Fred J. and McNeely, John H. 1993. *The State and Higher Education: Phases of Their Relationship.* New York: Carnegie Foundation for the Advancement of Teaching.

Langfitt, Thomas W. 1990. The Cost of Higher Education. *Change* 22(6): 8–15.

Lenth, Charles S. 1993. *The Tuition Dilemma: State Policies and Practices in Pricing Public Higher Education.* Denver: State Higher Education Executive Officers.

Miles, Mathew B. and Huberman, A. Michael. 1994. *Qualitative Data Analysis: Expanded Sourcebook.* Newbury Park, CA: Sage.

Mumper, Michael. 1996. *Removing College Price Barriers.* Albany: State University of New York Press.

Ostar, Allan W. 1987. State Tuition Policies and Public Higher Education. In Leonard E. Goodall, ed., *When Colleges Lobby States.* Washington, DC: American Association of State Colleges and Universities.

Rivera, Dylan. 1995. New Student Group to Fight Financial-aid Cuts. *Chronicle of Higher Education* (June 16): A28.

Savoca, Elizabeth, 1990. Another Look at the Demand for Higher Education: Measuring the Price Sensitivity of the Decision to Apply to College. *Economics of Education Review* (9)2: 123–134.

Simpson, William B. 1991. *Cost Containment for Higher Education: Strategies for Public Policy and Institutional Administration*. Westport, CT: Praeger Publishers.

Wallace, Thomas P. 1992. The Inequalities of Low Tuition. *Association of Governing Board Reports* (May/June): 24–27.

Western Interstate Commission of Higher Education. 1994. Access, Quality and Student Costs. *Reports on Higher Education in the West* (March): 1–11.

Yin, Robert K. 1989. *Case Study Research: Design and Methods*. Newbury Park, CA: Sage.

Zemsky, Robert and Massy, William E. 1990. Cost Containment. *Change* 22(6): 16–22.

Collective Bargaining

Allan M. Hoffman, Randal W. Summers, and
Yvonne Thayer

The literature that addresses collective negotiations, or collective bargaining, in higher education can be viewed from several perspectives. For the purpose of this brief review, the literature will be considered from a process perspective. Since bargaining is a process that is utilized to facilitate an outcome—the resolution of worker and management needs in an organization—it is useful to look at higher education negotiations with the eye of an outsider who is not involved in this process. The following questions may be asked to guide this viewing: What is the context in which collective bargaining functions in higher education? What issues arise around organizing for bargaining? What is the emerging role of higher education management and leadership during this process? How does third-party intervention, specifically mediation, affect negotiations? What has been the impact of collective negotiations upon higher education.

This review attempts to look critically at the literature, noting omissions that suggest a biased or limited picture of negotiations in higher education. However, several assumptions guide this review, from the perspective of the authors as well as other writers in this field. First, collective bargaining in higher education is a process that is followed to produce positive outcomes (Howe 1993). We, therefore, seek to find differences that have occurred because of the bargaining effort. Additionally, we believe that the bargaining parties believe in the concept of good-faith bargaining (DiGiovanni 1993). The negotiation process should be defined, refined, and institutionalized as a repeatable process that insures quality results. If the negotiation process has been refined, and positive outcomes are not forthcoming, the problem is with the people involved in the process, not the bargaining process itself (Howe 1993). As Howe states: "In short, collective bargaining is, by design, a means of peaceful reconciliation between interest groups which, because of differing perspectives, will have, quite naturally, divergent views concerning matters of common interest."

CONTEXTUAL PERSPECTIVE

In 1993, Begin reported that faculty union membership has changed over the past several years, with a loss of private institutional members offset by slow growth in larger, public institutions. He stated that faculty bargaining has not decentralized, and that workplace issues have not been transformed, as (1) the workplace environment has been stable, and (2) human relations practices, which may have been bargaining issues in other settings, have been incorporated into the higher education organization. Begin's conclusions suggest that a historical perspective of bargaining is needed to understand the current context in which bargaining occurs. Although this chapter will highlight data that begin to offer a wider view of the experience in higher education, detailed information can be found from several writers who monitor this field and report in a historical format. Collections include a legal history of collective bargaining (Newman 1984), a bibliography on bargaining (Lowe and Johnson 1993), information specifically for community colleges (Annunziato 1995c; Wiley 1993a), and a 20-year retrospective on bargaining in higher education (Johnson 1992). Data published since 1995 provide information on unionization among faculty, bargaining agents in higher education, faculty contracts, and graduate student bargaining agents (Annunziato 1995a, 1995c; Lanzerotti et al. 1995).

Although the development of collective bargaining can be traced back several decades (Hutcheson 1991), the mid-1970s appears to have fostered growth in unionization. In 1978, Gier wrote that faculty and teacher unions were growing dramatically at a time that membership in traditional union areas was decreasing. He found that in the 28 states allowing bargaining, 28% of higher education faculty was represented by unions. Additionally, he noted a positive attitude among faculty was overcoming resistance to unions, with a large majority of professors nationwide supporting collective bargaining. Burton and Thomason (1988) reported that public-sector union membership reached a high point in the mid-1970s of around 40%, and was able to maintain that level with only a slight decline of a few percentage points in the mid-1980s. In 1990, the National Center for the Study of Collective Bargaining reported that professors' membership peaked in the early 1980s at 30%. By 1994, unionization was still viewed as growing among faculties, in part due to successful collective bargaining elections and growth in existing bargaining units.

Compared to other state and local government contracts, colleges and universities negotiate well for their employees. The contracts that expired in 1995, which were bargained in 1993, yielded annual wage changes (including cost-of-living allowance payments) of 2.6% in state government contracts and 2.4% in local government contracts, compared to college and university employees who had the highest average gain, 3.6% (Sleemi 1995). Early studies of the 1970s looked at the impact of bargaining on faculty salaries. One study examined 30 institutions with agreements and matched them to similar institutions without agreements. Comparing salaries prior to and following unionization, the bargaining agreements were found to have little effect upon increases in faculty salaries (Marshall 1979). A second study considered data from a 1977 survey of faculty from 158 colleges and universities. The author estimated that the salary advantage to unionized faculty was less than 2% (Barbezat 1989). Additionally, the latter study found that unionization impacted faculty decision making by increasing a return to seniority and emphasis on publications and postdegree experience. In 1992, collective bargaining was credited as affecting pay raises when business professors moved ahead of engineers as the top wage earners at public universities (Magner 1992). A historical study of the effect of unionization in California's community colleges found that there appeared to be no long-term effect upon salaries (Wiley 1993b). During this 25-year period of bargaining, the highest number of faculty strikes were in the 1970s and have declined since, with the proportion of strikes in two-year colleges declining faster than four-year colleges (Annunziato 1995b). The first five years of the 1990s, faculty strikes were the lowest ever recorded (Annunziato 1994).

The context in which bargaining is conducted today is the result of efforts to negotiate with unions representing less than one-third of faculty. The impact of unionization upon faculty salary increases is unclear in recent years, but the decrease in strikes is worthy of note. Additionally, the possible loss of shared decision making in organizations with contracts should be examined. Many colleges and universities are attempting to embrace the notions of Total Quality Management and the ideals of W. Edwards Deming, who called for employee involvement and organizational goals rather than individual performance measures (Deming 1986). Other management experts call for workers to view organizations systemically, working as team members to learn together and to minimize competition among colleagues (Senge 1990). The relationship between collective bargaining beliefs and any movement toward collective learning and decision making may be at cross-purposes since they are based on very different assumptions about the roles of management and labor.

ORGANIZING FOR NEGOTIATIONS

Direction for those interested in organizing higher education may be found in publications that provide an overview for bargaining (Andersen

1991; Mannix 1993), as well as writing that relates specifically to part-time faculty (Rajagopal and Farr 1993), clerical and technical employees (Hurd 1993), two-year colleges (Annunziato 1995b), graduate-student organizing (Villa 1991), multicampus arrangements (Sicotte 1993), and women's issues (Cobble 1993). Since the cultures of industry and higher education are different, it is not unexpected that issues related to collective bargaining will be different in the two organizational settings. The unionization of professors presents conflict between the practices of labor negotiations within industry and the life of an academic community (Ping 1973). It may be helpful, therefore, to look at recent academic bargaining experiences for guidance on the organizing phase of the bargaining process, rather than reviewing work from industry.

Hurd (1993, 324–325) offers three lessons from organizing and bargaining experiences in higher education:

1. Clerical, technical, and professional employees in higher education feel disenfranchised. They form unions to gain an independent source of power.

2. Colleges and universities that face an organizing campaign among clerical, technical, or professional employees should consider seriously the option of neutrality. By adopting a position of genuine neutrality, the administration conveys respect for the employees' legal rights and their competence to make an independent choice.

3. Universities and colleges can benefit from bargaining partnerships with their white collar unions. Collective bargaining need not be adversarial. . . . Employee involvement programs and other forms of jointness contribute to employee morale and hold great promise as vehicles to improve productivity and quality.

Good planing and a review of the collective bargaining process are two strategies that have proven successful in implementation (Sicotte 1993). The process may include an advisory committee that may or may not include the college president. Sicotte (1993, 229) notes there are several advantages for a spokesperson to represent the chancellor's staff rather than utilizing an advisory committee:

Unions often believe that the direct contact with the spokesperson having full authority to make decisions during collective bargaining outweighs the extra committee process. . . .

This process places an added responsibility on the spokesperson to establish, well ahead of collective bargaining, the management position on all topics that will be discussed. . . . This process, although requiring more preparation, assists and provides for more streamlined and successful collective bargaining.

Howe (1993) believes that implementation of contracts has been neglected in the literature. After discussing at length the ratification process that follows the design of a contract, Howe is quick to note that living with a contract can be "a burden" because the contract is a requirement, it is somewhat restrictive, and it represents compromises not necessarily reached rationally. To implement the contract, administration must become management, and Howe requests a well-planned program of in-service education for all administrative officers whose responsibility it is to execute the contract.

MANAGEMENT AND LEADERSHIP

"Few activities in which university systems are involved require as much close communication and coordination as does collective bargaining with a systemwide faculty union" (Naples 1993, 193). The role of the administrator is critical to communication and coordination, but questions related to management and leadership issues emerge. Does the administrator insure the integrity of the contract, or does he or she build a relationship with those benefiting from the contract? How important is support from those stakeholders of the contract?

As universities and colleges face financial and other institutional challenges in the new millenium, the role of the contract administrator is ambiguous, with views supporting a centralized approach and others suggesting greater empowerment of employees. Hollander (1992) argues that strong collective bargaining can lead to strong institutional leadership and effective management, especially during times of fiscal constraints. Begin (1993) believes that during economic stress, the centralization of authority to administrators is needed because faculty tend to focus on their own disciplinary interests. Collective bargaining can be approached with appreciation and commitment, can become an effective tool for increasing communication (Figuli 1993), and, perhaps, a cooperative model for collective bargaining offers administration and faculty the greatest flexibility required in uncertain times (Gibbons and Ed 1991). Taken a step beyond cooperation, the notion of shared power in the academic community is also represented in the literature, with the possibility of increased collegiality through social exchange (Massengale 1995). This view can be supported with a developmental perspective of personnel that argues for a holistic and strategic view of human resource management (Mortimer 1993). Julius (1993, 151) reminds the administrators of the interdependence of their actions on each other and the importance of coordinated action between academic and nonacademic constituencies. "[No] approach, design, strategy, or plan will succeed unless those responsible for [contract administration] are sensitive to the many internal constituencies who truly believe they possess a stake in the mission of the university and, therefore, in the labor relations process." A change in the bargaining paradigm should follow a study of other models that have foreseen problems, such as morale and quality (Bennett and Quinlan 1992).

Begin (1993, 35–36) is one writer who directs leaders to move away from the traditional adversary bargaining model to one of *mutual gains bargaining*. He suggests the following tactics and strategies of mutual gains bargaining:

1. Do not bargain from positions. Rather, ascertain the underlying problems and mutually search for and evaluate alternative solutions to the problems.

2. Stop using negative, personal attributions to explain the behavior of the other side. . . . Rather, use positive attributions to help build cooperative relationships, and search for environmental explanations for events. In short, be sensitive to the importance of language in setting the tone of the relationship. . . .

3. Be sensitive to the other side's needs, "listen" to what they are saying, and ask questions. A competitive "we-they" relationship impedes this type of communication.

4. Use objective information to evaluate alternative solutions. For example, jointly agree to the type and number of institutions that could be used as benchmarks for your own institution's policies. Jointly design and analyze surveys of employment issues.

5. Invent options for mutual gain by (a) dividing the agenda into distributive items involving a direct exchange of resources . . . and integrative items involving mutual gain, (b) separating the agenda by people . . . or by time, (c) fractionating the agenda by dividing into smaller, more easy to deal with pieces, (d) jointly brainstorming solutions to problems, and, (e) packaging items into related trade-offs made through tentative, exploratory proposals. . . .

6. Become expert in negotiating with your own constituents. Sense their interest, keep them informed, and adjust their expectations where necessary so that they are ready to settle when it is time. This internal negotiations process is facilitated by a cooperative bargaining relationship and made extremely difficult by a competitive relationship.

Negotiations do not always lead to an easy resolution of issues. It is advisable at times to seek the assistance of a third party, a mediator, who can implement a process that will not only resolve the situation, but teach the participants a process they can follow in subsequent impasse situations (Chandler 1993). "The mediator's approach depends on the situation, the parties, the issues, the place, the timing, and most of all, personalities" (Lobel 1993, 120). Chandler (1993) provides an overview of the mediator's task, specifically explaining how parties work with a mediator. Lobel (1993) describes the mediation process, how negotiations occur with a mediator, and the techniques mediators use. Understanding mediation is valuable to the leadership of an organization because mediation may be necessary when consensus and compromise cannot be achieved. Although negotiations should always be approached with the goal of settlement without the intervention of a third party, "it is important to request the presence of a mediator after the issues are resolved but before the parties are so entrenched that further compromise becomes impossible" (Lobel 1993, 125).

THREE DECADES OF COLLECTIVE BARGAINING IN HIGHER EDUCATION: WHAT HAVE WE LEARNED?

After several years of talking and signing contracts, we should be able to reach some conclusions about bargaining in higher education. Begin (1993) speculates on the transformation that he sees occurring in this setting. He notes the conclusions reached by Kochan et al. in *The Transformation of American Industrial Relations* as a foundation for discussing higher education. Among those conclusions, Kochan et al. (1986) find that labor membership is declining and, thus, weakening its influence on society; negotiations have been decentralized so that smaller units are bargaining for themselves; and workers are involved directly in workplace decisions. Given this context, Begin discusses the absence of growth in faculty union membership since the 1980s, and attributes this in part to the U.S. Supreme Court's *Yeshiva* decision (Begin 1993). This decision determined that faculty in private institutions with managerial authority were excluded from National Labor Relations Act protections. "Thus, the sole change in faculty union membership in recent years has been the loss of private institution membership offset in part by the slow growth of unionism in larger, public institutions—a growth that has been impeded in an important way by the slow extension of bargaining rights into states where large number of institutions remain unorganized" (Begin 1993; 31). Unlike the private sector, Begin finds that faculty bargaining structures have not been decentralized, that continuous bargaining does not appear to be increasing, but that there has been movement toward a mutual gains approach to negotiations. He also finds that workplace issues have not experienced the transformation noted in the private sector, with tenure remaining unchanged and recruitment policies stable. Changes due to unionization are noted in regard to grievance processes, and the areas of sexual harassment, Americans with Disabilities Act, retirement, pensions, and employment at will.

Julius and Chandler (1993) examined a 15-year Ford Foundation study of the sharing of authority in two-year and four-year colleges and universities. Their goals were to assess the extent to which faculty associations have negotiated labor agreements that penetrated traditional management functions, to determine the bargaining agent effect on traditional professional rights, and to develop predictors of contract language. They found that negotiators in the public sector are more "politically and legally circumscribed" than those in the private sector. Second, unionized private faculties have been unable to gain greater rights through the negotiation process. Finally, Julius and Chandler learned that union and management have been innovative in their adaptation of collective bargaining principles. Their study proposed the following future for faculty-administration bargaining:

In the coming years higher education will become increasingly product oriented. New clientele will be sought and new programs initiated in a competitive search for markets. Administrators will be pushed hard on matters the professorate considers to be appropriately within its rights and jurisdiction. Given the professional craft style of faculty unionism and the nature of the prospective issues of the mid-1980s, controversy over the rights issues is almost certain to intensify. (p. 353)

Finley (1991) surveyed a quarter of the full-time faculty at 20 union and nonunion colleges to determine job satisfaction. He found satisfaction levels higher among nonunion faculty on seven of the eight dimensions of the inventory used. Why could this be? In another study, a look at the interactions between the union and administrative bargaining teams over an eight-month contract negotiations period found problematic goals (vague, non-agreed-upon goals on both sides of the table), unclear technology (both parties uncertain about the bargaining process and the effects of outcomes on institutional functioning), and fluid participation (bargaining team members in and out of meetings) (Birnbaum 1993). Based on his inclusion in this experience, Birnbaum offers the following recommendations to improve bargaining:

1. Use third-party (mediator) to intervene and clarify discussions in the process.
2. Improve record keeping by developing a process for tracking paperwork.
3. Use computer spreadsheets during salary negotiations.
4. Increase training in the process of negotiations to reduce unrealistic expectations, diminish reliance on ideology, and help participants understand behaviors during negotiations.

A decade after the California Higher Education Employer-Employee Relations Act (HEERA), some observations have been made about the experience at the University of California (Kramp 1993). Some aspects of management have been easier: (1) management rights are delineated and are more extensive than other labor agreements provide; (2) after negotiations are concluded, management no longer meets with union representatives on a weekly or monthly basis; (3) equal sharing of arbitration expenses has created fewer grievance arbitration sessions; and (4) contractual and policy provisions are generally clearer. While the contracts have been favorable to management, HEERA has been expensive. Increased lawsuits, unfair practice charges, and the like have been costly to defend. The transition to bargaining has been smooth, with few work stoppages and demonstrations. Kramp makes other observations:

1. Stronger unions have been successful with statewide contracts.
2. Political intervention has impacted the bargaining process, sometimes appearing more effective than bargaining.
3. Health care bargaining has been conducted in an environment where increases for health care employees must be balanced against state-funded employees.
4. Nonexclusively represented employees have received wage increases and benefits that closely approximate negotiated salaries and benefits.
5. Separate bargaining units and contracts have been able to address needs of particular employees—for example, nurses.

The research in organizational culture points to the differences in institutions based on their assumptions, their traditions, how they learn, and how their leaders behave (Schein 1985). The culture of industry and the culture of higher education—including how their governance is structured—are different, academic freedom being one notable difference. How does academic freedom play into the bargaining process? A small study at eight universities found that faculty chose to limit their bargaining to issues involving money, job security, and the grievance procedure, rather than issues related to academics (Ponak et al. 1992). In the case of *Lehnert v. Ferris Faculty Association*, the Supreme Court affirmed that local unions can charge nonmembers for certain activities. While a number of questions remain to be answered after *Lehnert* (Bryant 1993), this decision may weaken academic freedom by forcing faculty to participate in union activities (Russo et al. 1992). In order to protect the role of the academician and to maintain interest in academic issues, governance structures, and university traditions, institutions can pursue voluntary bargaining. In states where there is no legal framework for collective bargaining in the public sector, voluntary bargaining may be an option worth pursuing.

There are at least three reasons why a public university might choose to bargain with an exclusive representative in the absence of enabling legislation. There may be a de facto employee representative who demands collective bargaining and who has the muscle to call an effective strike if demands to bargain go unheeded. The university's governing board or the political powers governing the university may, as a matter of public policy, choose to encourage collective bargaining. The university may perceive some advantage to bargaining collectively with employees (Harrison 1993, 196).

Voluntary bargaining can encourage self-reliance on solving problems identified during bargaining discussions, creating more emphasis on compromise and less emphasis on third-party participation. However, in the absence of legislation and policies, contested issues, such as the scope of bargaining, may be difficult to resolve (Harrison 1993). "There is not enough evidence yet to determine if the nature and quality of the labor management relationship is any different under a policy voluntarily enacted or under a comprehensive collective bargaining statute" (Harrison 1993, 206).

REFLECTIONS

Although collective bargaining in higher education does not seem in jeopardy, it does not appear to be growing in a formalized way. The notion of voluntary bargaining is very interesting because it suggests a value to bargaining that can be duplicated without the legal parameters applied by laws or policy. The lesson to be learned from mediation is that resolution to problems and difficult issues can be found when properly facilitated. Whether the bargaining parties can themselves fill the role of facilitator, as Chandler (1993) suggests, remains a question. The objectivity required for mediation and facilitation seems unlikely when a bargaining representative is following a stated agenda. However, the suggestion that working together is the best way to find common ground and resolution is encouraging. During an era of rhetoric regarding shared decision making and empowerment, any discussion of collective negotiations should reflect on the power structure of organizations and the historical basis for negotiating in organizations.

REFERENCES

Andersen, C. J. 1991. Academics Bargaining Collectively: Some ABCs. *Research Briefs, American Council on Education* 2(2):14.

Annunziato, F. R. 1994. Faculty Strikes in Higher Education: 1966–1994. National Center for the Study of Collective Bargaining in Higher Education and the Professions (hereafter NCSCBHEP) *Newsletter* 22(4):10.

Annunziato, F. R. 1995a. *Directory of Faculty Contracts and Bargaining Agents in Institutions of Higher Education*, Vol. 21. New York: NCSCBHEP, Baruch College, City University of New York.

Annunziato, F. R. 1995b. Faculty Collective Bargaining at Exclusively two-year Colleges. NCSCBHEP, *Newsletter* 23(2):10.

Annunziato, F. R. 1995c. Unionization Among College Faculty—1995. NCSCBHEP *Newsletter* 23(1):13.

Barbezat, D. A. 1989. The Effect of Collective Bargaining on Salaries in Higher Education. *Industrial and Labor Relations Review* 42(3):443–455.

Begin, J. P. 1993. Transformation of the U.S. Collective Bargaining System: The Impact on Higher Education: 29–38. In D. J. Julius, ed., *Managing the Industrial Labor Relations Process in Higher Education*. Washington, DC: The College and University Personnel Association (hereafter CUPA).

Bennett, L. and Quinlan, M. 1992. Universities and Enterprise Bargaining. *Australian Universities' Review* 35(1), 23–27.

Birnbaum, R. M. 1993. Negotiating in an Anarchy: Faculty Collective Bargaining and Organizational Cognition: 129–147. In D. J. Julius, ed., *Managing the Industrial Labor Relations Process in Higher Education*. Washington, DC: CUPA.

Bryant, D. T. 1993. Chargeability After "Lehnert." *Journal of Law and Education* 22(1), 19–25.

Burton, J. F. and Thomason, T. 1988. The Extent of Collective Bargaining in the Public Sector. *Public Sector Bargaining*. Washington: BNA Books.

Chandler, M. K. 1993. Dispute Resolution: Making Effective Use of the Mediation Process: 113–118. In D. J. Julius, ed., *Managing the Industrial Labor Relations Process in Higher Education*. Washington, DC: CUPA.

Cobble, D. S., ed. 1993. *Women and Unions: Forging a Partnership*. Ithaca, NY: ILR Press, School of Industrial and Labor Relations, Cornell University.

Deming, W. E. 1986. *Out of the Crisis*. Cambridge, MA: MIT Center for Advanced Engineering Study.

DiGiovanni, N. 1993. The Concept of Good Faith Bargaining and the Unilateral Implementation of Last Offer. 81–102. In D. J. Julius, ed., *Managing the Industrial Labor Relations Process in Higher Education*. Washington, DC: CUPA.

Figuli, D. J. 1993. The Responsibilities of Trustees and Presidents: 49–58. In D. J. Julius, ed., *Managing the Industrial Labor Relations Process in Higher Education*. Washington: CUPA.

Finley, C. 1991. The Relationship Between Unionization and Job Satisfaction Among Two-Year College Faculty. *Community College Review* 19(2), 53–60.

Gibbons, J. A. and Ed, B.H.J. 1991. Collective Bargaining in Higher Education: Leadership in Uncertain Times. In *19th Annual Conference of the National Center for the Study of Collective Bargaining in Higher Education and the Professions*, New York.

Gier, N. 1978. The Phenomenal Rise of Faculty Unions. *Rendezvous* 13(1), 23–32.

Harrison, S. L. 1993. Collective Bargaining With Public University Employees: Before and After Enabling Legislation: 195–208. In D. J. Julius, ed., *Managing the Industrial Labor Relations Process in Higher Education*. Washington, DC: CUPA.

Hollander, T. E. 1992. Can Collective Bargaining Help Institutions During a Period of Constrained Resources? *Education and the Professions Newsletter* 20(3), 1–6.

Howe, R. A. 1993. The Collective Bargaining Process and the Potential for Productive Outcomes: 59–72. In D. J. Julius, ed., *Managing the Industrial Labor Relations Process in Higher Education*. Washington, DC: CUPA.

Hurd, R. W. 1993. The Unionization of Clerical, Technical and Professional Employees in Higher Education: 315–328. In D. J. Julius, ed., *Managing the Industrial Labor Relations Process in Higher Education*. Washington, DC: CUPA.

Hutcheson, P. A. 1991. "Reform and Representation: The Uncertain Development of Collective Bargaining in the AAUP, 1946–1976." Dissertation, University of Chicago.

Johnson, B. H. 1992. The Impact of Collective Bargaining on Higher Education: A Twenty Year Retrospective. 20th Annual Conference, New York (April 13–14).

Julius, D. J. 1993. Effective Contract Administration: 183–194. In D. J. Julius, ed., *Managing the Industrial Labor Relations Process in Higher Education.* Washington, DC: CUPA.

Julius, D. J. and Chandler, M. K. 1993. Academic Bargaining Agents in Higher Education: Do Their Achievements Differ?: 329–373. In D. J. Julius, ed., *Managing the Industrial Labor Relations Process in Higher Education.* Washington, DC: CUPA.

Kochan, T. A.; Katz, H. C.; and McKersie, R. B. 1986. *The Transformation of American Industrial Relations.* New York: Basic Books.

Kramp, Gregory. 1993. The California Higher Education Employer-Employee Relations Act: The UC Experience 10 Years Later. In D. J. Julius, ed., *Managing the Industrial Labor Relations Process in Higher Education.* Washington, DC: CUPA.

Lanzerotti, R. et al., eds. 1995. *Directory of Graduate Student Employee Bargaining Agents and Organizations.* New York: NCSCBHEP, Baruch College, City University of New York.

Lobel, I. B. 1993. Mediation in the Resolution of Collective Bargaining Disputes: 119–128. In D. J. Julius, ed., *Managing the Industrial Labor Relations Process in Higher Education.* Washington, DC: CUPA.

Lowe, I. B. and Johnson, B. H., eds. 1993. *Collective Bargaining in Higher Education and the Professions, Bibliography no. 21.* New York: NCSCBHEP, Baruch College, City University of New York.

Magner, D. K. 1992. Business Professors Become Top Wage Earners at Public Universities, Supplanting Engineers. *Chronicle of Higher Education* (10 June): A11–A13.

Mannix, T. M. 1993. Collective Bargaining for Employees of the State University of New York, An Effort at Labor/Management Cooperation: 209–216. In D. J. Julius, ed., *Managing the Industrial Labor Relations Process in Higher Education.* Washington, DC: CUPA.

Marshall, J. L. 1979. The effects of Collective Bargaining on Faculty Salaries in Higher Education. *Journal of Higher Education* 50(3): 310–322.

Massengale, J. D. 1995. Shared Power Through Negotiation in Higher Education. *Quest* 47(1), 64–75.

Mortimer, K. P. 1993. The Context of Collective Bargaining in American Colleges and Universities: 19–28. In D. J. Julius, ed., *Managing the Industrial Labor Relations Process in Higher Education.* Washington, DC: CUPA.

National Center for the Study of Collective Bargaining in Higher Education and its Professions. 1990. *Newsletter* 18(3, A).

Naples, C. J. 1993. How to Organize the Administration of a Multi-Campus System for Bargaining: 183–194. In D. J. Julius, ed., *Managing the Industrial Labor Relations Process in Higher Education.* Washington, DC: CUPA.

Newman, C. M. 1984. A Legal History of Collective Bargaining in Private Higher Education. Dissertation, DA8416011: Boston College.

Ping, C. J. 1973. On Learning to Live with Collective Bargaining. *Journal of Higher Education* 44(2), 102–113.

Ponak, A. et al. 1992. Collective Bargaining Goals of University Faculty. *Research in Higher Education* 33(4), 415–431.

Rajagopal, I. and Farr, W. D. 1993. Mediative Roles for Management: Collective Bargaining with Part-time Faculty. *Journal for Higher Education Management* 8(2), 67–81.

Russo, C. J., et al. 1992. Agency Shop Fees and the Supreme Court: Union Control and Academic Freedom. *West's Education Law Quarterly* 1(3), 277–283.

Schein, E. H. 1985. *Organizational Culture and Leadership*. San Francisco: Jossey-Bass.

Senge, P. 1990. *The Fifth Discipline*. New York: Doubleday Currency.

Sicotte, J. 1993. Collective Bargaining/Contract Administration for the Oregon Multicampus System of Higher Education: 227–236. In D. J. Julius, ed., *Managing the Industrial Labor Relations Process in Higher Education*. Washington, DC: CUPA.

Sleemi, F. 1995. Collective Bargaining Outlook for 1995. *Monthly Labor Review* (January).

Villa, J. 1991. Graduate Student Organizing: Examining the Issues. *CUPA Journal* 42(4), 33–40.

Wiley, C. 1993a. The Effect of Unionization on Community College Remuneration: An Overview. *Community College Review* 21(1), 48–57.

Wiley, C. 1993b. A Historical Look at the Effect of Collective Bargaining on Faculty Salaries in California Community Colleges. *Journal of Collective Negotiations in the Public Sector* 22(2), 157–172.

Student Development: Its Place in the Academy

Denise C. Ottinger

INTRODUCTION

The notion that there is more to a collegiate education than classroom learning has long been recognized. The emergence of student personnel as a profession became more and more evident as colleges and universities evolved. As the role of the United States in world events changed, the importance of advanced education increased. As colleges and universities grew, so, too, did the needs and expectations of students. As a result, specialized services emerged to address these new demands and developed, over time, into full-fledged divisions of student affairs.

In this chapter, there will be an effort made to encapsulate the emergence of student affairs as a prominent player within the college/university environment. First, an historical overview of the student personnel movement will be provided. A discussion will follow about the concept of student development and its role in the college environment. Third, information will be provided about organizational development and planning issues in an age where consumer expectations and the notion of continuous quality improvement are regular topics of conversation. Finally, leadership and management issues for the student affairs practitioner will be addressed.

HISTORICAL OVERVIEW

In early America, the first colleges to emerge were colonial-based and were influenced greatly by religious missions. Because of the focus on religion, good citizenship, and moral development, student "services" (e.g., tutoring, housing) were handled by the president and faculty (Fenske 1980; Miller and Winston 1991). Fenske (1980, 5) noted the following:

> Surely the religiously oriented college that predominated the American higher education scene for two-thirds of its history provided a setting in which student services, although not yet differentiated and professionalized, were at their apex, in the functional sense that they involved all participants and were inseparable from the academic program.

Due to the locations of these early institutions of higher learning, lodging became a necessity. "Dormitories" were created to ensure supervision and control. A concern for students' life experiences was a unique characteristic of the early American colleges "What the student did before, after, and between his academic studies was viewed as important, perhaps even paramount, to the educational mission involved" (Miller and Winston 1991, 6). This interest and concern separated American colleges from their European counterparts and led to the eventual creation of the student personnel movement (Miller and Winston 1991).

Student behavior and discipline were guided by strict rules and regulations during this time. Close supervision by the faculty resulted in a familial relationship; thus, the use of the term *in loco parentis* (Garland 1985; Miller and Winston 1991). Peer influence, however, was also recognized in the early beginnings as a motivator for behavior. As is true today, this influence resulted both in positive and negative outcomes (Miller and Winston 1991; Rudolph 1962).

Students began to make their influence known by creating activities to fill their time and to meet some unsated needs outside the classroom. Class distinctions (e.g., freshman, sophomore) provided the first opportunities to "rush" and "haze." Literary and secret societies began to emerge; so did theatrical and singing groups. Fraternities soon followed. As these organizations grew in popularity, colleges made efforts to gain some control (Rudolph 1962; Miller and Winston 1991).

During the early- to mid-1880s, America saw many changes. So, too, did institutions of higher learning. In 1833, Oberlin College became the first coeducational institution in the country. Women's colleges were also being founded (Miller and Winston 1991). The movement away from a strong religious emphasis was also noted. Trustees were laymen, administrators were not of the cloth, and "students became more concerned with higher education as a means to worldly advancement than as a means to spiritual salvation" (Fenske 1980, 6).

By the mid-19th century, higher education was responding to societal trends. Public institutions became alternatives to private, religious ones. Following the Civil War, land-grant colleges were created as a result of the

Morrill Act of 1862 (Fenske 1980; Miller and Winston 1991). With their establishment, it was only a matter of time before public higher education would grow in leaps and bounds. In addition, other types of public institutions (i.e., normal and professional schools, junior colleges, and technical institutes) began to emerge. In response to these changes, presidents were delegated more control of institutional operations (Fenske 1980). At the same time, faculty were becoming more specialized. "Tired of his responsibilities for student discipline, enlivened by opportunities to conduct research and pursue scholarship, the academic man of the late 1800s sought to rid himself of the more onerous responsibilities associated with student life" (Garland 1985, 4).

"Student life" continued to evolve, however. Secret societies and Greek organizations became prominent groups on college campuses. It became evident that extracurricular activities "needed to be reinstitutionalized as an integral part of the higher education enterprise" (Miller and Winston 1991, 9). As faculty became more involved with research and less involved in the development of their students, administrators and practitioners were employed (Garland 1985; Knapp 1969; Fenske 1980). As more administrative positions were created, student services became a separate entity, functioning apart from the academic units (Fenske 1980).

As the 1920s arrived, American higher education was faced with new challenges: growth leading to issues of impersonalization, diversity of students, and the need for reform (Miller and Winston 1991). The foundation for modern higher learning was grounded during this time (Fenske 1980). The student personnel movement also began to grow as changes occurred. Some of the services that evolved following World War I included student health, student counseling and testing, placement, and intramural and intercollegiate sports (Brubacher and Rudy 1976; Fenske 1980; Miller and Winston 1991). In addition, several positive things occurred during this time, including "the popularity of a supportive educational philosophy, concern by leading figures in higher education for reintegration of the academic and social development of students, and vigorous, self-confident organizational growth by student service professionals" (Fenske 1980, 18).

The Depression proved to be a setback for the student personnel movement. Many services were eliminated during this time, allowing institutions to survive. "These moves not only were consistent with financial survival but also coincided with a new philosophical emphasis on an old theme, that of the overriding value of the intellect in higher education as opposed to character or personality development" (Fenske 1980, 21). The profession rebounded, however, immediately preceding and following World War II. During this time, a professional identity was solidified, and services became more sophisticated (Garland 1985).

Following World War II, there was a major explosion in enrollment at public institutions of higher learning. This was due, in part, to the Serviceman's Readjustment Act (i.e., the GI Bill). "These colleges and universities were more responsive to the urgent need to accommodate on short notice the many hundreds of thousands of young men who wanted higher education and who were reluctant to postpone their opportunity until a later semester or year" (Fenske 1980, 10). The postwar interest in higher education did much to revive and alter student services. There was an increased need for advice and assistance in many areas (Fenske 1980). Of all service areas available, student housing probably experienced the greatest growth and change. Design shifted from small residential colleges and units to large residence halls. Married student housing was also constructed for the first time (Schneider 1977; Miller and Winston 1991).

To meet growing enrollments and increased federal involvement, new student services were created and "housed" within divisions of student affairs. By the middle of the twentieth century the student personnel movement had matured into an emerging profession" (Miller and Winston 1991, 10). Several studies were conducted and documents were created during the first half of the century, lending credence to the professionalization of the field. One of the most important of these documents was *The Student Personnel Point of View* (American Council on Education 1937). Miller and Prince (1976) identified four basic assumptions that were covered by these important works:

(1) the individual student must be considered as a whole: (2) each student is a unique person and must be treated as such; (3) the total environment of the student is educational and must be used to achieve his or her full development; (4) the major responsibility for a student's personal and social development rests with the student and his or her personal resources. (4)

Growth of higher education continued well into the next decades. Many veterans who had taken advantage of their GI loans in public institutions chose to send their children to these institutions as well (Fenske 1980). Due to the increasing numbers of students seeking admission to institutions of higher learning, the federal government found it necessary to provide assistance. This assistance was covered, in part, by several pieces of legislation, including the National Defense Act of 1958, Higher Education Facilities Act of 1963, and Higher Education Act of 1965 (Fenske 1980).

By this time, "the participation of faculty in what are now called student services functions changed from total involvement to detachment" (Fenske 1980, 12). Not surprisingly, the number of student service functions continued to grow. In response, more and more professionals were hired by colleges and universities as areas became more specialized. Because of the increased specialization and the lack of involvement on the part of the faculty, it became more difficult to integrate student services with the academic component of the institution.

The historic development of the student services profession has resulted in a large, highly diversified field of student-related activities that has been and continues to be in a continual identity crisis. . . . From the point of view of many faculty, the present arrangement is satisfactory, because it relieves them of many student-related chores. However, there seems little doubt that at present most student services professionals view their segregation from primary academic functions as a troubling issue that continues to evade solution. (Fenske 1980, 22)

Growth in college/university enrollments continued during the 1960s and 1970s. This led to a demand for more services, resulting in further specialization (Garland 1985). This was also a period in which the very fabric of American higher education was challenged as a result of the student protest movement. *In loco parentis*, the guiding force of institutions, was ruled null and void. "Student personnel staff were caught in the awkward position of having to react to rapid changes without a guiding philosophy" (Garland 1985, 6). As a result of this challenge to a rapidly growing and increasingly specialized profession, there was a need "to establish its theoretical and operational base and to embrace a philosophy to guide its efforts within the institution" (Garland 1985, 6). During this time, the profession began a transition away from the student personnel/services model to that of the student development movement (Garland 1985; Miller and Winston 1991). "[A] result was the commitment to student development (the theories of human development applied to postsecondary education) as a guiding philosophy, if not theory, and the continued attempt to ensure that the development of the whole person was an institutional priority" (Garland 1985, 6).

STUDENT DEVELOPMENT

The essence of intentional student development is the interaction between the student and the educational environment so that all aspects of students' lives are attended to and the environmental resources both challenge students and give the support needed to meet these challenges so that more advanced levels of development result (Miller and Winston 1991, 11).

The transition in philosophy and change to a student development approach were aided, in part, by new areas of study. As early as the 1960s, behavioral scientists began investigating the actions of college students. Others became interested in developmental processes, growth measures, and the assessment of student concerns (Saddlemire 1980). A report prepared by the Committee on the Student in Higher Education (1968) challenged institutions of higher learning to "take specific steps to educate the whole student, to recognize the wide diversity within the student body, and to stress the development of native talents as well as of areas in which a student might be relatively weak" (Saddlemire 1980, 29–30). It was suggested that curricular and cocurricular programs be presented in a manner that would consider the total development of the student (Saddlemire 1980).

As the term "student development" became part of the working philosophy and part of the daily lexicon of the profession, human scientists voiced concern that professionals were not prepared to "walk the talk," lacking a knowledge of developmental psychology and its applications. As a result, preparation programs were forced to reevaluate their offerings. In addition, attempts were made to provide professional development workshops for those individuals already in the field who lacked the theoretical framework (Saddlemire 1980).

In recent years, the amount of research and information related to student development issues has grown at such a rate, it has been almost impossible for the practitioner to remain current in the field. The merging of human development theory with the original student personnel point of view, however, has established a strong foundation for the profession (Miller and Winston 1991). "The field has moved rapidly from simply providing students with basic support services to intentionally facilitating holistic development as an integral part of students' formal educations" (Miller and Winston 1991, 11). New theories have evolved as societal trends have changed. These new ideas and models must be examined carefully, and the profession must adapt. A recent document, *The Student Learning Imperative: Implications for Student Affairs*, was developed "to stimulate discussion and debate on how student affairs professionals can intentionally create the conditions that enhance student learning and personal development" (American College Personnel Association Student Learning Project 1994, 1). Perhaps this document, more than anything else, will set the course for student affairs practitioners in the years to come.

Student affairs, as a profession, continues to evolve. Practitioners, researchers, and leaders in the field must be prepared to meet the challenges. As Saddlemire (1980, 42) so aptly stated:

The dynamic nature of the field is evident: To adapt to increasing change, every aspect of the work, programs, and campus interrelationships must be constantly scrutinized and updated. The future of student services will be shaped by emphasis on holism, humanism, pragmatism, development of students at all ages and from many cultures, sensitivity to needs, accountability, new research and theoretical contributions, and growing professionalism.

ORGANIZATIONAL DEVELOPMENT AND PLANNING ISSUES

The current environment of higher education is forcing every institution to reexamine its relationships with students and other constituencies. . . . Public and private institutions alike face microscopic examination and questioning of long-held assumptions, beliefs, and even cherished values. Traditional goals and specific purposes are being reexamined, redefined, and restated. Also the organizational structure and functions of many institutions are being re-evaluated and redesigned to attain greater effectiveness which is often judged by criteria traditionally alien to higher education. (Shaffer 1991, 6)

Changing demographics, societal trends, and the increase of public criticism directed at higher education mean that it is no longer business as usual for our nation's colleges and universities. Some of the issues facing institutions of higher learning include changing demographics, growing state and federal intervention, rising costs, rapidly changing technology and information streams, doing more with less, recognizing and addressing increased disabilities and dysfunctional behaviors, litigation, consumerism, demand for increased accountability, and underprepared students. These issues and more will force colleges and universities to revisit their missions—those blueprints that will set them apart as being uniquely different from their counterparts.

In recent years, many institutions of higher learning have looked to quality management models for improvement. A number of states have created incentives and recognition programs to identify outstanding quality efforts in education. In addition, efforts are currently under way to establish an education category for the Malcolm Baldrige National Quality Award, first established in 1987. An education pilot has been established with the following purposes in mind:

- to help improve school performance practices by making available an integrated results-oriented set of key performance requirements;
- to facilitate communications and sharing of best practices information within and among schools of all types based upon a common understanding of key performance requirements;
- to foster the development of partnerships involving schools, businesses, human service agencies, and other organizations; and
- to serve as a working tool for improving school performance, planning, training, and institutional assessment (National Institute of Standards and Technology 1995, 3).

Hart and Bogan (1992, 4) noted that the Baldrige model does not attempt to define quality. It does, however, "define total quality management by identifying a full landscape of areas where organizations will want to be proficient in order to ensure their success and continuous improvement." Hubbard (1994, 3) stated that "quality is a perception, and it is the customer's perception that counts. Quality is always defined by the customer."

While opponents argue that corporate principles and processes cannot cross over into academe, it is obvious that a movement is under way to apply continuous improvement efforts to daily operations. Such efforts require that there is a change in thinking and a change in the way things are done. Student affairs divisions can learn from the quality movement and incorporate organizational strategies that will enhance their effectiveness.

Before any department or division can begin to organize itself and function to meet the needs of the institution and its "customers," it must have an understanding of the college or university mission, usually incorporated within a brief statement. The distinctiveness and uniqueness of the institution is established and described within such a statement (Lyons 1993). The mission statement provides a framework for making realistic decisions and evaluating achievements. In addition, it provides an understanding of purpose—where one fits in the big picture. This enhances the practitioner's self confidence and, ultimately, results in better service to the student (Hubbard 1992; Shindell 1993). The mission "should be straight forward and factual. . . . It should represent a collective commitment setting forth what the institution wishes to maintain or to become" (Hubbard 1992, 109).

It is important, then, that student affairs practitioners know and understand the institution's mission:

we must know our tasks, which flow from many sources, including both our students and our institutions . . . student characteristics, needs, and differences; administrative processes and procedures; and the knowledge and skills essential to the creation of strong student affairs programs. . . . One essential element that shapes our work . . . [is] the institutional mission. (Lyons 1993, 3)

Once the student affairs division has studied the institution's statement of mission, it should develop or revisit its own. This statement and related goals should be aligned to or flow from that of the college/university. The statement of mission must "provide guidance . . . on how . . . work is linked to the larger educational enterprise and what goals student affairs and the institution share" (Barr 1988a, 13). The process of creating and/or revising a mission statement is not a simple task. It is time-consuming and requires the input of all members of the student affairs team. It "clearly articulates the overarching goals of the enterprise and provides a blueprint for staff work" (Barr 1988a, 13).

Again, it is critical to reinforce the notion that the student affairs mission statement aligns with that of the institution. A clear understanding of the mission will provide a better opportunity for a successful student affairs program (Lyons 1993, 3). Once the mission for the division is in place, it is important to revisit it often. It is also critical that everyone within the division understands the mission and agrees with it. This is where the notion of employee and institutional fit becomes paramount.

Planning becomes the mechanism for managing change and the achievement of the institution's mission. With rapid change being a constant, the ability to plan strategically also becomes a necessity. The planning process must be one that works. In addition, it must be viewed as an essential procedure by those within the division/unit (Barr 1988a). Effective strategic planning involves continuous environmental scanning (assessing the external and internal environment). It is a process that enables us to identify issues, anticipate problems, and develop appropriate and timely responses. Shindell (1993, 178) indicated that because of limited resources, the planning process must also become the basis of establishing priorities and conducting financial planning. With effective strategic planning the institution can respond to user needs and at the same time maintain its integrity in respect to it's philosophy, goals and limitations.

Every institution has or should have a planning model or process in place. The following is just one example of how an institution and the respective units within that institution prepare for the future. Northwest Missouri State University (1994) incorporates a seven-step model in its planning process. Once a department has developed a statement of mission—one that is aligned with the university's mission—it begins the planning steps as outlined below.

CULTURE OF QUALITY SEVEN-STEPS

1. Identify key quality indicators (KQIs).
2. Validate them with the customer.
3. Develop goals and establish a strategy to accomplish them.
4. Formulate an assessment strategy to track performance.
5. Establish baseline data, and track trends.
6. Benchmark superior processes at other institutions when weaknesses are identified.
7. Set stretch goals.

This planning process is an on-going one. It is important to revisit the key quality indicators periodically and begin the process anew.

A key quality indicator is "quality in the customer's words." It is an essential metric or mark "that signifies . . . the presence of a quality attribute" (Hubbard 1994, 3). Northwest has identified 11 institutional KQIs: communications competencies; problem-solving competencies; critical/creative thinking competencies; computer competencies; self-directed learning competencies; competence in a discipline; personal/social development; teamwork/team-leading competencies; multicultural competencies; cultural enrichment; and an attractive, well-maintained, safe, orderly, and healthy environment. In addition, each unit/department has the opportunity to identify its own KQIs—those that are consistent with its mission.

Once the KQIs have been identified, they must be validated by the customer. This ensures that the KQIs actually address real needs and expectations. Once the validation process has occurred, goals are developed; and strategies to accomplish them are prepared. Ongoing assessment tracks performance in the achievement of said goals. Information obtained from the assessment process is used to establish baseline data, track trends, and make comparisons. When deemed appropriate, benchmarking superior processes at other institutions can be helpful in improving quality efforts and, thus, can be helpful in improving outcomes. At this point in the process, it is important to set stretch goals, which will move the division/unit beyond expectation (Northwest Missouri State University 1994).

For divisions of student affairs to succeed, they must align themselves closely with the institutional mission. In addition, they must have immediate and long-range plans that focus their efforts. As chief student affairs officers become more familiar and comfortable with quality management theories, they will begin to recognize the need for "new organizational models that are leaner, more flexible, flatter, and more responsive to changing conditions. No longer is the management culture based on control over others. It is now directed toward empowerment of employees, delegation of responsibility, and creation of a sense of ownership" (Shindell 1993, 176).

LEADERSHIP/MANAGEMENT ISSUES

"Failure on the part of student affairs administrators and their staffs to engage forcefully and competently in their institution's deliberations is an abdication of professional responsibilities" (Shaffer 1991, vii). In order to involve themselves in a competent manner, chief student affairs officers and their team members must have certain abilities in order to succeed. Garland (1985, vi) identified eight abilities for student affairs professionals:

1. assess the environment of the institution; 2. comprehend institutional issues and internal politics; 3. develop professional credibility with faculty; 4. become experts on students' expectations, needs, and interests and be able to articulate them to others in the institution; 5. be able to explain the goals of student affairs and student development to others in the institution in terms that are meaningful to them; 6. contribute to the quality of the academic experience; 7. contribute to the effective and efficient management of the institution and be prepared to take leadership in the formulation of institutional responses to changing conditions; and 8. develop appropriate skills.

While the list of necessary behaviors and skills for the student affairs professional is a long one, information will be provided about chief student affairs officers (CSAOs) in the following areas: as leaders, as managers, as politicians, and as educators. Certainly, the skills and behaviors identified as necessary for CSAOs, are also important for the student affairs practitioners regardless of their position within the organization.

CSAOs AS LEADERS

"From a student affairs perspective, effective leadership must marshal resources to accomplish tasks of enhancing cognitive and personality development in students" (Douglas 1991, 616). As leaders, CSAOs must articulate the philosophies of the profession, the institution, and the division. They must also interpret and relay the institutional culture and values to their teams and other constituents (Stamatakos 1991).

Stamatakos (1991, 679) stated the following:

The extent to which the CSAA [chief student affairs administrator] has been enculturated into the profession, has accepted its basic assumptions and beliefs, and has made an occupational commitment to it will greatly determine the administrator's effectiveness in transmitting the important mission of student affairs within the division and its various constituencies.

Somewhere within the student affairs mission, the importance of the optimal development of each student must be stressed. CSAOs must be vocal in reminding others of the significant role the division can play in enhancing student involvement and, thus, the overall quality of the collegiate experience (Garland 1985; Study Group on the Conditions of Excellence in American Higher Education 1984).

Effective CSAOs encourage open communications, welcome student and faculty involvement, and appreciate being kept up-to-date on issues and concerns (Ambler 1993; Sandeen 1991). In addition, they "must demonstrate commitment to building relationships, set priorities, purposely involve staff, and take responsibility to assure that attention is paid to this important aspect of student affairs administration" (Sandeen 1993, 312).

CSAOs AS MANAGERS

While many student affairs professionals have received extensive academic preparation, many truly do not learn how to manage the enterprise until they have been on the job. Generally, one learns to develop a management style that is comfortable by the application of theory and by trial and error. Regardless of how one learns the necessary skills, it is critical that CSAOs be responsible managers. Upcraft and Barr (1988, 1) defined student affairs management as "the process of organizing available human and fiscal resources to meet institutional and program goals in an efficient, effective, ethical, and fiscally responsible manner."

Human Resources

A professionally trained, competent team builds the foundation for an effective student affairs program (Barr 1990; Sandeen 1993; Stimpson 1993). "Student affairs is a very people-intensive enterprise, and our greatest strength, as well as our greatest potential liability, lies with staff members who work with students and design programs and services for them" (Barr 1990, 160). As such, it is critical that CSAOs devote sufficient time to the selection, training, supervision, and evaluation of personnel.

Given the growing complexity and specialization within the profession, student affairs practitioners must be both managers and educators. Progressive institutions must have student affairs professionals who support their overall missions by understanding student development theory as well as managing its highly complex facilities (Shindell 1993). Management skills that should be considered in the hiring process and/or in training/ professional development sessions include the following: planning; budgeting; information management; human relations; research, assessment, and evaluation; policy determination; organizational development; and politics and diplomacy (Garland 1985; Miller and Winston 1991). "The student affairs professional—today and in the future—must integrate the traditional student affairs roles of disciplinarian, custodian, and student development educator with the roles of environmental scanner, market, analyst, legal advisor, development officer, and manager" (Garland 1985, 8–9).

Given the complex nature of student affairs positions, job descriptions and search processes must be developed that truly delineate the wants and needs of the institution. Up front, CSAOs must identify what their minimal expectations are prior to hiring new team members. In addition, they must determine what their responsibilities are to provide on-going, professional team development for their current and future employees. Resources should also be provided for involvement in professional organizations, conferences, and seminars. Moreover, CSAOs must determine the appropriate amount of supervision that is necessary; this will vary from employee to employee and will also be dependent upon the CSAOs' leadership style. Finally, an appropriate performance evaluation process should be created and implemented. Members of the student affairs team should be provided the opportunity to assist in developing the assessment tool and should understand the purpose of the evaluation process.

The ultimate success of a collegiate institution, as well as its student affairs program, is predicated upon the abilities of executive-level officers to develop staff teams who possess the capabilities to initiate those critical interrelationships that lead to cooperative and collaborative educational activities of such impact that a rich collegiate experience is assured for all students. (Stamatakos 1991, 699)

Financial Resources

Managing fiscal resources is essential for a student affairs division to be effective in its efforts. In times of limited resources, student affairs and other student support services are most likely to suffer cuts first because they are not viewed as central to the institution's mission (Barr 1988c). Consequently, it is essential that resources are managed well.

This means that programs should be operated efficiently, that resources are audited carefully, and that requests for increased funding are justified in a reasonable way (Douglas 1991).

Woodard (1993, 245) remarked that "budgeting should be viewed as a dynamic, creative, consensus-building process that involves key decision makers in an effort to set priorities that best serve students and societal needs." The budgeting process is a means for identifying goals and setting priorities that are consistent with the missions of the division and institution. It also provides an accountability check for resource flow throughout the fiscal year (Woodard 1993). To view the budgeting process as a means to steer the course and to manage fiscal resources in an efficient, practical, and ethical manner speaks well for CSAOs and their divisions. "The successful student affairs administrator . . . has a thorough understanding of the institution's budgeting process, has the capacity to inform others of the importance of student affairs, and utilizes technical management skills to acquire resources essential to accomplish its mission" (Douglas 1991, 618).

Within the section entitled "Human Resources," several skills were identified as being important for the student affairs professional. A few of these will be touched upon in slightly more detail at this time.

With the age of the information highway and advanced technology well under way, it is important for CSAOs to recognize the importance and applicability of information systems to their programs. "By using modern computer and information technology . . . student affairs organizations can enhance the delivery of student services, activities, and programs and increase the overall effectiveness and efficiency of the administrative functions" (Baier 1993, 183). Consequently, CSAOs and their teams must continue to learn about new technology, especially as it can be applied to their respective duties within the division (Baier 1993).

In addition to technological skills, CSAOs must also have skills in the area of research, assessment, and evaluation. "Like any profession, student affairs should be able to offer proof of effectiveness for any ongoing program. It may not mean that every program has to be assessed all of the time, but that positive evidence has been collected recently" (Erwin 1993, 238). With rapidly changing societal conditions and with a growing focus on continuous quality improvement, it is critical that divisions of student affairs assess their programs, policies, and activities regularly to ensure that they are having a positive effect.

The assessment of student outcomes should be a central focus of CSAOs. Sandeen (1991, 174) suggested that assessment be ongoing and independent to avoid internal bias. Effective student outcome assessment "can improve quality, provide guidance for planning, and enhance the acceptance of programs on the campus as a whole."

CSAOs AS POLITICIANS

CSAOs must understand the process of decision making. They "must be able to identify not only those individuals or groups who have legitimate decision-making power but also those who have the power to influence decisions" (Barr 1988a, 10). From a political perspective, CSAOs must take steps to ensure that they are perceived by others in the organization as competent and dedicated to their units or divisions. It is only then that CSAOs can be in a position to influence decisions in the organization (Moore 1993).

Thus, it is important for CSAOs to position themselves in such a way that they can and will make decisions—that are in the best interest of the students—without compromising their ethical standards and values (Upcraft 1988).

"Clearly, an understanding of institutional decision making must be a priority for all those who hope to make and influence policies affecting their work and institutions" (Moore 1993, 152). For student affairs to be an integral, respected part of the campus community, it is critical for CSAOs to understand the unique characteristics of institutions of higher learning that influence decision making and to build strong linkages to administrative and academic units.

To establish themselves as credible professionals, CSAOs must increase their visibility and become more involved in all areas of the institution. Political and diplomatic skills are crucial in implementing change and in gaining influence among colleagues. These skills also enhance CSAOs' ability to be successful advocates for students (Garland 1985). It is essential that CSAOs create a network whereby they develop support on various issues. They must not only have insight into the manipulative strategies of others, but also embark upon creating a collaborative environment that nurtures the negotiation and bargaining process.

Exhibiting political savvy is not a bad thing. In fact, one would have a difficult time surviving the college/university environment without political acumen. "The astute professional learns responsible politics as one method for achieving resolution on issues and managing the inevitable conflict within the institution" (Barr 1988b, 60). Barr identified three behaviors that are important for one to become a good campus politician: "demonstrating respect, gathering information, and learning to observe and analyze both individual and organizational behavior patterns" (p. 60). Respect should be shown for all individuals connected with the college or university. It is important to understand a unit's way of thinking or of responding to a specific incident; this takes time. Lines of communication must be open and information shared (Barr 1988b). Gathering information is an important ability for the political practitioner to possess. In order to understand what is occurring throughout the institution and to fit the puzzle pieces together, it is important to obtain information from a variety of sources (Barr 1988b). It is also essential to understand behavioral patterns within the organization and among individuals. It is important to recognize "that elements or issues that appear independent are often linked" (Barr 1988b, 61).

For CSAOs, an understanding of the political nature of the institution is essential if they wish to be effective leaders. It is critical for CSAOs to establish strong relationships with the president. Moore (1993) indicated that CSAOs should engage in a variety of endeavors that would secure their relationship with senior colleagues such as supporting, informing, training and protecting them. In addition to the president, it is important for CSAOs to establish good working relationships with other senior administrators. Without an element of teamwork, issues will become even more problematic (Moore 1993). The politically minded CSAOs select their approaches based on their colleagues' strengths and weaknesses, thereby strengthening their relationships and protecting their interests.

In addition to good working relationships with the president and senior colleagues, it is important for CSAOs to be well-versed in division operations and to anticipate trouble spots or areas of potential crisis or controversy. Moreover, it is necessary for CSAOs to have a good understanding of institutionwide issues as well as regional and national issues related to higher education (Moore 1993).

CSAOs should be visible on campus and in the community. They should be cognizant of the accomplishments of their team members; these accomplishments should be acknowledged and shared with the president and other senior administrators. In addition, CSAOs should be aware of their "public presence." "One needs to act, look, and see oneself as a major player in institutional decision making and leadership" (Moore 1993, 162).

CSAOs as politicians must deal with conflict; it is inevitable given the nature of higher education. Generally one's leadership style and values will come into play in approaching solutions to problems. Ultimately, integrity is the most significant characteristic to be considered. "[C]onsistent ethical behavior is the most important strategy. . . . To lose integrity is to lose claim to leadership and the support of the boss, staff, and students" (Moore 1993, 164).

CSAOs AS EDUCATORS

"The debate centers on the question of whether we are 'educators' with a systematic body of knowledge based on theoretical constructs or whether we are 'practitioners' just 'minding the store' of ancillary but necessary services for students" (Ambler 1980; 159). In recent years, a greater emphasis has been placed on the "educator" role of student affairs practitioners. A new call for a stronger focus on student learning may steer the profession on a more direct course in the years to come. Miller and Winston (1991) identified the attributes that CSAOs must have in order to successfully fulfill their educator role. CSAOs must:

- recognize American higher education as a unique institution,
- understand the organizational culture in which they work,
- have an in-depth knowledge of student development, and
- utilize relevant administrative/organizational theories to address the goals of higher education.

As an educator, CSAOs are concerned about both in-class and out-of-the-classroom experiences. Typically, student affairs efforts have been more aligned with cocurricular activities. "Student affairs has often defined itself as serving a complementary function to the formal curriculum, helping students overcome impediments to academic achievement and development of essential academic skills and attitudes" (Miller and Winston, 1991, xii–xiii). Winston (1990) suggested that student affairs practitioners must focus on creating certain environments for students, which would promote and nurture:

- intellectual development
- healthy personalities
- democratic ideals
- fundamental justice
- wholesome lifestyles
- a set of moral, ethical, and/or religious values

Changing conditions in education, however, require a more collaborative effort by student affairs and academic units. A major goal should be that of integrating the efforts of both parties to provide a truly holistic, seamless experience for students (Garland 1985). As Garland (1985, 60–61) stated, "Responses to changing conditions offer opportunities for student affairs to maintain its professional goals while building stronger bridges within the institutional community, which can be accomplished most notably through cooperative efforts aimed at resisting decline."

If CSAOs are to serve effectively as educators, they cannot be reactionary (Sandeen 1991). Sandeen (1991, 152) argued that CSAOs "must have strong convictions about what they want students to learn—both academically and in a broader sense—as a result of their experiences." In addition, the CSAO must have goals and processes for achieving these goals in mind. Successful programs can be accomplished through collaborative efforts with faculty and academic colleagues. Successful CSAOs believe that the student outcomes they seek are as worthy as those being sought in classroom experiences. In addition, they are capable of communicating this to their faculty colleagues. Moreover, effective CSAOs are visible and active participants in academic activities on campus. They regularly provide input on academic priorities and new programs (Sandeen 1991).

CSAOs must also have an in-depth understanding of all areas of the college/university environment in order to advise and refer students in an appropriate manner. In addition, they must educate student affairs teams so they, too, can best serve the student constituencies (Stamatakos 1991). According to Stamatakos (1991) student affairs teams cannot function properly without a thorough understanding of the basic requirements of their positions, the institution's policies and procedures, and the responsibilities they have to other staff, faculty members, their administrative offices and programs.

In addition to educating students and team members about the institution, CSAOs are often called upon to serve as official spokespersons for their student bodies (Stamatakos 1991). Because of the training and knowledge base, CSAOs are perceived as "experts" on student behaviors and are faced with "teachable moments" when crises/issues arise on their campuses or on campuses elsewhere in the country.

Educating students is the primary purpose of student affairs. Thus, all efforts must be directed to growth, development, and life-long learning (Sandeen 1993). CSAOs can be good leaders, managers, and politicians. If they are not involved in educating their students, however, they have ignored their primary professional duties (Sandeen 1991). CSAOs will rally respect and support for the division "only to the extent that [they have] developed successful programs of educational activities which both enhance students' growth toward freedom, maturity, restraint, and responsibility and project an honest image of the student affairs division as manifesting similar characteristics" (Stamatakos 1991, 694).

CONCLUSION

Student affairs has evolved as a profession over time. The real momentum began during the first half of the 20th century. With the advent of student development as a philosophical foundation, the profession has continued to legitimize its existence at institutions across the nation. As postsecondary education has grown in popularity, the administration of student affairs programs has become increasingly complex.

Today, CSAOs and their teams regularly interact with students, manage resources, create policy, manage existing facilities and coordinate the construction of new ones, manage crises, and deal with social and educational change (Barr 1993). Consequently, it is critical that they possess the necessary skills that will enable them to be successful leaders, managers, politicians, and educators. Silverman (1980, 12) stated the following:

Our uniqueness . . . rests on our ability to fashion significant educational environments, using the resources, values, norms, and opportunities of the variety of constituencies on our campuses. To the extent that we are successful in our innovative work, we will be respected, not because of position, but as a result of the impacts we have on campus life.

Today, CSAOs and practitioners alike must strive hard to make a difference in the lives of their students. They must work collectively and collaboratively with others on campus to provide the best living-learning experience possible. To do less is unacceptable.

REFERENCES

Ambler, D. A. 1980. The Administrator Role: 159–174. In U. Delworth, G. R. Hanson and Associates, eds., *Student Services: A Handbook for the Profession*. San Francisco: Jossey-Bass.

Ambler, D. A. 1993. Developing Internal Management Structures: 107–120. In M. J. Barr, ed., *The Handbook of Student Affairs Administration*. San Francisco: Jossey-Bass.

American College Personnel Association Student Learning Project. 1994. *The Student Learning Imperative: Implications for Student Affairs*. Washington, DC: American College Personnel Association.

American Council on Education. 1937. *The Student Personnel Point of View. American Council on Education Studies*: Series 1, Vol. 1, No. 3. Washington, DC: Author.

Baier, J. L. 1993. Technological Changes in Student Affairs Administration: 183–196. In M. J. Barr, ed., *The Handbook of Student Affairs Administration*. San Francisco: Jossey-Bass.

Barr, M. J. 1988a. Managing the Enterprise: 5–20. In M. L. Upcraft and M. J. Barr, eds., *Managing Student Affairs Effectively*. New Directions for Student Services, No. 41. San Francisco: Jossey-Bass.

Barr, M. J. 1988b. Managing Important Others: 51–64. In M. L. Upcraft and M. J. Barr, eds., *Managing Student Affairs Effectively*. New Directions for Student Services, No. 41. San Francisco: Jossey-Bass.

Barr, M. J. 1988c. Managing Money: 21–37. In M. L. Upcraft and M. J. Barr, eds.,

Managing Student Affairs Effectively. New Directions for Student Services, No. 41. San Francisco: Jossey-Bass.

Barr, M. J. 1990. Growing Staff Diversity and Changing Career Paths. In M. J. Barr, M. L. Upcraft, and Associates, eds., *New Futures for Student Affairs: Building a Vision for Professional Leadership and Practice.* San Francisco: Jossey-Bass.

Barr, M. J., ed. 1993. *The Hand Book of Student Affairs Administration.* San Francisco: Jossey-Bass.

Brubacher, J. S. and Rudy, W. 1976. *Higher Education in Transition.* New York: Harper & Row.

Committee on the Student in Higher Education. 1968. *The Student in Higher Education.* New Haven, CT: Hazen Foundation.

Douglas, D. O. 1991. Fiscal Management: Background and Relevance for Student Affairs: 615–641. In T. K. Miller, R. B. Winston, Jr., and Associates, eds., *Administration and Leadership in Student Affairs: Actualizing Student Development in Higher Education,* 2nd ed. Muncie, IN: Accelerated Development.

Erwin, T. D. 1993. Outcomes Assessment: 230–241. In M. J. Barr, ed., *The Hand Book of Student Affairs Administration.* San Francisco: Jossey-Bass.

Fenske, R. H. 1980. Historical Foundations: 3–24. In U. Delworth, G. R. Hanson, and Associates, eds., *Student Services: A Handbook for the Profession.* San Francisco: Jossey-Bass.

Garland, P. H. 1985. Serving More Than Students: A Critical Need for College Student Personnel Services. *ASHE-ERIC Higher Education Report No. 7.* Washington, DC: Association for the Study of Higher Education.

Hart, C.W.L. and Bogan, E. E. 1992. *The Baldrige: What It Is, How It's Won, How To Use It To Improve Quality in Your Company.* New York: McGraw-Hill.

Hubbard, D. L. 1992. *Crafting a Statement of Mission: Some Observations Regarding Meaning, Form, and Content. A Collection of Papers on Self-Study and Institutional Improvement,* 1992: 108–115. Chicago: North Central Association of Colleges and Schools.

Hubbard, D. L. January 6, 1994. What Is a Key Quality Indicator? *Northwest This Week:* 3.

Knapp, D. 1969. Management: Intruder in the Academic Dust. *Educational Record* 50: 55–65.

Lyons, J. W. 1993. The Importance of Institutional Mission: 3–15. In M. J. Barr, ed., *The Handbook of Student Affairs Administration.* San Francisco: Jossey-Bass.

Miller, T. K. and Prince, J. S. 1976. *The Future of Student Affairs: A Guide to Student Development for Tomorrow's Higher Education.* San Francisco: Jossey-Bass.

Miller, T. K. and Winston, R. B., Jr. 1991. Human Development and Higher Education: 2–35. In T. K. Miller, R. B. Winston, Jr., and Associates, eds., *Administration and Leadership in Student Affairs: Actualizing Student Development in Higher Education,* 2nd ed. Muncie, IN: Accelerated Development, Inc.

Moore, P. L. 1993. The Political Dimension of Decision Making: 152–170. In M. J. Barr, ed., *The Handbook of Student Affairs Administration*. San Francisco: Jossey-Bass.

National Institute of Standards and Technology. 1995. *Malcolm Baldrige National Quality Award: Education Pilot Program*. Gaithersburg, MD: National Institute of Standards and Technology.

Northwest Missouri State University. 1994. Culture of Quality Seven Step Planning Process. Maryville: Northwest Missouri State University.

Rudolph, F. 1962. *The American College and University: A History*. New York: Random House.

Saddlemire, G. L. 1980. Professional Developments: 25–44. In U. Delworth, G. R. Hanson and Associates, eds., *Student Services: A Handbook for the Profession*. San Francisco: Jossey-Bass.

Sandeen, A. 1991. *The Chief Student Affairs Officer: Leader, Manager, Mediator, Educator*. San Francisco: Jossey-Bass.

Sandeen, A. 1993. Developing Effective Campus and Community Relationships: 310–312. In M. J. Barr, ed., *The Handbook of Student Affairs Administration*. San Francisco: Jossey-Bass.

Schneider, L. D. 1977. Housing: 125–152. In W. T. Packwood, ed., *College Student Personnel Services*. Springfield, IL: Charles C. Thomas.

Shaffer, R. H. 1991. Foreword: V-X. In T. K. Miller, R. B. Winston, Jr., and Associates, eds., *Administration and Leadership in Student Affairs: Actualizing Student Development in Higher Education*, 2nd ed., Muncie, IN: Accelerated Development, Inc.

Shindell, W. G. 1993. Facilities Management Issues: 171–182. In M. J. Barr, ed., *The Handbook of Student Affairs Administration*. San Francisco: Jossey-Bass.

Silverman, R. J. Fall, 1980. The Student Personnel Administrator as a Leading Edge Leader. *NASPA Journal* 18: 10–15.

Stamatakos, L. C. 1991. Student Affairs Administrators as Institutional Leaders: 673–705. In T. K. Miller, R. B. Winston, Jr., and Associates, eds., *Administration and Leadership in Student Affairs: Actualizing Student Development in Higher Education*, 2nd ed., Muncie, IN: Accelerated Development.

Stimpson, R. F. 1993. Selecting and Training Competent Staff: 135–151. In M. J. Barr, ed., *The Handbook of Student Affairs Administration*. San Francisco: Jossey-Bass.

Study Group on the Conditions of Excellence in American Higher Education. 1984. *Involvement in Learning: Realizing the Potential of American Higher Education*. Washington, DC: National Institute of Education.

Upcraft, M. L. 1988. Managing Right: 65–78. In M. L. Upcraft and M. J. Barr, eds., *Managing Student Affairs Effectively*. New Directions for Student Services, No. 41. San Francisco: Jossey-Bass.

Upcraft, M. L. and Barr, M. J. 1988. Editors' Notes: 1–2. In M. L. Upcraft and M. J. Barr, eds., *Managing Student Affairs Effectively*. New Directions for Student Services, No. 41. San Francisco: Jossey-Bass.

Winston, R. B., Jr. 1990. Using Theory and Research Findings in Everyday Practice: 35–36. In D. D. Coleman, J. E. Johnson, and Associates, eds., *The New Professional: A Sourcebook for New Professionals and Supervisors in*

Student Affairs. Washington, DC: National Association of Student Personal Administrators.

Woodard, D. B., Jr. 1993. Budgeting and Fiscal Management: 242–259. In M. J. Barr, ed., *The Handbook of Student Affairs Administration.* San Francisco: Jossey-Bass.

Managing with Diversity in Colleges and Universities

Amer El-Ahraf and David Gray

Every organization is diverse. No organization has a hundred matched pairs of people who are alike in age, gender, ethnic orgins, life experience, education, or worldviews. With the growing diversity of our nation and several decades of proactive programs to make organizations more representative of the general population, organizations in the academic community are markedly more diverse than they have been in the past. The makeup of the population itself has become far more diverse since the early 1980s, and successful affirmative action programs have brought this diversity into academic organizations in a significant manner. Many colleges and universities have become associations of people with different backgrounds in which there is no longer a dominant majority. These recent developments have spanned a sizable genre of literature that is centered on the concept of "managing diversity." We think this perspective is an inappropriate starting point for an exploration of the impact of diversity on organizations. We believe diversity cannot be managed. Diversity is imbedded in the fundamental makeup of people that creates their sense of identity. No amount of management improvement will alter the identity of the people who participate in the organization. We believe the emphasis in organizations that are highly diverse must be on creating a climate in which people with a dissimilar sense of identity can work together in a way that makes diversity an asset. We think a more useful perspective is "managing with diversity."

No doubt some of our readers will think this is a distinction without a difference. We think it is fundamental because it puts emphasis on creating an environment in which people of diverse life experiences can be comfortable and successful. It concentrates attention on the similarities of the members instead of their differences. It is based on the conviction that there is a broad band of human experiences that is generic to all of the members of the organization, and within that band there is the basis for a cooperative enterprise that can make diversity an advantage. The focus of this chapter will be on identifying conditions and perspectives that can foster that result.

There is an ancient chinese curse, "may you live in interesting times." As a nation we are learning the meaning of that cryptic message. We are indeed living in interesting times, where the breadth and depth and pace of change are affecting various major segments and millions of individuals in our society differently. We wonder if the broad consensus of American society that has made self-government possible is still here. Some individuals are withdrawing into enclaves divided by religion, politics, gender, ethnicity, sexual orientation, lifestyle, or economics. It is in this context that many colleges and universities are trying to build an academic community with a diverse membership.

Manning Marable, Director of the Institute for African-American Studies at Columbia University, has said "establishing a multicultural democracy is the main task of the 21st century." That statement is a challenge to every American; it particularly resonates with academic communities.

Daniel J. Boorstin (1994, 28), a distinguished scholar and former Librarian of Congress, wrote, "The menace of America today is the emphasis on what separates us rather than what brings us together—the separations of race, of religious dogma, of religious practice, of origins, of language. I'm wary of the emphasis on power rather than on a sense of community. Community is not dependent on government. It is dependent on the willingness of people to build together."

These timely reminders of the need to establish a multicultural democracy, on the need to emphasize the things that bring us together not what separates us, and the need to build a community together are recurrent themes in this chapter. There are reasons to be hopeful that we can be successful. We will need renewed tolerance for transformation to get us through the impending changes in academic organizations. Colleges and universities have a role to play as world citizens who model successful diverse communities that recognize, foster, respect, and value individual differences.

DIVERSITY IN THE WORKPLACE

There are four particularly influential megatrends that are remaking the American workplace:

- adjustment to a global economy
- adoption of sophisticated technology

- abandonment of the traditional organization
- development of a multicultural/multiethnic workforce

All of these megatrends are represented to some extent in academic institutions.

Each of these changes would be a major event in the creation of new ways of working. Collectively they guarantee an extended period of uncertainty, ambiguity, tension, and even conflict in the American workplace on the one hand, and creativity, improved efficiency, more effective use of collective intelligence, and the possibility of a better working life on the other hand. It is this combination of problems and responsibilities that makes this era so fascinating.

The focus of this chapter is on the fourth megatrend in our list: development of a multiethnic/multicultural workforce—but it will be useful to review the other three because they all influence each other.

First, let us consider some of the implications of *involvement in a global economy*. The most obvious implication is that we must compete with other nations of the world in the provision of products and services on the world market. This places on us the necessity of providing products and services of acceptable quality at competitive prices. This requirement has generated major changes in the way we design and produce goods for sale on the world market. We have had to improve our quality and cut our costs. We have also had to become familiar with cultures where our goods are for sale, to key our designs to the expectations of our intended customers, to deliver acceptable quality, and to compete on price. We could not do these things and maintain a "business as usual" approach in our organizations and operations. Some collegiate institutions have enough foreign students that they are competing directly in the global economy, where there is growing evidence that international competition for students is rising.

The second major trend has been widespread *adoption of sophisticated technology*—primarily computer technology. With the advent of competent and inexpensive personal computers (PCs) and workstations and marketing of a wide range of business-oriented software, the long-delayed payoff for investment in individual computers occurred. Many of the tasks previously undertaken by middle management personnel can now be done by a few people using PCs. When those computers are networked they become a powerful communication system capable of transmitting and receiving e-mail, making calculations, accessing data banks for information, and facilitating the work of the organization. Computers also speed the work of design and perform hundreds of other functions that previously were done by hand. These innovations in technique soon produced an analog in the way the organization is designed and the way it functions. This process is going forward in many colleges and universities.

The third major trend is in part the product of the other two: *change in the theory and practice of organizing human endeavor*. Traditional ways of forming organizations went back thousands of years to the ancient Egyptians and the Roman legions who laid out the basic principles of hierarchy. Hierarchical organizations are still common in government and many other segments of our economy, but leading-edge corporations, particularly those involved in global markets, have altered traditional functional organizations in a hierarchical mode. They are experimenting with teams, teams of teams, task forces, temporary help, reengineering, Total Quality Management, learning organizations, and a host of innovative approaches. Gone are the traditional functional hierarchies; in are temporary organizations that draw together personnel with the skills to achieve the objective, do it, and then disband. Gone are the private offices and the private secretaries and in are office hotels, conference rooms for teams, powerbooks, and employees in the field working with customers. Alert colleges and universities are experimenting in this area. The outlook is for further modification of traditional academic organizations.

Fourth is the *multiethnic/multicultural workforce* that is already in being in some parts of academic organizations and beginning to join the team everywhere. This new complement of workers is an overlay on the three megatrends we have already discussed. They reinforce the processes of change. Each of these developments is highly significant in its own right; taken together they suggest a revolutionary change in working life for most Americans. Academic institutions will make their own adjustments to these developments.

A MULTICULTURAL/MULTIETHNIC WORKFORCE

The Labor Department issued its *Work Force 2000* project for the American workforce in 1985; it attracted considerable attention because it predicted dramatic shifts in the complement of workers by the turn of the century. Among other estimates the report predicted that 85% of the 25 million people entering the labor pool would be women, minorities, or immigrants. Only 15% would be white males and their share of the workforce was expected to drop from 51 to 45%. With minor statistical variations these projections have been confirmed by trends in the American labor pool over the intervening years. Similarly, according to a 1996 study by the California Community Colleges Board of Governors, the state labor force is going through dynamic changes. Today 6 out of every 10 workers are women and minorities. However, during the next 10 years 14 out of every 15 new workers added to the California workforce will be minorities and women.

The forces pushing diversification today are not only the goodwill gestures of the past because it is the "right thing to do," but also market forces.

The world is more diverse, markets are more diverse, customers are more diverse, and diverse workforces are a better "fit" for current conditions.

There are other forces pushing diversity. Among the best candidates available are often minorities or women in addition to those representing other segments of society. With alert organizations valuing the intellectual contributions of every staff member, they realize that an individual's gender, ethnicity, and culture influence the way he or she thinks about the work, and this broadens the "intellectual capital" the company has to work with if the workforce is diversified. The whole point of fostering diversity is to draw on the unique skills and perceptions of each employee. Among other things this consists of an even-handed approach to staff that assures minorities, women, and white males their contribution to the success of the enterprise is welcome, recognized, and appreciated. They must feel they have a future in the organization. They must feel personnel decisions are based on merit to keep them as involved and productive members of the organization.

The world of work is undergoing transformation at an unprecedented pace, a pace far more rapid than the transition from an agrarian to an industrial economy. The stresses and dislocations of these monumental changes are already evident in the economic, political, and social life of our nation and we are only partway through the adjustment process. We find technology is transforming the kinds of jobs available and the kind of work that is done; globalization is changing the kinds of products and services we offer and where the work is done; women's greater involvement is revising who does what in the American workplace; and empowerment of the poor and minorities is opening up new opportunities for careers once reserved for the privileged. This tsunami of change is creating great hardship for some people and great opportunity for others. Education is the key. Through education people learn how to change and how to adapt to the new environment and those are indispensable skills in the contemporary workplace.

In spite of early warning in the Labor Department projections and the optimistic projection about our ability to deal with change, development of diverse workforces has not gone as smoothly as anticipated. Human resource experts estimate only 3–5% of U.S. corporations are diversifying their workforces effectively.

It is clear there is a great deal of work to be done before the American workforce looks like the American population. We still have to realize the value of diversity in the workplace. The introspection of Ernest Drew, the chief executive officer of Hoechst Celanese, the chemical giant, speaks of his commitment to a more diverse workforce. He was attending a planning conference of employees that included 125 managers, mostly white men, and 50 supervisors who were women and minorities. The group was split into problem-solving teams and asked to consider how the corporate culture affected the business and how it could be changed to improve results. As he listened to the reports he was impressed. It was so obvious that the diverse teams had the broader solutions. "They had ideas I hadn't even thought of," he reflected. For the first time he realized diversifying the staff improved their problem-solving skills. It was an important discovery (Reisch 1991, 21).

The National Association of Manufacturers, anticipating the year 2010, urges manufacturers to focus on skills and training, doubling their percentage of payroll that they spend on those activities (estimated average of 1.5%). They also suggest that firms focus on immigration and pay, greater attention to diversity issues (Miller 1997).

THE ACADEMIC EXPERIENCE

Throughout history, cultures flourished through contacts with others. People at the crossroads were more aware, more intellectually developed, more cosmopolitan, richer than people on the byways. Civilization developed at the crossroads.

Today urban universities are at the crossroads. They are more aware, culturally richer, more representative of the world than the neighborhood. They are conducting experiments in intercultural/interethnic community and, perhaps even more important, they are participating in and helping develop a great worldwide electronic crossroads that promises for the first time development of a world community—a community that brings together millions of people of all ethnicities and virtually all cultures in a worldwide communication network. This makes the dream of a world civilization a possibility. People on this network are laying down a record of humanity in the last days of the 20th century.

But our concerns here are not with the background of development of a world civilization but with the foreground of the daily experiences of people living and working in a multicultural/multiethnic community. It is from these communities that world citizens may emerge.

But even in sheltered academic institutions the diversity experience is not what we would like to report. In a wide-ranging report on "Race on Campus" *U.S. News and World Report* (1993) discussed race relations on campuses. It appears there is racial animosity between black and white students on many large university campuses and voluntary segregation in housing and out-of-class events is common.

In a *U.S. News & World Report* column (1993) John Leo discussed a study done at Stanford by John Bunzel (1992), former president of San Jose State University and now at the Hoover Institute at Stanford, who has written a book, *Race Relations on Campus: Stanford Students Speak*. His principal findings: no hard-core bigotry was reported. Surface relations between whites and blacks are very good but underneath there is a "pervasive racial anxiety." The survey found nearly two-thirds of all seniors thought "most people on campus are fair to all racial and ethnic groups." Very few whites had stereotypical views of black academic ability.

But there is another side to race relations at Stanford, Bunzel wrote: "A great many blacks, inclined to think of racism in institutional terms and therefore as firmly fixed in the university, insist that the real problem is oppression, not segregation. The more Stanford has tried to do—aggressive affirmative action, sensitivity training, ethnic theme houses, changing the 'Eurocentric curriculum'—the worse matters have become." One wonders how such well-intentioned efforts produced such undesirable results.

Some community colleges, such as Orange Coast College in Southern California, have approached diversity as a strategic choice and a necessary planning element of its overall college plan. In addition to active recruitment of underrepresented groups, the college's general education program includes a requirement in American cultural diversity and lists multiple courses from ethnic studies to women's literature from which students are able to choose. Additionally the college is developing new courses and course modules with emphases on internationalization. Segments of the Bulletin are written in Vietnamese or Spanish, reflecting the increased numbers of these students and sensitivity to their needs.

There are many ethical reasons to develop diverse communities. Among them is the American ideal of recognizing each human being as an individual who is a unique blend of qualities, including a physical and mental endowment, abilities, learning, and experiences that collectively constitute one's sense of personal identity. This developmental process can best be fostered in a diverse community where the perceptions of a multiethnic/multicultural world can be nurtured.

There are also many pragmatic reasons for development of diverse academic communities. Among them, these reasons are prominent:

- the United States is increasingly diverse.
- College students are increasingly diverse.
- College faculty and staff are increasingly diverse.
- The American workforce is increasingly diverse.
- The United States is involved in a global market.
- Multiculturalism is driven by market forces.

To see what has happened to the population of Southern California, anyone need only look out the window on a drive through Los Angeles. In the signs and buildings, the clothes and the features of the people, the evidence of multiethnic and multicultural people is everywhere. It is in the Los Angeles basin that many of the adaptations to this experiment in multicultural community are being worked out. The telephone companies are finding ways to link ethnic groups, the supermarkets stock a dizzying array of specialty foods, the schools are learning to cope with students who speak more than 80 languages and dialects but no English. Government must deal with citizens whose life experience make them suspicious of all public institutions. The colleges and universities are enrolling the sons and daughters of these new Californians, and these campuses have been seeking ways to provide programs and instructional methods that will enhance their learning potential.

THE DOMINGUEZ HILLS EXPERIENCE

R. C. Richardson, Jr. (1990a) demonstrates how state and institutional policy leaders influence colleges to move through three stages of adaptation to racial diversity. These stages influence access and achievement. In stage one, barriers to college participation are removed, allowing entering classes to reflect the ethnic compositions of the service area. In stage two, underprepared minority students are given assistance in adapting to institutional expectations, to increase their retention and graduation rates. In stage three, the institution becomes more responsive to students of diverse backgrounds by developing academic programs that better reflect a multicultural society. "As institutions move through the stages, their definition of quality changes from an emphasis on reputation and resources that excludes diversity to the recognition that any definition of quality must incorporate diversity to be meaningful in a multicultural society." A comprehensive study by Petrus Hendrikus Van Hamersveld (1994) indicated that Dominguez Hills has reached that status and students consider it to be a quality university.

California State University, Dominguez Hills is a teaching and learning community dedicated to excellence and committed to preparing students of diverse ages, cultural backgrounds, and interests—for lives of accomplishment in a world of unprecedented challenge and change. The campus is strategically located in the heart of a major technological, industrial, and transportation complex. Moreover, it is central in a population that is international and multiethnic, and the people of this area are genuinely heterogeneous; cultural pluralism is a major characteristic of the university.

A fundamental condition of this university's existence is the multiethnic and multicultural nature of its setting. It seeks to enhance that pluralism in programs and in the makeup of the student body, faculty, and staff. It invites international perspectives, cultivates programs that serve students from other nations, and encourages students to participate in studying in other countries.

California State University, Dominguez Hills is an effective case history of a diverse institution. The campus is among the most ethnically diverse universities, not only in Southern California, but also in the country. Furthermore, the university is generally credited by its internal constituencies

Table 10.1
Ethnic and Gender Distributions, CSU, Dominguez Hills

Ethnic Category	Faculty	Staff
White	75.6 % (204)	41.7 % (249)
Black	8.1 % (22)	32.2 % (249)
Asian	8.5 %	14.9 % (89)
Hispanic	7.8 %	11.2 % (67)
Gender Category		
Male	46.2 % (320)	41.9 % (250)
Female	53.8 % (373)	58.1 % (347)

and by external opinion as providing a successful cultural diversity experience. In the 1995–96 academic year the student population was 31.5% white, 29.5% African-American, 25.2% Hispanic, 13% Asian, and 8% other ethnicities. The 1995 figures for the ethnic and gender distributions of the faculty and staff are depicted in Table 10.1.

Students on the campus represent about 85 countries. The ethnic distribution of American students does not represent a clear majority of any particular group. This, in addition to possible self-selection, may explain the results of recent surveys of student opinion of the campus environment. The studies show that a positive interethnic/intercultural environment prevails at Dominguez Hills. Generally, relationships between races on campus are characterized by harmony.

It is estimated that 50% of the faculty have made adjustments in traditional classroom management or curriculum design to help multicultural students be successful and comfortable in classes. In addition, the university orientation class is designed specifically to help students from cultures other than the United States to understand and use the variety of support services available to them. The course often serves as a bridge experience to help students adjust to university life. It is conducted with a pattern of open communication that permits students from other cultures to explore things that seem odd in a nonthreatening environment.

Some professors conduct multicultural classroom exercises as a means of opening communication and illustrating valid but different perspectives that cultures bring to consideration of common human experiences. Professors have found that many minority or foreign-born students lack the self-confidence to participate in the classroom. Students often use alternate communication systems that they find more comfortable. Some professors use e-mail to carry on dialogues with students who are reluctant to raise questions or participate in class discussions.

The university is also carrying out a process of continuous improvement in its teaching and classroom management practices. With the aid of a federal grant, observers are visiting classrooms to see what works and what doesn't work among professors' teaching methods. Their observations are cataloged and suggested guidelines are written to increase the effectiveness of current methods. In some classes more than half of the students are multilingual. Faculty members have adjusted their teaching styles to help these students learn.

The university is continuing to expand its multicultural resources center and faculty members plan to introduce a more diverse body of literature and textbooks into the classroom. Surveys of American literature, for example, would be expanded to include writings by African-American authors; and the literature produced by Latino authors will be increased. The Institute for the Study of Cultural Diversity and Internationalization is building a reference center on Cultural Diversity and International Issues.

The university has conducted workshops in classroom assessment techniques designed to help faculty obtain useful feedback on how much and how well their students are learning. Depending on the information obtained in assessment, faculty members can refocus their teaching and help students make their learning more efficient and more effective.

On the campus the faculty are following several strategies to make students from diverse backgrounds more comfortable. They all stress communication. Getting multiethnic students to talk is the surest way to improve everyone's classroom experience. Professors are using "cooperative learning" groups in classes and electronic mail systems to promote interaction. Some professors also use assignments that involve work in groups and classroom presentations as a means of stimulating interaction of class members and generating dialogues among the students.

Diversity among the faculty and staff members is also fostered. A vigorous affirmative action program has been pursued for several years. Among the faculty, recruitment of a fully representative membership is in progress but not yet achieved. In the nationwide arena where faculty must be recruited, the competition for minorities and women in many disciplines is very strong. The university has not always been able to retain the services of individuals it would like to have as members of the faculty. Nevertheless, there has been progress and the university is working on the problem.

Among the staff there are a large number of diverse people. The university has a very good record in minority appointments. It has also excelled in another aspect of staff development. The California State University system has a generous program of enrollment in courses related to work and career development that can be taken by employees without fees. Many staff members have used this program to complete bachelor's and master's degrees.

A development of widespread interest is the California Academy of Mathematics and Science (CAMS), which is located on the campus of the university. The academy began in the 1989–90 academic year and encompasses 9th through 12th grades. Its first graduating class (1994) consisted of about 120 students. Students are drawn from eight school districts and 60 middle schools in Southern California. Applicants must present a "portfolio or other evidence of interest in mathematics and science." Typically, from a total of 700–800 applicants, two students are selected from each school. The academy has achieved its objective of reflecting the student demographics of the Los Angeles basin, which is highly populated by minorities. The student body of 500 plus is 52% female and it is balanced ethnically with 29% Hispanic, 25% African-American, and 7% underrepresented Asians (Cambodian, Vietnamese, etc.). The remainder of the student body is 18% Asian, 20% Caucasian, and 1% Native American.

The academy has almost no attrition; for all reasons including family relocation the rate is less than 3%. Absenteeism is also less than 3%. All 116 members of the 1995 graduating class are attending college. The members of this class will collectively receive an estimated $500,000 in grant and scholarship aid. Eleventh-grade students typically take one or two college courses on the Dominguez Hills campus. They compete well with college freshmen and score an exemplary 3.2 mean grade point average; the freshmen average is 2.48.

Science classes are held in university laboratories and CAMS students also use the university's physical education facilities, foreign language labs, computer labs, and food services facilities. This cooperative arrangement has been beneficial to CAMS and the university. The academy adds a unique overlay to the diversity of the university campus.

Campus leaders have also undertaken a substantial effort to promote diversity within the university and in the communities the university serves. In April 1994 the university announced formation of the Institute for the Study of Cultural Diversity and Internationalization. The linkage between cultural diversity and international commitments is in recognition of the special role of the United States as a culturally diverse society and a major player in the international community. The institute was established to promote an understanding of the dynamics of cultural diversity and to encourage or heighten international activities and awareness. It has developed a program that devotes its resources to:

- sponsoring an annual cultural diversity conference;
- establishing a campus repository of educational resources relating to cultural diversity and internationalization;
- developing resources for faculty, students, and staff who are committed to enhancing cultural diversity and internationalization;
- providing encouragement, support, and communication linkages for campus programs related to the enhancement of cultural diversity and internationalization.

A recent annual conference was conducted under the appropriate title, "Enhancing Community Through Cultural Diversity." The all-day confer-

ence featured nationally known writers and educators who focused on providing teachers with well-defined approaches to cultural diversity that can
be used in the classroom. The positive intercultural/interethnic environment
at Dominguez Hills is fostered by the campus community and its administrative leadership. The campus president issued a planning guide that
states: "To encourage and heighten international activities and awareness
we should bring more international activities to our campus, encourage
international curricular content and academic programs, strengthen study
abroad programs, stimulate student and faculty international exchanges
and foster other enterprises that encourage awareness and respect for diverse cultural groups" (Detweiler 1994).

CAMPUS CLIMATE AND CULTURAL DIVERSITY

In 1992 Dominguez Hills participated in a national survey of student
opinion about cultural diversity on campus (Blischke 1992). The study
yielded some valuable insights about how students experience a multicul-
tural/multiethnic institution. The study was conducted in a three-stage
model of the relationship between underrepresented minorities and institutions of higher learning. The first stage was based on barriers to access;
the second stage involved development of a support system to help students
succeed; and in the third stage alterations were made in the institution itself
to make it more responsive to the needs of minority students.

In the first stage Dominguez Hills reached "parity" in African-American
representation. One type of parity was the ratio of students of a particular
ethnic background to the numbers of that minority resident within the
university's service area; the second type of parity was the ratio of graduation to numbers of students of each minority group within the student
body. The university did not quite reach parity in Latino students, which
was the most rapidly growing group. Graduation rates reached parity for
both African-Americans and Latinos, which was an unusual achievement.

In an effort to understand why so few institutions reached parity in graduation statistics, a few institutions were picked as a national sample of
successful institutions; Dominguez Hills was chosen in this group. In the
third-stage institutions are asked to change their methods and services to
fit these nontraditional students. At this stage faculty become involved and
they begin to modify instructional methods to serve a more diverse group
of students. Only three institutions in the national sample, including Dominguez Hills, were judged to be at stage three.

The student survey was designed to gather data on attitudes that permitted institutions to reach stage three. The data were sorted into four
ethnic groups—Asian, African-American, Latino, and Caucasian. The sample included about 500 respondents. The first question asked whether the

respondent valued interaction with other ethnic groups. Overall, three out of four students responded affirmatively.

Question number two dealt with diversity. Almost 90% of respondents indicated diversity is good for Dominguez Hills and should be actively promoted by students, staff, faculty, and administrators.

In question number three an effort was made to determine whether the Dominguez Hills experience had influenced the very positive response to question two. It asked whether sensitivity to other racial groups had increased since they had become part of the campus community. Approximately half of each group thought the university had contributed to their increased sensitivity.

The university asked for an overall assessment of this vital area in question four. Between 7 and 8 students in every 10, in every ethnic group, rated their total experience highly.

The university closed the questionnaire with two very tough questions: the first was how often had the respondent experienced racial discrimination on the campus. Some 83% answered "rarely" or "never." The second question attempted to get at behavior among ethnic groups; it asked to what extent respondents thought their group was integrated with other ethnic groups on the campus. This question generated a wider set of opinions. A small percentage strongly agreed the groups were integrated; about half of the respondents were on the positive end of the scale, about a fourth were neutral, and about a fourth said their group was segregated.

One might conclude from these results that there was an extremely positive mind-set when this survey was taken, but there is a gap between attitudes and behavior. The university concluded that there may be a self-selection of students who value a diverse environment who attend this university. This is a campus without a majority ethnic group, each of the four groups is of considerable size, and its members do not feel isolated, and diversity has been valued on the campus for many years. Multiculturalism is part of the institutional mission statement and it is frequently reflected in the language and behavior of its members.

MANAGING WITH DIVERSITY

There is considerable attention in the literature these days to "managing diversity." As discussed in the beginning of this chapter, we think use of the term "managing" puts the wrong connotation on building an effective community with diverse members. There are things management can do to foster diversity, of course. Some of the things listed in the previous pages were designed to make the university more responsive to the needs of a multicultural/multiethnic community. But the administration cannot will harmony. Harmony may be nurtured by management attitudes, policies, and practices but it cannot be mandated. There are some doubts that it can be programmed. Given this perspective on diversity, what should the university do to encourage diversity and build a community that diverse members are comfortable with and one in which they can be successful?

Should a university undertake fostering effective diversity programmatically, as Stanford has done?

Should the university conduct sensitivity training, help ethnic-oriented living groups, alter the curriculum to speak to ethnic sensibilities, seek ethnic representation on university councils, conduct ethnic orientation in introductory workshops for entering students, or conduct aggressive recruitment programs to make the university reflect today's diverse society? Depending on an alert administration and willing faculty and staff, a university might pursue many of these initiatives. But is it more effective to provide help that fosters similarities or differences? These are difficult questions and there are no easy answers. The guiding principle is, "Does the proposed program promote diversity or community?" If the answer to that question is, "it promotes community," the program is probably appropriate in an academic setting.

The following factors are what is needed to work in a multiethnic/multicultural setting:

- a sense of fairness
- tolerance for differences
- recognition of similarities
- sensitivity to feelings of co-workers,
- the desire to learn,
- open communication
- getting beyond stereotypes to know individuals,
- realization that cultural loading may alter perceptions of messages,
- a sincere desire to create a successful multiethnic/multicultural community

An organization that produces an environment that can support these sensibilities is on the right track.

Diversity must be honored; it is important to be clear about one's own set of social values, but in a diverse group other people may have a profoundly different and equally valid social orientations. In interacting with people of different backgrounds, one must always be aware of the law of unintended consequences. Well-intended but insensitive initiatives can damage the sense of community. A guiding principle is to be inclusive rather than exclusive in planning changes. We all have much to learn from one another. While all of the points noted above are self-explanatory, it is important to elaborate on the first point—a sense of fairness that is so essential to successful diversity programs and the sense of community.

FAIRNESS

A central and recurrent concept in satisfactory accommodation of diverse membership in an organization is "fairness." The question "Is it fair?" or often the allegation "It isn't fair" have been with the human race for thousands of years and they are with us now, perhaps more frequently than in any other period of history. We have built endless codes of law and provided courts to adjudicate claims to assure fairness. We have provided systems in organizations to hear complaints and render judgments about fairness of proposed actions and still we hear the complaint, "It isn't fair." Certainly the world needs better methods to divide things fairly.

Some universities are conducting research on decision making with emphasis on reaching fair conclusions. Mathematical modeling is one approach. Researchers have already validated some things that work. For two people the "birthday cake" system—where one person cuts the cake into two pieces and the other person chooses first—works well but it cannot be successful with more than two people or with something that cannot be divided equally. The most difficult decisions involve matters of personal significance that are highly emotional.

Concepts of fairness are highly related to the individual. What seems fair to one person is unfair to another person. No system of reaching controversial decisions can please everyone. Yet concepts of fairness are central to development of a successful diverse community. For some members an open process is enough; for others the decision must go their way. For some members consultation before decision is enough, particularly if the decision is based on data or factual evidence.

Given this volatile condition in perception of fairness, sensitive decisions should be approached with caution. Several strategies to improve the acceptability of major decisions have been widely used. Among them the most obvious is the system of law and the courts, but decisions in academic institutions rarely go this far. Internal decisions use various methods to improve decision making, including prior discussion to determine opinion and emotional involvement before decision, solicitation of expert advice, committee review and recommendation, committee decision, group vote, levels of review with recommendations prior to decision, and so on. These strategies may improve the possibilities of reaching decisions that will be perceived as fair by participants.

Value-laden decisions are the most difficult. One system under review in research is determination of alternatives and assignment of points to each person attested by the outcome. Each participant is given 50 points, which may be assigned to the various alternatives as their values may suggest.

Assignments of the participants are totaled for each alternative and the one with the highest score is selected. Researchers suggest this system is widely regarded as fair and it has been successful in trials.

How elaborate a decision process must be to be regarded as fair depends on the significance of the issue and how emotional it is. Some decisions affect everyone. Some affect a single individual. Some key decisions generate hundreds even thousands of follow-on decisions. A decision to inaugurate a new major, for example, opens a series of ensuing decisions about time, place, funding, equipping, staffing, promoting, recruiting, program design, and so on. Key decisions of this kind are so important to everyone involved that great care needs to be taken in reaching them. In the cited instance, near unanimous consent would be necessary for such a decision to be regarded as "fair."

THE OUTLOOK FOR DIVERSITY

Diversity is not something that will happen in the future; it is here now. It has been developing since the creation of the United States as a nation, but it has become more prominent in national life in this century and an item of wide current interest in the 1990s decade. If one were organized to collect clippings from the daily newspaper that have significant content on diversity, one would have a voluminous file in a month and a drawer-full in a year. What makes diversity so prominent at this time is that it has become highly visible during a period of uncertainty and volatility in American economic, political, and cultural development. It is a period when belief in the "American dream" of a better life for one's children has faltered and the future has turned ambiguous. Affirmative action programs have been challenged at a number of universities, starting with the most famous action taken by the Board of Regents of the University of California. There is agreement in universities and colleges that with or without affirmative action programs a successful model of diversity in California is essential as higher education faces 700,000 additional students in the next 15 years. Many of them will add to the multicultural student bodies that already exist on California campuses. For most workers in California, diversity in the workplace is a common reality. For most students in school, multicultural classmates are the norm, not the exception. As a result most young people come to college with multiculturalism as an expectation, not a surprise. The necessity of providing for these new students is the motivation to communicate across cultures. Communication is the beginning of community.

Even with these environmental developments as a backdrop, the picture of race relations in the workplace, where relationships are personalized in individual relationships, is good. In a Los Angeles *Times* poll conducted in 1995, the results depict an American workforce in which there is more agreement about workplace diversity than the headlines suggest: 88% of the respondents to that survey said race relations were good to excellent in the workplace; 88% said relations between men and women were good to excellent, including 91% of the women. Race relations falter on stereotypes and blossom on personal contact. It is when we know each other as people that we get along together.

The outlook for increased harmony in intercultural, interethnic, intergender relations is good. The university is not unaware of social, economic, and political developments that would argue otherwise, but it seems to us we can overcome these problems and continue to build a community based on a worldview that anything less than harmonious relations in a diverse society is unacceptable.

People who are working in organizations where diversity is successful are tending the seed-beds of the new mentality. In the last few decades they have gained new insights about the power of human thought to create physical reality. The "new physics" is beginning to demonstrate to the scientific mind that people literally create external reality by the choices they make in their inner dialogue. They create internal reality based on thought systems and on internal paradigms about the world, about life, and about other people. This new world consciousness can be the source of a new world order. So what kind of paradigm do we need to support the development of diversity in a new world order? Here is a beginning:

- The world is diverse.
- We are all equal.
- We must look for the common good.
- Our similarities are much greater than our differences.
- Our differences are a source of creativity and growth.
- We must be inclusive rather than exclusive.

A picture of a multicultural multiethnic community is more like a mosaic than a painting. Each person brings the tile of personal identity to the image of community. Collectively they make up the picture but each person maintains a unique sense of self. No one is asked to sacrifice a personal sense of identity for the sake of community. In this multiethnic/multicultural world, learning to live together and work together is not a choice, it is a necessity; it is not in the future, it is now; it is not for someone else, it is for each one of us.

DEVELOPING COMMUNITY

The world "community" has interesting origins. It can be defined as "a group of people who reside in a specific locality, share a government, and often have a common cultural and historical heritage." What is new about the current effort to build community is that universities are bringing together people who do not have a common cultural and historical background. That is what makes efforts to build community so difficult and so fascinating. Community is the willingness of people to build together.

Many financial advisors recommend a diversified investment portfolio because diversification gains strengths from multiple sources and strengths needed to deal with an environment marked by continuing change. What is true of investments is also true of organizations. A diversified membership provides strengths to cope with an unpredictable tomorrow in a changing world. America not only is changing; it has changed. Guidelines that were acceptable in the recent past are not useful today, and nowhere is that more apparent than in the membership of successful organizations. In the early years of this century, America was thought of as a "melting pot," which held that immigrants to this country were expected to lose their culture and their individual identities and become Americans. As a nation we are now engaged in the greatest experiment in a multicultural/ multiracial society the world has ever seen. This new society embraces people with a wide range of cultures, perspectives, sensitivities, and insights that are gaining recognition for their value. The old view of diversity as a liability is changing to diversity as an asset, and the evolving view of our economy as worldwide is accelerating that transition. In a country marked by diversity competing in a diverse worldwide economy, the only rational strategy to maximize our human potential is to create organizations in which people of diverse heritages can feel comfortable, valued, and productive.

There is a growing recognition in the corporate world that diversifying companies is the right thing to do for the business. This recognition that making a place for a diverse workforce is both a good business decision and correct social policy is motivating rapid change in the corporate world. For many institutions there are solid business reasons to promote diversity. For all employers there are compelling social and philosophical reasons to foster diversity, and for most organizations there are important program reasons to employ a diversified workforce.

What is diversity? A dictionary definition says diversity is "the fact or quality of being diverse; difference. A point or respect in which things differ. Variety." Current usage goes far beyond the limits of this concept. Diversity is:

- a comprehensive method of building a representative work force
- a program in some institutions
- a way to assemble intellectual capital
- an ideal based on equality

- a way to build community
- a method of recognizing and respecting differences
- a system to parallel a workforce and a client base
- a program to understand the special characteristics of each individual and the value of nurturing those qualities
- a family of issues
- complexity
- an evolutionary process
- a way of communicating with a diverse population

Diversity is not:

- a numbers game
- tokenism
- confined to minorities
- a substitute for affirmative action
- easily defined
- a new management fad
- a quick fix

Diversity is not just a race and gender concept now; it is an effort to include everyone. It is based on fairness. It is a condition that permits members of the organization to continue learning, to continue improving, to contribute more to the success of the enterprise. Diversity doesn't leave anybody out. It is a culture based on a paradigm of inclusiveness, of continuous improvement of human development, of removing barriers, of growth, of advancement. It is a spirit that permeates all human resource systems. It is a pattern of people taking personal responsibility for their careers. It is a method that welcomes differences, that honors multicultural/multiethnic perspectives. Diversity stimulates problem solving, shares information, seeks a balance between professional and personal commitments, and permits flexibility in making adjustments.

There are valid reasons to support development of a diverse workforce based on the concept of "intellectual capital." In this competitive world we all live in, knowledge is an indispensable requirement. It is essential to discover, develop, and apply intellectual resources to the problems and possibilities that each institution faces. In an academic institution, faculty members are recruited for their intellectual and subject-matter competence. This clear mandate has not been so obvious on the administrative side of the organization, but administrative roles are increasingly complex; maintaining the emotional and intellectual equilibrium of the institution in this period of dramatic change requires sensitivities and administrative skills of a high order. Effective support services require identification and utilization of all of the intellectual capital the staff possess for the solution of administrative problems. No administration can afford less than full utilization of all of its talent. Full utilization requires a personnel system that identifies and recruits effective people, that does not put people in little organization boxes and accuse them of "working out of class" for venturing out. Full utilization also requires a clear commitment to being "fair." The perception of fairness is particularly important. Any suspicion that personnel actions are based on stereotypical reasoning can destroy cooperation.

In corporate America it is relatively easy for firms involved in international operations to justify a workforce that replicates the diversity of its customer base. Few people seriously challenge the customer-workforce match in international trade. However, this principle is not so obvious among companies involved solely in operations in the United States. A diverse customer base is somehow less compelling when its members are U.S. residents. Yet educating students to deal effectively with customer diversity on international and national levels is essential for their success as employees and the economic success of companies employing them.

In colleges and universities the need to match the ethnic, gender, age, and economic background of the staff to their client base is rarely considered. Consequently, foreign students and minority domestic students often see some staff as unyielding, rule-driven bureaucrats who rarely provide personal attention to their problems and are unimaginative in helping them comply with regulations. That is partly because staff are often more subject to rules and regulations developed outside of the university for a number of generic organizations that do not service students and faculty directly. That insensitivity to the values of the customer requires new approaches to management of the university, until new state rules governing actions of the staff in an educational context are developed. Total Quality Management or Quality Service represents an alternative means of providing program flexibility. Empowerment of staff to act beyond traditional roles is essential to providing support and understanding of current populations.

POTENTIAL PROBLEMS

Diversity can be a social issue, a moral issue, and an institutional issue. White males can be concerned about affirmative action quotas; women can worry about being promoted on merit not on gender; people of color can feel they are up against a double standard; and older employees can feel they are not as valued as their younger counterparts. Given these and other possibilities for real and imagined grievances, it is a wonder that newly formed diverse organizations do not have more personnel problems than they do. If they have sensitive leadership both in the workers and the managers, a reasonable accommodation to these multiple perspectives can be

worked out. In this process the informal organization may be as potent or
more potent than the formal organization. When a viable working arrangement has been worked out, it must be fostered by maintaining a sense of
fairness, by resolving grievances promptly, and by celebrating successes.

Diversity in the workplace produces concerns that go beyond race, gender, and ethnicity to include age, physical disabilities, and lifestyle. Effective
resolution of issues that arise from different cultural traits from person to
person, from different life experiences, and different worldviews requires a
broad understanding of multicultural community and tolerance. It cannot
be done by quoting rules or demanding conformance to some arbitrary
standard. Curing these issues requires treatment with the balm of mutual
understanding. They cannot be ignored. Diagnosis begins with the question
"What is the right thing to do?" and ends with doing it.

COMPETITION INVADES THE ACADEMY

To some extent colleges and universities drawing students from the same
market niche have always been competitive. For many institutions enrollment is the primary source of financial resources and competition for enrollment is very real. What has been is only a faint image of what will be.
Failure to recognize students as clients, to systematically collect and analyze
student opinion about services, and to add just services to meet their needs
all cast doubts about the long-term fiscal viability of institutions in highly
competitive markets. Competition appears in many guises. It comes from
other traditional institutions that are sharpening their marketing and improving their services. It comes from abroad as the competition to attract
international students heats up. It comes from marketing companies that
gather rights to courses from traditional institutions and market them via
television. It comes from the business sector where for-profit companies
develop courses and curricula, seek accreditation, and grant degrees. Many
of these vendors are unburdened by the traditions of institutions of higher
education. They have no campus, they have no tenured faculty, they have
no committees, they have no fixed schedules. What they have is a viable
program based on market research and response to customer needs and
preferences. They do not schedule required courses Monday, Wednesday
and Friday at 9:00 a.m. They make it convenient to take classes.

DIVERSITY RECRUITMENT

Any organization that aspires to future leadership must pursue diversity
in its customer base and in its workforce. The demographics are very clear.
Minority ethnic groups will grow. Americans will be older; more women
than ever will be enrolled in higher education; more companies will be
involved in the global economy; and so on. Any corporation providing a

service ignores these developments at its peril. And any college or university, particularly public institutions, must respond to the needs and interests of a diverse population. Representative distribution in students, faculty, staff, and leadership will be the symbol of institutional sensitivity and commitment to diversity. Planning into the 21st century must attract and hold these representative distributions. This is not quotas; it is not affirmative action as it has been practiced in the recent past; it is not even recruitment of people in any particular group. It is a vigorous effort to find and attract the best people available. If that is done effectively the student body, the faculty, the staff, and the administrators will be a representative group.

Companies that have been building a diverse workforce since the 1960s have learned it is not necessary to alter standards. There is a growing awareness of the value of a diverse staff with different points of view, different perspectives, and different cultural and ethnic backgrounds. They have also learned that having a diverse staff improves decision making because the decision makers bring to problem solving much wider perspectives and the alternatives identified offer a wider range of options. The discussions are more comprehensive and the data on customer preferences are often first-hand from personal participation in conversations with customers. Decisions reached in this process have proved to be longer range and better tuned to the needs of the corporation. There is no reason to believe that this process that has served the corporate world so well will be any less successful in academic institutions. In many alert colleges and universities this process has already been adopted.

In academic institutions there is no substitute for clear and consistent commitment to diversity articulated by its administrators and practiced in its daily activities. The goal is to have a competent workforce as diverse as the people the institution serves. When such a commitment infuses the strategic planning of the organization, it becomes a clear competitive advantage. Every major decision in an effective college or university must be taken with attention to the long-term development of the institution and service to diverse constituencies must be a prominent component of these decisions. The inference of this necessity is that diverse members of the administration must be involved in the decision-making process. Listening to students and other constituencies and to members of the faculty and staff is an essential first step in planning for the future. It must be followed by creative strategic planning and by taking reasonable risks. One of the major benefits of a diverse academic community is to demonstrate the ideas and methods that make it successful.

LEARNING TO WORK TOGETHER

One of the most significant developments in contemporary life in the United States is that we have become a multiethnic/multicultural nation.

More than a third of our people are ethnic minorities at the end of the 1990s, and the forecast is for that figure to become 52% of the population by 2005. Demographic changes of this magnitude have significant implications for higher education. For most colleges and universities, multicultural membership in the student body and the faculty and staff is already a reality and the outlook is for increasing diversity of ethnic groups and increasing numbers of members in each group. Adjusting to these changes is essential to the effectiveness of academic institutions. Realizing the inherent advantages of a multicultural organizations will require some changes in traditional practice. The first step is recognition that change is necessary. It is characteristic of the human condition that the cultural values and practices one learned as a child are the "natural" ways to live in the world; any departure appears deviant. It requires some sophistication to realize that different people have different childhoods and different perspectives on these matters. Thus, each individual has cultural "loading" and no claim to authenticity is stronger than another. Each institution may have several minority groups represented among the students and the staff. How can their multiple views be accommodated in institutional processes?

In considering the importance of multicultural sensitivity it is essential to develop accelerated changes in traditional behavior in members of the administration and the staff. The key word is sensitivity. The beginning is awareness. It requires effort to put multicultural sensitivity into practice. Effective service to a multicultural student body is unlikely until sensitivity is practiced. Service must take into account the cultural values of the client to provide effective service. Particularly in the classroom, students of different cultures reflect different learning patterns. Minority students exhibit reluctance to participate in class discussions. To encourage involvement it is necessary to be sensitive to this cultural condition and to alter traditional recitation practices to make participation easier. Working with a partner and later in a small self-directed group may be necessary before minority students feel comfortable in class discussions. In the traditional American culture, independence is a widely supported value, but in some Eastern cultures interdependence is preferred. Students who are just beginning their college careers are in a foreign land. Everything is bigger and more complicated than high school. They have to make and keep their own appointments, identity the information they need and find it, interpret catalog information, find their way around campus, and sometimes lead a solitary life. If they are away from home they have escaped daily regulation and support of their families. They have freedom they could not have imagined in the past and responsibility that is frightening. They do not speak the bureaucratic language. They have the right to success or failure on their own terms in an institution that will make judgments about their progress.

If these new students are ethnic minorities it is comforting to find members of the faculty and staff who share their ethnic background. They can serve as guides, advisors, even mentors in the first bewildering months in this new land. They can point the way and interpret the rules. They can provide support without compromising independence. Ethnic students have their own culture-related needs associated with adjustment to this new learning community. Multicultural sensitivity helps them accelerate that process and regain their confidence.

Multicultural sensitivity must begin with a commitment to be open to understanding other people's cultural values. Learning about other cultures requires an inquiring, nonjudgmental mind. It requires realizing what others have, not what they lack. It must grant dignity and self-worth to people of other cultures. It is an exploration, not a critique. It looks for broad areas of commonality not just differences. In the end it seeks community. The delivery of cultural sensitive services is a necessary and legitimate dimension of every college and university.

SELECTED READINGS AND REFERENCES

Blischke, William. 1992. Campus Climate and Cultural Diversity Survey. Memorandum for the California State University, Dominguez Hills Executive Committee and Personal Communication.

Boorstin, Daniel. 1994. The Age of Negative Discovery. *The American Enterprise* 5(6): 28.

Bunzel, John, H. 1992. Race Relations on Campus: Stanford Students Speak. *Publishers Weekly* 239 (April 20): 19.

California Community Colleges Board of Governors. 1960. *The New Basic Agenda: Policy Directions for Student Success*. Sacramento, March 14.

Clark, Kathleen. 1996. California Academy of Mathematics and Science. Personal Communication.

Detweiler, Robert, C. 1994. Planning Guide—California State University, Dominguez Hills. A Memo to the Campus Community form President Robert C. Detweiler.

El-Aharaf, Amer; Gray, David; and Naguib, Hussen. 1995. Partners for Quality in a University Setting: California State University, Dominguez Hills and Xerox, Corporation: 164–198. In Allan Hoffman & Daniel Julius, eds., *Total Quality Management: Implications for Higher Education*. Maryville MO: Prescott.

El-Aharaf, Amer and LaCorte, John, eds. 1994. *Enhancing Community Through Cultural Diversity Approaches for Educators*. Institute for the Study of Cultural Diversity and Internationalization. California State University, Dominguez Hills.

El-Aharaf, Amer; Levine, Gary; & Alkhafaji, Abbass, eds. 1995. *Internationalizing the University Curriculum: Strategies and Opportunities*. Apollo, PA: Closson Press.

Elfin, Mel and Burke, Sarah. 1993. Rage on Campus (Race Relations on College Campuses). *US News & World Report* 114, (April 19): 15.

Fact Book—1994. California State University, Dominguez Hills. Office of Institutional Research. With appreciation to Dr. Kenneth Gash and Mr. Petrus Hendrikus Van Hamersveld.

Leo, John. 1993. Separatism Won't Solve Anything (Segregation of Black and White Students on Campus). *U.S. News & World Report* 114 (April 19, 1993): 65.

Lively, Kit. 1996. University of California's Professional Schools—Plan to Abolish Racial Preferences in Admissions Spurs Debates over Fairness, Questions on Procedures. *The Chronicle of Higher Education*, March 22.

Marable, Manning. 1950. *Black Leadership*. New York: Columbia University Press.

Miller, William H. 1997. Forget 2000! Worry about 2010. *Industry Week* 246: 64.

Reisch, Marc S. 1991. Hoechst Celanese's Drew Assesses Firm's Growth, Sketches Future Plans. *Engineering News* 69(35): 21.

Report of Institutional Self Study for Reaffirmation of Accreditation. 1996. Orange Coast College, Costa Mesa, California.

Richardson, R. C., Jr. 1990a. *Minority Achievement Counting on You: The State Role in Promoting Equity* (June). Denver: Education Commission on the States.

Richardson, Richard C., Jr. 1990b. Shared Vision: Transformational Leadership in American Community Colleges. *Change* 22 (Sept./Oct.): 50–53.

Van Hamersveld, Petrus Hendrikus. 1994. Racial Diversity and Student Perceptions of Educational Quality on CSU Campuses. Dissertation. California State University, Dominguez Hills.

Wilson, Catherine. 1996. Department of Human Resources, California State University, Dominguez Hills. Personal Communication.

Managing Evaluations in Higher Education

John C. Ory

As in any organization, evaluation can be used to direct and assist decision making in institutions of higher learning. This chapter will demonstrate how an internal evaluation office (Office of Instructional Resources, OIR, at the University of Illinois at Urbana-Champaign, UIUC) designs and manages evaluation programs and program evaluations for a variety of campus decision-making purposes. Whether the evaluation information is used for course or curriculum improvement, personnel reviews, or policy analysis, evaluation serves many different purposes by providing relevant and useful information. Following examples of OIR evaluation efforts is a set of "lessons" our staff has learned about conducting internal evaluations in a university setting.

OIR EVALUATION ACTIVITIES

Among other responsibilities, including faculty development, instructional computing, and media utilization, the Office of Instructional Resources is responsible for the development and management of several evaluation programs as well as the conduct of ad hoc evaluations of selected campus programs. Following is a brief description of a few of these evaluation activities.

Evaluation Programs

Instructor and Course Evaluation System (ICES)

ICES is a computerized-based system for obtaining student ratings of instructors and courses. ICES serves three major purposes: (1) to provide information to instructors who desire to monitor and improve their instruction, (2) to provide information that departments might use in promotion and personnel decisions, and (3) to provide information to students to help in course selection.

Faculty can select evaluation items from a catalog for inclusion on their ICES questionnaires. Two global items and five open-ended questions are printed on each questionnaire. The two global items are "Rate the instructor's overall teaching effectiveness" and "Rate the overall quality of the course." Departments have the option of including a set of items (the departmental core) on the forms of all faculty in the department. Faculty can also elect to include a set of six items (the student core) for which results are printed in a student publication.

Faculty administer the questionnaires during the last two weeks of class. Results are presented in a computer-generated ICES instructor report distributed to faculty after grades are posted. A comparison of the instructor's global item ratings with the normative ratings of other faculty within the instructor's department and within the university as a whole are provided. Faculty receiving exceptionally high ICES ratings are included on a list of "Excellent Teachers" that is printed in the student newspaper. Faculty can obtain a "Longitudinal Profile" of all of their course ratings while at UIUC for use in promotion and annual reviews.

Managing ICES. Each year over 200,000 ICES questionnaires are collected in approximately 10,000 course sections. Each semester's ICES results are stored in a database for easy retrieval and norms are recalculated each year. There have been several redesigns of the ICES forms and final reports over the years to maximize faculty understanding and campus use. The office is currently studying the possibility of discipline differences in ICES results and ways to aggregate ICES results within a department for unit review purposes. Last year several focus groups were conducted with faculty and administrators to learn of any misunderstandings and recommendations for change. A recent review of the ICES catalog resulted in the deletion of seldom-used items and the addition of new items in the area of instructional technology and active learning.

Placement and Proficiency System (P&P)

UIUC administers a variety of placement and proficiency tests for new freshmen in a precollege testing program. Examinations are administered on Saturday test dates each spring. The major purpose of the system is to help place students in the most appropriate course in each of several subject matter areas and to award proficiency where appropriate. Locally developed tests are administered in mathematics, chemistry, foreign languages, and rhetoric. Scores from the placement tests are used with admission test scores for academic advising and program planning purposes. Proficiency exams are used to award credit and/or exemption from university requirements.

Managing P&P. Each year P&P results are made available to freshmen and their advisors prior to registration. Results are also provided annually to departments to help them plan the type and number of course offerings. Reviews of current exams are conducted periodically to determine the appropriateness of test content. A new mathematics exam and new foreign language exams have been developed. The student score report was also revised to improve its readability and to make it more informative.

Administrator Evaluation System (AES)

The Administrator Evaluation System is a cyclical evaluation of campus department chairs, directors, and deans. The purposes are to deliver a useful and trustworthy evaluation to the administrator to whom the person being evaluated reports, to provide information to administrators with the intent of helping them better understand their competencies as leaders, and to promote a more productive working relationship between the unit faculty or staff and the administrator being evaluated.

The information collected should relate to the effectiveness of the administrator. Effectiveness can be defined as the extent to which the administrator performs assigned and expected responsibilities and tasks. For example, information should be collected about how well the department chair or unit head recruits new faculty, handles the promotion process, and communicates faculty needs to the dean or vice-chancellor. The information should include opinions of the faculty and demographic data, such as unit success in receiving grants, student enrollment patterns, and ability to recruit new faculty. Effectiveness can also be measured by rating the administrator's style—namely, how does an administrator behave in carrying out his or her responsibilities? *The AES Catalogue of Items* includes items that cover both definitions of effectiveness.

Managing AES. OIR maintains the evaluation schedule and notifies administrators of their scheduled review. An evaluation committee is appointed by the supervisor of the administrator being evaluated. OIR also provides evaluation materials to the committee and offers to meet with them to discuss evaluation procedures and/or to review evaluation instruments. Responsibilities of the committee include meeting with the administrator being evaluated, developing an evaluation plan, designing instruments for data collection, collecting and interpreting data, and preparing a written evaluation report. The evaluation committee also meets with the supervisor to discuss contents of the evaluation report and to develop a plan to communicate to the unit faculty or staff the procedures used in the evaluation and, at its completion, a summary of the findings.

International Teaching Assistant (ITA) Assessment and Training Program

In 1987 the state legislature passed State of Illinois law 1516, which requires all state universities to "establish programs which will ensure that all their classroom instructors will possess oral proficiency in the English language." To respond to the law, we have initiated an assessment program for international students in which all graduate students who are not native English speakers and who are planning to teach at UIUC are required to pass a test of spoken English and attend a teaching-skills orientation program before they begin providing instruction. For this evaluation program, the Test of Spoken English (TSE), developed by the Educational Testing Service, or its institutional version, SPEAK, is administered. Student feedback surveys and classroom observations are also conducted.

Managing ITA. Each semester OIR administers the SPEAK exam on campus. OIR-trained raters score the taped exams and results are maintained in a computerized database. Students failing to score 230 or higher may appeal to a committee consisting of faculty, graduate college staff, OIR staff, and undergraduate students.

Individuals who fail to demonstrate oral proficiency are required to participate in at least one semester of ongoing campus improvement activities before they can retake the SPEAK.

Individuals who demonstrate oral proficiency must attend a week-long campuswide teaching skills orientation before they begin teaching. Once in a teaching assignment, the international teaching assistant must be monitored by the academic unit in which he or she is hired. ITAs are also required to distribute and collect student feedback surveys at the end of the first three weeks of the first semester in which they provide instruction. OIR conducts the training orientation, assists units in the monitoring of teaching assistants, and supports the collection of student feedback.

PROGRAM EVALUATIONS

Evaluation of SCALE

UIUC received a three-year $2.1 million grant from the Alfred P. Sloan Foundation to establish the Sloan Center for Asynchronous Learning Environments (SCALE). The center is expected to profoundly affect how students are taught. The center focuses on how faculty can use computers and electronic communication to supplement traditional classroom instruction.

Asynchronous learning, a method of teaching using computer networks, allows course instructors and students to access course information and participate in discussions on their own time.

During the academic years 1995–1998, the Sloan Center supported the restructuring of up to 15 courses. The electronic format was used in engineering, science, and humanities classes to supplement classroom, library, and laboratory work. The first of these classes became available in fall 1995 and approximately 15,000 students were able to take advantage of the redesigned courses. Students in the redesigned classes use one of several commercially available software packages, such as "PacerForum," "FirstClass," or "LotusNotes," to communicate with each other over the computer network. Students also use software tools such as NCSA Mosaic to access electronic documents, course materials, and lecture notes on the World Wide Web.

Managing the Evaluation of SCALE

The evaluation measured the success of each new asynchronous learning (ALN) course as well as the success of the overall project. The evaluation attempted to address both the impact and process of implementing ALN technologies. Impact was defined in two ways. First, the evaluation was designed to measure impact in terms of each of the specific outcomes that were of special interest to the Sloan Foundation: decreased time-to-degree (TD); increased retention (RE), including fewer dropouts; decreased faculty time (FT), including decreased time spent in lectures, office hours, and meetings and overall increased student access to faculty; and the economics of instruction (EI), including more efficient use of TA support and increased student/faculty ratio.

Second, impact was judged in terms of whether faculty and departmental expectations about the possible benefits of ALN technologies were met and whether they help students to learn better, faster, and more efficiently. The evaluation paid special attention to issues related to faculty acceptance of ALN, and the added value of ALN approaches to faculty in carrying out their teaching. Evaluation focused on faculty time spent teaching, productivity, and quality of life (such as decreased number of routine staff meetings, and the ability to work from home during convenient hours).

Evaluation of the Campus Honors Program

The Campus Honors Program is designed to foster close collaborative relationships between top students and distinguished faculty. This occurs through the small honors classes, through each student's sharing academic and research interests with his or her faculty mentor, and through the many informal contacts that grow out of the program's extracurricular offerings. An evaluation was conducted after the end of the first year of the program, which collected information about the motivational characteristics of the honors students, their academic and nonacademic experiences, and the types of activities in which they participated while enrolled at UIUC.

Managing the Evaluation of the Honors Program

The College Student Experiences Survey (CSES) was administered to learn how students spend their time—in course work, in the library, in contacts with faculty, in extracurricular activities, in various social and cultural activities, and in taking advantage of other facilities and opportunities that exist in the college setting. SPECTRUM was used to measure the motivational characteristics of the honors students. This instrument measures four basic motivational factors: accomplishment, recognition, power, and affiliation. Also administered were group interviews and an opinion survey, both designed to assess student opinions regarding academic and personal development, attitudes toward school, and judgments of the honors program. Evaluation results were given to the program administrator to indicate program strengths and weaknesses and to suggest areas for improvement.

Senior Survey Evaluation

Every three years a Senior Survey is sent to all graduating seniors at UIUC. The survey results are intended "to give us a way to measure the success of our efforts to provide an excellent undergraduate education in an environment that is rich in opportunity and contributes to personal growth. The Senior Survey seeks information about the respondents and their postgraduate plans. It also asks about senior satisfaction in 7 broad categories, including campus environment, teaching and education environment, services, programs, facilities, achievement of educational goals, and overall undergraduate experience.

Managing the Senior Survey

OIR is responsible for administering the survey, tabulating responses, and making results available to interested stakeholders. Each administration's results are maintained in a database that can be accessed to create longitudinal summaries that compare results over time. Survey items are reviewed before each administration and modifications are made based upon past item performance or new campus interests.

Discovery Program Evaluation

The UIUC Discovery Program is an experimental one designed to develop greater interaction between faculty and first-year students. Discovery courses are offered in a number of formats, but regardless of format, the courses share important features: they are faculty-taught; they are interactive; enrollment is limited to no more than 20 students; most, if not all, of the students are freshmen. The aim of the program is offer freshmen the opportunity to develop intellectual skills, personal attitudes, and social relationships that will enrich their educational experience throughout their years of undergraduate study.

Managing the Discovery Program Evaluation

Evaluation of the Discovery Program involved short questionnaires administered at the end of the fall and spring semesters. The questionnaires asked students about their Discovery experience. End-of-course questionnaires as well as focus groups with students and faculty were also utilized. The Senior Survey responses (see previous section) on selected items were compared between students who did and did not enroll in Discovery courses. The intent of the comparison is to assess long-term effects of Discovery course participation on the student' attitudes about their undergraduate experience at UIUC.

LESSONS LEARNED

The previous section reveals the scope and variety of evaluation activities conducted by OIR. All of our evaluation efforts follow a multiple-purpose, criteria, source, method approach (Ory 1989) to provide decision makers with credible and useful information. However, some activities are more successful than others. Some activities are more difficult to conduct than others. Some activities are more enjoyable to conduct than others. Why? Through the years OIR has learned several lessons about conducting evaluations within the university organization. We have learned to appreciate the difficult, schizophrenic role of the internal evaluator. These lessons are described below.   .

We Have to Live with These People

Conducting evaluations or coordinating evaluation systems is only one of many services provided by OIR. On a weekly basis, OIR staff interact with hundreds of faculty and staff in many units on campus. We try to work cooperatively with the campus as a whole. Oftentimes we help other units and they help us, making both of our jobs easier, more efficient, and/or less costly. One could could argue that most campus units follow a model of cooperation rather than competition, despite the pressures of declining budgets.

This cooperation model can be greatly affected when one unit (e.g., OIR) is often assigned the task of evaluating the work of another. Our staff members continually remind themselves that program evaluation is making judgments about some "thing." Internal evaluation is making judgments about some "thing" that happens to belong to a colleague or friend. It is picking through the neighbor's garbage or peering through their half-closed curtains. It is learning how much they earn and how they spend their money. In brief, our staff recognizes the threat of evaluation.

We have tried to acknowledge and minimize our colleagues' concern over their program's evaluation by:

- discussing with them the purposes and goals of the evaluation as determined by the administration;
- seeking their help in the design of the evaluation;
- stressing the confidentiality of information;
- periodically sharing results with them to demonstrate our openness, to verify results, and to build credibility; and
- inviting them to respond to the final evaluation report.

Our evaluation of the Educational Opportunities Rhetoric courses is an excellent example of our efforts to get units involved in their evaluation. After extended negotiation with the Rhetoric Department about valid and reliable assessments of writing ability, we followed their recommendation to collect and evaluate portfolios of student writings rather than a single writing sample or essay test score.

It is no surprise that many of the behaviors described above are also recommended by Patton (1978) and others (Braskamp and Brown 1980; Weiss 1982) as ways to enhance the utilization of evaluation results. In essence, we are trying to demonstrate credibility and earn the trust of our colleagues while giving them some ownership of the evaluation. When asked to evaluate the work of others at UIUC, we realize that we will be "living" with these same people when the evaluation is over. Regardless of the evaluation results, we want to have the same relationship with the unit being evaluated after the evaluation as before.

Make the Most of Insider Information

In comparison to external evaluators, internal evaluators should always have a better understanding of the evaluation setting, including key decision makers, stakeholders, recurring campus problems, and typical decision-making processes. In our situation we have an inside track on watching how the campus uses our evaluation systems. We sit on committees using ICES information to make campus awards. We speak on the phone with parents and advisors who are reading and interpreting our P & P score reports. We observe and train ITAs with different SPEAK scores.

We continually use our insider information to design and/or modify OIR evaluation systems. For example, we developed the "Longitudinal Profile," which lists a professor's career of ICES results as a result of promotion committees struggling with varied and idiosyncratic summaries of instructors' student ratings. The P & P student report was modified after we saw first-hand how advisors struggled interpreting some of our original reports. Often we don't have to ask clients for changes because we are in a position to observe their difficulties.

Know When to Say No

OIR is a campus support office that provides many help services in addition to conducting evaluations. Our mission is to support instruction on campus. We want faculty and departments to feel comfortable coming to us with their instructional problems. We cannot build barriers between our office and the rest of campus. Sometimes it is in our best interest (and the campus') to refrain from conducting an evaluation. For example, several years ago OIR was approached to help evaluate how departments were training their teaching assistants. Campus administration expressed interest in having OIR conduct a survey wherein departments reveal their training strategy, or lack of one. It was obvious to us that the "surveyors" could be viewed as the campus TA police. If so, the same departments that we would want to have come to us for help would be afraid of telling us of their problems! We obviously refrained from conducting the survey. There are times we need to see the big picture and know when to say no.

Conduct Efficient Evaluations

If our evaluations are intrusive, time consuming, and costly to those requesting the evaluation and/or those being evaluated, they are less likely to be asked for in the future. One of the best ways we have learned to keep our evaluations efficient is to have a complete working knowledge of all campus databases and sources of information. There is no need to collect data that already exist or to design evaluations without first thinking about available sources of information. We have learned that a data analyst with a complete knowledge of and ability to access all campus databases is invaluable.

Matching Campus Expectations, Needs, and Wants

As internal evaluators we are once again in an excellent position to know what our decision makers want in an evaluation. By working with them on a weekly, sometimes daily, basis we have gained first-hand knowledge of our client's expectations, needs, and wants. We have learned which clients prefer quantitative rather than qualitative evidence. We know when less is better than more. Or, as we think of it, when to deliver a Dodge evaluation instead of a Cadillac. We also know the politics of the environment and can tailor our design to address the needs of important stakeholders, or to get some stakeholders more involved than others in the initial design of the study. There are times when a faculty advisory committee lends credibility to an evaluation and other times when advice is more credible coming from staff persons who are in the trenches dealing with campus problems.

The Sloan and Discovery evaluations are good examples of how we have tailored our evaluations to the expectations or needs of our clients. Our provost has said on more than one occasion, "I come from the chemical sciences and have an appreciation for hard, quantitative data." It just so happens that the Sloan Foundation shares this preference. Thus, while qualitative data will certainly be collected, we have emphasized the collection of quantitative data in our evaluation design.

The Discovery Program has received a considerable amount of positive attention. While we are planning a more thorough and comprehensive evaluation in the future, we realized how much the administration wants to know the "early returns" right now. Consequently, we conducted a small-scale evaluation immediately following the first semester of Discovery classes. We continually attempt to use our familiarity and understanding of our clients and the campus environment to produce useful and utilized evaluations.

Build in Flexibility and Be Accomodating

When designing our evaluation programs we have always tried to build in system flexibility to accommodate the broad range of campus requests. ICES is an excellent example of a flexible evaluation system. Faculty can select their rating items from a large catalog covering multiple areas of instruction. Periodically we place additional items in the catalog to address new instructional topics. The open-ended items on the back of the ICES forms leave space to accommodate additional concerns of the instructor. We also help departments develop their own "core" of items to help tailor ICES to the particular interests of the unit.

At the same time system flexibility is important, so too is staff flexibility in administering the system. When the last college chose to abandon their own student rating system and to adopt ICES, they made many requests unique to their traditional way of evaluating courses. Rather than to refuse their requests and inform them of "the one and only way" that ICES operates on campus, we chose instead to modify our operations to accommodate their college needs. We have learned to accommodate unique requests as long as they do not compromise the quality of the evaluation program. In the process of doing so, we please our campus colleagues and provide a more desirable and useful evaluation.

Make Sure the Purpose of an Evaluation Is Identified

One of the greatest sources of evaluation anxiety is the failure of the individuals being evaluated to understand the purpose of the evaluation. When we are asked to evaluate a particular program within another unit, the individuals being evaluated want to know: Why are they being evaluated? Are cuts going to be made? Are people complaining about the program? Are other programs also being evaluated? Seldom do their inquiries assume positive rather than negative consequences. To most people, evaluation or accountability means only one thing: possible cuts in funding or staff.

We have found it most useful for the administrator requesting the evaluation to directly communicate its purpose to the individuals responsible for the program. We cannot have the same credibility as the administration in conveying the purpose of an evaluation. We were once asked to evaluate a program for purposes of expansion rather than extinction. The administration was quite pleased with the quality of the program, but wanted some evidence to support recent requests for its expansion. Regardless of what we said and did, the staff of the program being evaluated was reluctant to offer much help in the evaluation because they were convinced we were only trying to find reasons for cutting the program. Since that time we have asked the administration to clearly inform units about the purpose of an evaluation, even if it means arranging a meeting between them.

SUMMARY

The purpose of this chapter was to demonstrate the variety of evaluation activities performed by an internal evaluation office at a large university and to explain how experience has shaped the way in which the activities are conducted. Our experiences are not unlike those of other internal evaluation offices wherein we are concerned about the quality of our work as well as our working relationships within the large organization. We try to take advantage of our insider knowledge of the university, including availability of information, familiarity with decision makers, and awareness of campus needs for information. We try to watch and to learn how our clients are using our evaluations and what we can do to make them more useful. We have learned to avoid evaluating other units within the university without their complete understanding (and, we hope, approval) of the evaluation's purpose, design, conduct, and reporting mechanism. In essence, the way in which we conduct our evaluation programs and our program evaluations reflects our understanding of how important it is to satisfy our clients as well as to get along with our neighbors.

REFERENCES

Braskamp, L. A. and Brown, R. D., eds. 1980. *Utilization of Evaluative Information*. San Francisco: Jossey-Bass.

Ory, J. 1989. A Role for Assessment in Higher Education Decision-Making. In P. Gray, ed., *Achieving Assessment Goals Using Evaluation Techniques*, New Directions for Higher Education, No. 67. San Francisco: Jossey-Bass.

Patton, M. Q. 1978. *Utilization-Focused Evaluation*. Beverly Hills, CA: Sage.

Weiss, C. H. 1982. Measuring the Use of Evaluation. In E. House, ed., *Evaluation Studies, Review Annual* No. 7. Beverly Hills, CA: Sage.

Evaluating Collegiate Administrators

Richard Miller and Peggy Miller

Improving administrative performance is the main reason for evaluating adminstrators as is the case for faculty. This basic theme, however, does not preclude finding weak areas of performance that may require extra work, and, even more rarely, finding that the overall work performance does not warrant the individual's continuance with the institution. Administrator evaluation should have these basic purposes:

- Finding areas for improvement should be the focus; and complimenting areas of strength can be that "spoonful of sugar that helps the medicine go down!"
- Clarifying relationships and consistencies between the individual's goals and objectives with those of the institution can be an outcome of administrator evaluation. Related is the compatibility of the individual's administrative style and skills with those of the position and institution.
- Improving internal communication almost always happens in a well-defined and -managed administrative evaluation system.
- Resources can be facilitated through the administrative assessments. The road to better uses of human resources can be through systematic administrative assessments.
- Rewarding outstanding administrative performance is a logical outcome if the institution has a merit system for administrators or other ways of recognizing excellence.
- Validating the institution's interest in vigorous and effective administrator evaluation and improvement can be gained and sustained by a well-defined and -managed system. The institution's governing board will be pleased to have evi-

dences of a systematic system for evaluating college administrators, even if their own company does not have such a system.

- Answering the general public's interest in administrator evaluation as well as faculty evaluation can be facilitated by having these systems operations.

CHARACTERISTICS OF EFFECTIVE ADMINISTRATOR EVALUATION SYSTEMS

- Regular administrative evaluation takes place on a known schedule.
- The system is standardized and its policies and procedures are readily available.
- The system is based upon a positive approach: To assist administrators to improve their professional performances.
- Opportunities for professional improvement are available for administrators.
- The system has a grievance procedure.
- The administrative evaluation system is evaluated every third year by an ad hoc committee established by the chief executive officer (CEO).
- The evaluation system is taken seriously because it is a searching effort and positively motivated.
- Some positive instructional personnel adjustments have resulted from the system.

EVALUATING THE STATUS OF ADMINISTRATOR

A number of questions should be raised in an effort to determine the status of administrator evaluation at your college as well as to determine its qualitative dimensions questions, such as:

- What is the status of administrator evaluation at your college? What is the credibility of your policies and procedures and/or system?
- Do these policies and procedures allow for a fair, searching, yet appropriately confidential system?
- Are the formal evaluation processes and procedures carried out on a regular, and known, schedule?
- Are the evaluation results discussed with those who are evaluated, with written record (notes) made of the conversations?
- Is an appeals procedure available?
- Has the system been scrutinized by a lawyer who is familiar with postsecondary institutions?
- Is the efficiency and effectiveness of the policies and procedures for the administrative personnel evaluation system reviewed on a periodic basis?
- Have you evaluated your evaluation system within the past two years?

OPERATIONAL GUIDELINES FOR ADMINISTRATOR EVALUATION

Many lists and rationales for administrator evaluation have been developed, although almost none of them have been tested by research or developed from a research base. Successful use has some de facto validity and reliability, but these types of "validations" by practice should not be confused with controlled, statistical research. One of the very few research studies, by Arthur Vorhies (1985), found that nine criteria had reliability when tested for evaluating college deans: administering, communicating, encouraging, facilitating, financing, innovating, organizing, prioritizing, and solutionizing. The reliability of these findings has not been tested for chief academic officers, but it is reasonable to believe that no major differences would be found if the criteria were also used for these groups. (The question of validity was not tested by Vorhies.)

Performance is measured against stated criteria for the position. These criteria require that a position description exists with sufficient definition so the component parts can be used as criteria for judging performance.

Objective and subjective measures are used. Since evaluation forms can be useful for evaluating faculty performance, it is logical that forms can be a useful aspect of evaluating administrative performance. But in both cases, subjective evaluations, including self-evaluations, also need to be used.

The degree of confidentiality is agreed upon. Some states have inclusive open records laws, which preclude almost all types of confidentiality; but even in these states a college can establish some reasonable degrees of confidentiality. In any case it is important that only bona fide and proper documentation be placed in the personnel files. Institutions that are unsure of the practical and legalistic limits of confidentiality in their state should consult a lawyer who has postsecondary experience. In unionized states and institutions, these matters almost always are spelled out in detail.

An annual schedule for faculty and administrator evaluations should be used. The schedule should be published annually within a three-year overall schedule. This pattern reduces possible confusion, adds respectability to the process, and allows other schedules to be adjusted to these evaluations. Such scheduling is especially important if a computerized section of the administrator evaluation system is used because of the necessary coordination of computer time needed for processing with other needs.

GUIDELINES FOR DEVELOPING ADMINISTRATION SYSTEMS

Systems for evaluating the chief executive officer (president, chancellor) are the prerogative of the governing board, and the board should not be challenged on this right and responsibility; however, it is fairly common to have an academic (instructional) affairs committee of the board that will ask for input from the chair of the faculty governing/coordinating board such as a faculty senate.

Have support of the CEO. Administrative systems that have intentionally or inadvertently bypassed the CEO will eventually run into trouble. It is best to seek the views and support of the CEO very early in the process, and keep him or her briefed at appropriate intervals.

Work with, not around, the other college evaluation systems. Administrator evaluation is no more or less important than the evaluation systems for students and for faculty. Occasionally, a group of faculty will attempt to develop an evaluation system to "get" a chief academic officer (CAO) or a dean. Such negative efforts can only tarnish the credibility and eventual value of the current or emerging plan.

Positive motivation is important. Administrator evaluation systems are to assist in performance improvement—the same positive evaluation that also must be evident in developing systems for evaluating faculty and students.

Discrete openness should be built into the system. Massive public disclosure of results of administrator evaluation usually serves little useful purpose. If the overriding purpose of the system is performance improvement, then the evaluation results will not need to be disclosed except under unusual circumstances.

On a related topic, one can find a handful of colleges that have developed catalogs of student evaluations of classroom teachers. In the late 1960s some college administrations did concede to this process as a result of student pressures, but a number of lawsuits by professors, most of which they won, discouraged the wider use of this approach. Evaluation systems should not be popularity contests but serious efforts to improve performance. However, occasionally the systems will uncover misfits between job descriptions and/or unacceptable levels of performance.

Approaches to the evaluator-evaluated system should be determined. Two approaches are used. The top-down approach is most common, partly because it is easier to administer. It can be effective. The CEO evaluates the vice presidents, the vice-presidents evaluate their deans or division heads, and the division heads evaluate their unit heads/chairs.

The "wrap-around" system is more complicated and takes more time to complete. Using the academic area as an example: The CEO and the instructional deans both evaluate the CAO; the CAO and the appropriate unit heads both evaluate the deans; and both the deans and representative groups of the unit's faculty evaluate the unit heads/chairs. This method does allow a more complete evaluation but it is also more time consuming.

PROBLEMS IN DEVELOPING ADMINISTRATOR EVALUATION SYSTEMS

Defining administration. Keeping the campus quiet usually is the number-one objective of the CEOs during times of unrest, and it rates very near the top at all other times also.

One can find countless treatises, books, and articles on leadership and administration. The nine elements for dean evaluation that were mentioned earlier may have some generic value. Also, the institutional circumstances and conditions at any particular time may be important factors in these evaluations. For example, it takes a somewhat different set of human skills and techniques to terminate faculty positions as compared with increasing them. Or a CEO who takes on the challenge of diminishing deep institutional indebtedness will need some different skills as compared with those needed during a growth period. There are no pat answers to these types of questions, but they are real factors in administrative evaluation.

Delineating the ways in which administrators work is another dilemma in evaluations. For example, it has been said that power is like money in the bank; the more of it you use the less you have! That leaves persuasion as a key modus operandi. The uses of administrative power does have its place, and there are other times when successful administrators *practice logical obscurantism,* which is saying clearly and precisely, nothing, but saying it with eloquence and conviction! In other words, sometimes administrators need to be ambiguous.

INDIVIDUALIZING EVALUATIONS FOR KEY ADMINISTRATORS

Evaluations for each key administrative position should be based, first, upon special considerations and unique elements that are related to that particular position, then upon questions that are crafted to meet these factors. Some generic questions relating to special considerations for each position should be developed.

Chief Executive Officer (chancellor/president)

Special considerations:

- Spends one-fourth to one-third of time on academic matters; even less time in large community colleges.
- Does many things quietly.
- Serves at the pleasure of the board. Two-year CEOs are closer to this reality than are their four-year counterparts because of their monthly board meetings.

- Demanding nature of the position. Particularly in public colleges and universities, everyone feels that he or she has a right to a "piece" of the CEO. Saying "no" gracefully but definitely is an art not a science, but an important one.

Unique considerations:

- Effective and close working relationships with board(s). The local board is of primary importance but state boards also are important.
- Delegated overall campus responsibility, which must be shared with trusted and competent assistants, it is hoped.
- External relations is a major time commitment.
- Projects the institutional image.

Chief Academic Officer

While not usually directly involved in the day-to-day evaluation efforts or in an annual performance review of faculty, except in sensitive or problem cases, the CAO does have very important dimensions included in his or her overall role as instructional leader:

- Espousing, facilitating, and monitoring academic quality makes everyone's work with academic personnel matters easier and more satisfying. This Pollyanna-like statement will be nothing more unless an espousal of quality is consistently backed by actions that, over time, enhance quality.
- Seeing that institutional promotion and continuing appointment policies and procedures protect institution as well as individual rights requires some legal expertise and sometimes much thought and consultation about appropriate strategies.
- Monitoring the institution's promotion and continuing appointment policies, procedures, and practices is an important function.
- Anticipating difficult academic personnel problems can decrease surprises. CAOs do not like surprises! It is estimated that 25% of the promotion and continuing appointment problem cases take 75% of the time that the CAO devotes to this area.
- Seeing that faculty recruitment policies, procedures, and practices are as effective as possible in putting the institution's best foot forward.

Special considerations:

- Serves at the pleasure of the CEO.
- Holds the most vulnerable of academic administrative positions
- Provides overall academic direction through personnel and budget recommendations.
- The demanding nature of the position.

Unique considerations:

- Responsible for overall academic planning and evaluation.
- Effective and close working relationships with the CEO.
- Effective and close working relationships with other vice presidents.
- Effective and close working relationships with academic deans.
- Effective and close working relationships with faculty leadership.

Academic Dean (coordinates and leads several instructional units)

Special considerations:

- Represents primarily the departmental interests yet needs to support institution-wide interests.
- Needs to maintain academic credibility while administering in an even-handed manner.
- Makes academic budget to the CAO recommendations for the respective instructional units.
- Serves as dean at the pleasure of the vice president for academic affairs.

Unique considerations:

- Maintains effective and close working relations with the departmental chairpersons.
- Maintains effective and close working relations with the CAO.
- Maintains effective working relations with faculty members in the academic unit.
- Provides academic leadership and planning for the academic unit, within an institutionwide context.

Department Chairpersons

Special considerations:

- The "front trench" academic administrative position.
- Usually needs to be both a practicing academic and an administrator.
- Makes basic personnel recommendations based upon recommendations by chairpersons.
- Communicates and implements unfavorable news and decisions without casting aspersions toward other upward administrative levels.

Unique considerations:

- Maintains effective and close working relations with departmental faculty members.
- Maintains effective and close working relations with the dean.
- Stays close to student views and needs.
- Makes equitable and legally defensible academic personnel decisions and recommendations.

To Terminate or Not to Terminate?

The most agonizing academic decisions concern recommending termination of individuals from the institution. But, first, all options need to be examined. The following taxonomy has that process in mind.

A. What is the nature of the inadequacy problem?
   1. Sudden
   2. Developing
   3. Specific
   4. Not clear
B. Can it be remedied?
   1. Through personal counseling
   2. Through reorganization
   3. Through enhancing professional competence
   4. Through changing the position description
   5. Through other means
C. Is the remedy worth the effort?
   1. Does the individual have sufficient expertise and/or promise to make the effort worthwhile?
   2. Is the individual loyal to the institution and will he or she make a concerted effort to change/improve?
   3. What will be likely consequences of a decision to terminate? Will the individual "make waves"? Will the best interests of the institution be served by a termination decision?
   4. Other considerations
D. Termination
   1. Sudden
      a. Usually for a major problem or irregularity
      b. Precipitous terminations without compelling reason usually create more problems than they solve.
      c. Campus reaction may be quite unpredictable.
   2. Planned termination
      a. Best interests of the institution should be the highest priority.
      b. Respect for the dignity and professional future of the individual are important and should be considered.

    c. Completely confidential meetings and correspondence are usually better. If secretarial leaks are a distinct possibility, use long-hand notes.

    d. Give general reasons, but if requested, specific reasons.

        i. Incompetence, such as:

- lack of preparation
- immaturity
- technical deficiencies
- indifference
- untrustworthy

        ii. Incompatibility of administrative styles and/or personalities

        iii. Poor human relations

        iv. Irregular behavior

        v. Failure to keep confidence

    e. Some ways to accomplish the termination

        i. Sabbatical/research leave before returning to faculty

        ii. For an agreed upon time, move into a position more compatible with interests and talents.

        iii. Reorganize, but this approach may create other problems that may not have been planned.

        iv. Provide continuing employment for a period of time.

        v. Give the individual a special project, with full pay and credible surroundings, with an agreed-upon finish time.

        vi. Give the individual an opportunity to resign.

DEVELOPING AN ADMINISTRATOR EVALUATION SYSTEM

The following outline sets forth a usable structure for developing and evaluating an administrator evaluation system.

A. Purposes of the evaluation system

B. Structure

    1. Who should evaluate whom?

    2. Selection of evaluation techniques

        a. Survey instrument

        b. Interviews

        c. Review of literature

        d. Benchmarking (check with other similar institutions)

        e. Other

C. Operationalizing the process

    1. Time schedule

    2. Gathering data

    3. Analyzing and evaluating data

        a. Use of normative references

      4. Feedback
      5. Follow-up

D. Uses of results
      1. Conference with immediate supervisor
         a. Format for conference
         b. Follow-up after conference
         c. Rebuttal grievance procedures
         d. Uses of conference results
      2. Conferences with others

ASSESSING AN ONGOING ADMINISTRATION EVALUATION SYSTEM

Rarely do we evaluate our evaluation systems. Somehow we assume that because it is an evaluation system it must be good by virtue of just being in existence, but evaluation systems, as systems of any sort, are good, average, or poor. It is just that they are rarely evaluated.

A. Charge for the evaluation given by CEO

B. Ad hoc committee is established.
      1. Balance among administrators, faculty, students, and/or external participants
      2. No factional domination or majority
      3. Committee members appointed by the president, based upon recommendations from appropriate groups.

C. The new committee should begin with a detailed review of the current system.
      1. An appropriate literature review is desirable.
      2. Successful models should be solicited from a few other colleges/ universities.

D. Time allocated for study
      1. Time-action-plan (TAP) is developed.
         a. Time frame for the study
         b. What actions will be needed?
            i Deadlines established for each phase of the study
         c. Checkpoints set up for determining progress toward deadlines.
      2. Developmental schedule for the system should include at least one open hearing.

A SIX-STEP PROCESS FOR EMPLOYEE-EMPLOYER ASSESSMENT

A systematic, step-by-step process can help diminish the normal anxieties that are almost always associated with personnel evaluation-both for the evaluated and the evaluator.

Step 1: At the designated time, both the evaluator and evaluated fill out the appropriate rating scales and/or other forms.

Step 2: The evaluatee submits a self-rating scale along with another form that includes narrative descriptions that includes these categories:

A. Position description

B. Unusual aspects of work-related activities since the previous evaluation

    1. Unexpected developments/happenings
    2. Most positive work-related happenings
    3. Most negative work-related happenings
    4. Problems to be solved, with possible solutions/ameloriations
    5. Possible changes in position description

C. Professional development needs/aspirations for the future.

This report is submitted to the evaluator one week in advance.

Step 3: A one-hour conference is scheduled between the employee and the employer. No particular structure for the conference is recommended. The conference discusses employee and employer responses on the rating scales in addition to the employee's narrative responses, as well as any narrative reports by the supervisor. The conference should conclude with some developmental, next steps, even for the superior-rated employee, under the assumption that when "you're through learning, you're through!"

Step 4: The evaluator submits to the employee, within one week, a summary statement of the conference, concluding with a developmental section.

Step 5: The employee signs the employer's report to the effect that he or she has *read* the report. The employee can attach a rebuttal and/or comments on an addendum to the report if the employee so wishes.

Step 6: If differences about aspects of the report exist, a follow-up conference may be desirable, or a prior meeting between the academic dean and the supervisor may be desirable before a follow-up employer-employee meeting.

An administrative evaluation system should be simple in form and structure, consistent in use, open in intent and operation, and both formative and summative in function.

REFERENCE

Salamone, Ronald E. and Vorhies, Arthur. 1985. Just rewards: Ensuring equitable salary reviews. *Education Record* 66(3), 44–47.

Index

About the Editors and Contributors

ALLAN M. HOFFMAN is dean and professor of the College of Health Sciences at Des Moines University—Osteopathic Medical Center and director of the Center for Prevention of Community Violence. He has provided consulting services on violence prevention to schools, colleges, and business organizations worldwide; has served in teaching and administrative capacities for many universities; and is a member of the North Central Association's Academic Quality Improvement Project. Among his numerous awards and honors he received a Certificate of Special Congressional Recognition from the U.S. Congress. His most recent books are *Schools, Violence and Society* (Praeger, 1996) and *Violence on Campus: Defining the Problems, Strategies for Action* (1988).

RANDAL W. SUMMERS is an adjunct professor in the Business Administration Program at the University of Phoenix, Southern California campus; director of Learning and Development at Informix in Menlo Park, CA; and a general partner in the consulting firm of Summers and Associates. Affiliated with Fortune 100 companies, he has specialized in human resource, organizational, and curriculum development. He has contributed most recently to *TQM: Implications for Higher Education* (1995), *Schools, Violence and Society* (Praeger, 1996), and *Violence on Campus: Defining the Problems, Strategies for Action* (1998).

RICHARD ALFRED is an associate professor in the School of Education, University of Michigan.

RANDY L. ARMSTRONG is associate professor of communications and director of student publications at Hardin Simmons University, Abilene, Texas.

J. VICTOR BALDRIDGE is president of Pacific Management Company and program director of the Center for Strategic Leadership at the Univeristy of San Francisco.

FRANK H. BESNETTE is executive director, Arizona Board of Regents, Arizona State University, Tempe.

AMER EL-AHRAF is head of the degree-granting division of the International Education Corporation, which is entrusted with realizing the vision of establishing the multicampus Southern California International University.

ROBERT H. FENSKE is professor of higher education in the division of Educational Leadership and Policy Studies at Arizona State University.

DAVID GRAY is the past vice president of Administration at California State University, Long Beach.

DAVID S. HONEYMAN is a professor in the Department of Education Leadership, College of Education, University of Florida, Gainesville.

DEAN L. HUBBARD is president of Northwest Missouri State University.

RANDALL J. ISAACSON is a graduate of the higher education master's degree program student affairs at Texas Tech University.

STEPHEN M. JORDAN is president of the Graduate Program in Public Administration at Eastern Washington University.

DANIEL J. JULIUS is associate vice president for academic affairs at the University of San Francisco, a senior fellow at the Stanford Institute for Higher Education Research, and past president of the College and University Personnel Association and the Academy of Academic Personnel Administrators.

JOHN S. LEVIN is associate professor of higher education and director of the Community College Institute, the Center for the Study of Higher Education at the University of Arizona.

PEGGY MILLER is a lecturer in the Management Systems Department at Ohio University.

RICHARD MILLER is professor of higher education at Ohio University.

JANA NIDIFFER is an assistant professor in the School of Education at the University of Michigan.

RONALD D. OPP is associate professor of higher education at the University of Toledo, Ohio.

JOHN C. ORY is director of the Office of International Resources and associate professor of educational psychology at the University of Illinois at Urbana-Champaign.

DENISE C. OTTINGER is dean of student services at West Shore Community College in Scottville, Michigan.

JEFFREY PFEFFER is the Thomas D. Dee II Professor of organizational behavior at the Stanford University Graduate School of Business.

SCOTT ROSEVEAR is an associate in the Information Technology Division at the University of Michigan.

ALBERT B. SMITH is professor and coordinator of the Higher Education Program at Texas Tech University.

GLORIA A. STEWART is director of Institutional Research at the University of Houston-Downtown Campus and a doctoral student in the Higher Education Program at Texas Tech University.

YVONNE THAYER is a policy analyst for the Virgina Department of Education in Richmond.

ISBN 0-89789-645-9

EAN

9 780897 896450

HARDCOVER BAR CODE